UNDERSTANDING HUMAN NATURE

Alfred Adler (1870–1937), Viennese psychologist, contemporary of Sigmund Freud and Carl Jung, and the father of Individual Psychology, remains one of the most influential figures in modern psychology and psychotherapy.

Among Adler's most significant contributions are: his emphasis on holism, arguing that one must study and treat the patient as a 'whole person', the central role he gave to equality in preventing psychopathology, and the importance of developing democratic family structures to the raising of children. His most famous concept is the inferiority complex, which addresses the problem of self-esteem and its negative compensations. Other seminal theories include the importance of birth order in the formation of personality, the impact of neglect or pampering on a child's development, the ability to work with others for a common good (social interest) as the hall-mark of sound mental health, and the idea that individuals develop a story about themselves in early childhood, a 'life style', that guides their perceptions and choices throughout life. Adler was also among the first psychologists to stress the importance of feminism, arguing that the power dynamics between men and women (and associations with gender) are crucial to an understanding of human beings.

After serving as a medical doctor in World War I, Adler founded a system of child-guidance clinics that spread throughout Europe. He was personally involved in training teachers, social workers, doctors and psychiatrists in his techniques, and lectured widely in America, where he moved in 1935. Adler died in 1937, leaving more than 300 articles and books on child psychology, marriage, education, and the principles of Individual Psychology. His best known works include *Understanding Human Nature*, *Understanding Life*, *What Life Could Mean to You*, and *Social Interest* (published by Oneworld) and *The Practice and Theory of Individual Psychology*.

Colin Brett is an accredited Adlerian counselor and former Training Officer of the Adlerian Society of Great Britain. He is the transla-tor of *Understanding Human Nature*, *Understanding Life* and *Social Interest*, and the editor of *What Life Could Mean to You*.

UNDERSTANDING
HUMAN
NATURE

alfred adler

A New Translation by Colin Brett

ONEWORLD

OXFORD

1/7/10
Lan
£29.95

A Oneworld Book

First published in English in 1927
First published in this new translation by Oneworld Publications 1992
First published in trade paperback 2009

ISBN 978-1-85168-667-4

Typeset by Jayvee, Trivandrum, India
Cover design by www.fatfacedesign.com
Printed and bound in Great Britain by
Bell & Bain, Glasgow

Oneworld Publications
185 Banbury Road
Oxford OX2 7AR
England
www.oneworld-publications.com

Learn more about Oneworld. Join our mailing list to
find out about our latest titles and special offers at:

www.oneworld-publications.com

CONTENTS

FOREWORD *by Dr James Hemming*   9
PREFACE   15
INTRODUCTION   16

PART ONE: FUNDAMENTALS OF CHARACTER DEVELOPMENT

1 WHAT IS THE PSYCHE?   27
  The concept of consciousness   27
  The function of the psyche   27
  Our purpose and goal-directedness   28

2 SOCIAL ASPECTS OF MENTAL LIFE   34
  The absolute truth   34
  The need for communal life   35
  Security and adaptation   36
  Social feeling   38

3 THE CHILD AND SOCIETY   39
  Infancy   39
  The effect of obstacles   41
  The individual as a social being   45

4 THE WORLD WE LIVE IN   47
  Our mental universe   47
  The way we see the world   49
    Perception   49
    Memory   50
    Imagination   51

5 **ASPECTS OF UNREALITY** 57
    Fantasy 57
    Dreams: general considerations 59
    Empathy and identification 59
    Influence, suggestion and hypnosis 61

6 **THE INFERIORITY COMPLEX** 66
    Early childhood 66
    Compensation: The striving for recognition and superiority 68
    The graph of life and the cosmic picture 74

7 **PSYCHOLOGICAL CHARACTERISTICS** 83
    Preparation for life 83
    Attention and distraction 85
    Criminal negligence and forgetfulness 87
    The unconscious 87
    Dreams 94
    Intelligence 102

8 **MALE AND FEMALE** 104
    Men, women and the division of labour 104
    Male dominance 106
    The alleged inferiority of women 110
    Rejecting the woman's role 114
    Tension between the sexes 122
    What can we do? 124

9 **THE FAMILY CONSTELLATION** 126

PART TWO: THE SCIENCE OF CHARACTER

10 **GENERAL CONSIDERATIONS** 135
    How do we become who we are? 135
    Social feeling, community spirit and the
        development of character 139
    How character develops 142
    The old school of psychology 148
    Temperament and endocrine secretion 149
    To sum up 155

11 AGGRESSIVE CHARACTER TRAITS 157
Vanity and ambition 157
Playing God 175
Jealousy 178
Envy 180
Greed 183
Hate 185

12 NON-AGGRESSIVE CHARACTER TRAITS 188
Withdrawal 188
Anxiety 189
Timidity 192
The detour syndrome 194
Absence of social graces 199

13 OTHER EXPRESSIONS OF CHARACTER 202
Mood and temperament 202
Manner of speech 204
Schoolroom behaviour 204
Pedantry and prejudice 205
Submissiveness 206
Imperiousness 209
Bad luck 209
Religiosity 210

14 FEELINGS AND EMOTIONS 212
Disjunctive feelings 213
Anger 213
Grief 216
Disgust 217
Fear 217
The misuse of emotion 219
Conjunctive feelings 220
Joy 220
Sympathy 221
Humility 221

15 GENERAL REMARKS ON CHILD-REARING
AND EDUCATION 223

CONCLUSION 229

GLOSSARY OF KEY TERMS   231
BIBLIOGRAPHY   233
INDEX   234

FOREWORD

It is very good news indeed that Oneworld Publications has embarked on publishing new translations of the works of Alfred Adler, the least known, but most relevant to our times, of the three great psychologist/philosophers: Freud, Adler and Jung. Perhaps I should begin this introduction by outlining the contributions of Freud and Jung in order to show the unique approach of Adler.

Freud courageously established the importance of unconscious drives in general, and the sexual instinct in particular, as dynamic elements in the development of the individual: no mean feat in the aftermath of Victorian prudery. Now, however, Freud's influence is waning because his focus of attention was the individual, studied as an isolated being. Society, to Freud, was nothing more than the stern suppressor of human impulses. It placed an intimidating NO! in front of human desires. Freud almost entirely ignored the positive role of human relationships, which are now coming increasingly to the forefront of attention.

Jung opened up a territory all his own. He explored the formative influence of the personal and collective unconscious. Whereas Freud saw the unconscious mind as being mainly an explosive confusion of urgent, often unfulfilled, instinctual impulses, Jung described it as the universal source of creative energy in the psyche, shaping people, societies and history. Jung's work lives on because people recognize a reality behind his ideas that needs continued exploration.

Adler's approach was different again. His central aim was to help people to live effectively. He was, in consequence, more immediately practical than either Freud or Jung. His focus of attention was the person in the world, shaping and being shaped by relationships with others. 'What are we?' 'What is our nature and our role?' 'Where are we going and why?' It was the psychodynamics behind these central questions that engaged Adler's attention. Because of his psychosocial approach, Adler's work has become ever more relevant as the years have passed.

We now know that individuals are nothing without social relationships, while society is nothing without the contributions of the individuals that compose it. The solution to the world's present problems lies in social interest: concerned relationships between people and groups. Adler's last book, *Social Interest*, deals with exactly this point. How to increase social concern is indeed the challenge of our times, a challenge that becomes greater with every year in which selfishness, and the waste and confusion it creates, dominate the affairs not only of humankind but of all life. It is Adler's emphasis on the importance of social feeling that marks his work as being of profound importance today.

So important is it that Adler's unique contribution should be understood that I hope the reader will forgive me if I devote much of this introduction to a brief outline of his central insights. This understanding is all the more important because there was for many years a conspiracy of silence – or, worse, distortion – in academic circles to block out Adler's work as inconvenient to those professionally identified either with Freudian theories or behaviourism.

The great strength of Adler's teaching is its challenging simplicity. Adler agreed with Freud that the early years are powerfully formative in building the individual personality. Freud then became tangled up in elaborate theorizing about infantile sexuality, while Adler asked: 'What does the world seem like to a young child?' His answer was that we all begin our lives small and weak in a world of adult giants, so that the first message of the environment to the child is: 'Overcome your weakness! Make your mark! Be someone who matters!'

We can expect, therefore, that, from the start, striving for significant self-fulfilment becomes children's unconscious aim. This is a powerful activating component in children's psyches, and all to the good, provided that their experiences build courage and confidence as they explore the surrounding world and make contact with the people in it. But suppose confidence is not built up, what then? If the children's blundering efforts to be recognized as people in their own right are greeted by inadequate understanding or by positively hurtful criticism – by lack of love, in brief – then children must be driven to the conclusion that they are not as good as others and are flawed in some dreadful and dispiriting way.

At that point the child's personal authenticity is put at appalling risk because the message is: 'You are no good as you are. You must put up a show of being different.' And that tempts children to turn from accepting their experiences and relationships as the source of self-esteem, and to depend instead either on retreat into a fantasy world of dreams or a compensatory pretence of some kind.

To the extent that most of us were subjected to at least some rejection when we were small, we are all to a greater or lesser degree caught up in this quandary. How far can we depend on our developing encounter with life to give us a sense of personal worth? How far do we feel the need to add something extra in order to impress?

Let us notice at this point that personal effectiveness, not personal perfection, is the aim of striving. Indeed, as the famous Adlerian, Dr Rudolf Dreikurs, used to tell his patients: we must have the courage to be imperfect. Life is about courageous striving, not about attaining perfection. Perfection would be a static condition with no future, whereas life is about movement – movement 'from a minus to a plus' as Adler used to say.

So we see that early in childhood we pick up the idea that we have or have not got what it takes. If, through love, encouragement and understanding from those around us, we acquire a confident feeling of our own personal value and capacity, then we shall embark upon making the most of our abilities within the context of real life and open relationships with other people. If, on the other hand, we are led by neglect, rejection and criticism to distrust what we are, then we shall turn to any of various phoney means intended to impress others, whom we may even regard as a threat.

The point is that whichever life style we pick up unconsciously when we are small and vulnerable we shall tend to cling to throughout life, unless something happens to switch our life style from the mainly ostentatious or illusory to the mainly genuine.

What can be done about it? 'Encourage the young child', Adler used to tell people, and 'Help the young child to come out on the useful side of life'. In what areas? In all areas, ultimately: in work, friendship, love and marriage. But it must be right from the start, in day-to-day living of all kinds, in courageous encounter with the world outside.

At this point we hit a snag because some adults think: 'We must give children everything and then they will become secure and happy adults'. Not true! Life is not about all giving on the one hand and all taking on the other. It is about sharing. The over-indulged child is as ill-equipped for life as the over-criticized one. The pampered child's erroneous life style is the built-in assumption that the best of everything is a proper reward just for existing. When faced with the real world, 'spoilt' children may crumble miserably. The magic has stopped working and they cannot see why. The child is, indeed, 'father to the man' with a nature powerfully conditioned by early self-evaluation – either in a positive or negative direction. For most of us it has been some of each.

So Adler saw us all as striving to become our fullest selves. He recognized, however, that if we had a disruptive start in life we could well go the wrong way about it, while all of us can benefit from honestly examining our motives. Anything unnaturally excessive in behaviour or emotional response suggest a faulty element in our life style. There is no harm in some faltering here and there – that's inevitable – so long as we learn from our mistakes instead of fretting about them over-much or taking flight from challenge. Of course, we all hate our gaffes and failures because they regenerate those feelings of inferiority that most of us carry through life as a residue from our earliest thwarted yearnings to be a success.

I should make it plain that it does not have to be the parents' fault if the child loses confidence and acquires a false life style. Circumstances often take a hand too. A case was brought to my notice of a girl showing decidedly antisocial tendencies. She had excellent parents who were very upset by what they saw as their failure. Actually the trouble arose because the girl was the youngest of three sisters. The first two were pretty children with handsome figures and curly golden tresses. The third was squat and plain, with a straggle of nondescript straight hair. One can understand why such a child acquires an unconscious compulsion to get her own back on life.

It is appropriate to point out here that compensation for inferiority feelings can assume enormous proportions. Both Hitler and Alexander the Great had rather uncertain childhoods. What was their compensatory drive for this early loss of face? Nothing less than to conquer the world! In his bunker, when the end was in sight, Hitler could see no error in his ways. He blamed the German people for what had happened. The strutter went on strutting to the last.

These cases lead up to one of Adler's most penetrating insights, what he called 'organ inferiority'. One thing we cannot do much about is the physical equipment we are born with. If this is deficient in any obvious way – both Hitler and Alexander were on the short side – a child may be extremely conscious of it and seek to compensate for it. This can go both ways. Small men are notoriously 'cocky'. Their message to the world is: 'I may be small but I'll make an impression all the same'. The positive side of 'organ inferiority' is the fantastic courage that handicapped people may show in surmounting their difficulties. In such cases a positive life style linked to the added incentive to overcome disability can lead to almost incredible achievements in spite of difficulties.

One of the best and most lovable headmasters I have ever had the good fortune to know lost his left arm as a boy owing to gangrene following injury in an airgun accident. He had a gentle, humane but down-to-earth mother. She resisted the temptation to cosset her injured darling after he returned from hospital. Her attitude was: 'Now you will have to learn how to live with one arm.' He did, with her help, and built a rich and varied life in spite of his loss. In the end one ceased to be aware of his handicap. But what if he had suffered the loss on top of rejection in childhood?

I would now like to broaden the perspective. The great value of the publication of *Understanding Human Nature* at this time is that it offers the wisdom of Adler when the world is most in need of it. At last we are beginning to get rid of the bullies and dominators. Autocrats are almost always show-offs and compensators. Why do they have to decorate themselves with medals and honours or build homes of outrageous ostentation, if not to reassure themselves about their personal worth? At last, at long last, we are beginning to spot the difference between the socially concerned leaders and the egocentric ones. People are also seeking ways to build genuinely participatory democracy in order to ensure a good future for the world. Yet, at the same time, the world is in desperate peril from the greed and destructiveness of those who neurotically pursue wealth as a source of personal importance. Adler's insights elucidate what is going on and indicate the direction change should take.

To secure the planet, and to release and enrich its resources in the service of an enhanced quality of life, person has to cooperate with person, group with group, and nation with nation. The future depends on the expansion of that very 'social feeling' of which Adler was the prophet. In his last book, Adler wrote: 'The justified expectation persists that in a far-off age, if mankind is given enough time, the power of social feeling will triumph over all that opposes it.'

That far-off age – only fifty years after Adler's death – is now. Such is the acceleration of recent events that we have been brought, with unexpected speed, to the point when we *must* run the world as a caring, interdependent whole, which was Adler's hope and vision. We all have a part to play in fulfilling that expectation, and it is good to have Adler's highly pertinent insights to help us in the struggle to transform life on Earth *in time*. We are moving inexorably towards the twenty-first century which, many writers have suggested, will be the make-or-break century for humankind. We today face a challenge of truly Adlerian scale.

James Hemming
Middlesex, England

NOTE TO THE 1998 EDITION
The intention behind this new, revised and updated edition is to offer a more accessible handbook of Individual Psychology that will appeal not just to Adlerian counsellors but also to students of psychology and interested laypersons. Consequently, sections of the text have been re-ordered to improve the flow of argument, subheadings have been added for greater clarity, and certain expressions have been updated in accordance with contemporary usage. Readers should also note that instead of using 'she' or 'he', the plural pronoun has been used where applicable.

PREFACE

This book is an attempt to acquaint the general public with the fundamentals of Individual Psychology. At the same time it is a demonstration of the practical application of these principles not only to the conduct of our everyday relationships with the world and our fellow human beings, but also to the organization of our personal lives. The book is based on a year's lectures to an audience of hundreds of men and women of all ages and professions at the People's Institute in Vienna. The purpose of the book is first to point out how the misguided behaviour of the individual affects the harmony of our social and communal life; second, to teach individuals to recognize their own mistakes; and finally, to show them how to adjust harmoniously to their social environment. Mistakes in business and science are costly and deplorable, but mistakes in the way we live our lives may endanger life itself. This book is thus dedicated to the task of illuminating humankind's progress towards a better understanding of human nature.

Alfred Adler

INTRODUCTION

'The destiny of man lies in his soul'
– Herodotus

The science of human nature should not be approached with too much presumption and pride. On the contrary, its practitioners are notable for exercising a certain modesty. The understanding of human nature is an enormous problem, whose solution has been the goal of our culture since time immemorial. It is not a science that should be pursued by a few specialists only. Its proper objective must be the understanding of human nature by every human being. This is a sore point with some academics who consider their research to be the exclusive property of a small group of experts.

Owing to the isolated lives we live, few of us know very much about human nature. In the past it was impossible for human beings to live such isolated lives as we do today. From our earliest childhood we have few connections with humanity. The family isolates us from the rest of society. Our whole way of life inhibits that intimate contact with our fellow human beings that is essential for the development of the science and art of understanding human nature. Insufficient contact with our fellow human beings estranges us from them. Our behaviour towards them is often misguided, and our judgements of them frequently incorrect. It is an oft-repeated truism that people walk past and talk past each other. They approach each other as strangers, not only in society at large but also within the very narrow circle of the family. Most parents complain at one time or another that they cannot understand their children, and most children claim that they are misunderstood by their parents. Our whole attitude towards another person is influenced by our understanding of him or her, and this understanding is therefore fundamental to any social relationship. Human beings would get on together more harmoniously if they had a better knowledge of human nature. Our social relationships would then improve, for we all know that most difficulties and disagreements stem from a lack of understanding, and this failure to understand each other properly can lead us to misinterpret or be misled by the façades that other people present.

We will now explain why we are attempting to approach the problem of human nature from a medical science standpoint, with the objective of laying the foundations of an exact science in this wide and hitherto inexact field. We will also examine the premises of this science of human nature, and determine what problems it must solve and what results may be expected from it.

In the first place, psychiatry is a field that demands a tremendous knowledge of human nature. The psychiatrist must gain insight into the mind of the disturbed patient as quickly and accurately as possible. In this field of medicine the practitioner can only diagnose, treat and prescribe effectively when quite sure of what is going on in the patient. Superficiality has no place here. Diagnostic errors are soon apparent, whereas a correct understanding of the disorder leads to successful treatment. In other words, our knowledge of human nature is rigorously tested. In everyday life errors in our judgement of another human being are not necessarily linked with dramatic consequences, for these consequences may occur so long after the mistake has been made that the connection between cause and effect is not obvious. We are frequently astonished when terrible misfortunes occur many years after a misunderstanding of another person. These unhappy events teach us that it is the duty of every human being to acquire a working knowledge of human nature.

Our study of nervous diseases has shown that the psychological disorders, complexes and delusions that are found in nervous diseases are fundamentally no different in structure from the behaviour of normal individuals. The same elements, the same premises, the same developments can be identified. The sole difference is that in the disturbed patient they appear more marked and are more easily recognized. The advantage of this finding is that we can learn from abnormal cases and be on the alert for related characteristics in the normal psyche. It is solely a question of applying the training, ardour and patience that are required by any profession.

The first great discovery was this: the foundations of the human psyche are laid in the earliest days of childhood. In itself this was not such a momentous discovery. Similar findings had been made by great thinkers through the ages. The novelty lay in the fact that we were able to link childhood experiences, impressions and attitudes, so far as we were capable of determining them, with the later phenomena of the psyche in one incontrovertible and continuous pattern. This in turn meant that we could now compare the experiences and attitudes of a person's earliest childhood days with the experiences and attitudes of the mature individual. In so doing we made the important discovery that single manifestations of the psyche must never be regarded as separate entities, and indeed could not be understood unless they were considered as parts of an indivisible whole.

We learned therefore that these single manifestations could only be evaluated when we examined and understood their place in the general behaviour pattern of individuals, in their whole mental universe, their 'life style'. When we did this, we were able to see that their secret childhood goals were exactly in accordance with their attitude in adult life. In short, it became astonishingly clear that, from the standpoint of psychological development, virtually no change had taken place. The actions and words that expressed these goals might have changed, but the fundamental aims and motivations, all directed towards the same psychological objectives, remained constant.

For example, a mature patient who has an anxious personality, whose mind is constantly filled with doubts and suspicions, whose every effort is directed towards isolating himself from society, shows identical character traits and psychological activity in his third and fourth year of life. The only difference is that such traits are more transparent and easier to interpret in small children, who have not yet learned to hide their real feelings. We made it a rule, therefore, to focus the greater part of our investigation on the childhood of our patients. In this way we were often able to infer the characteristics of a mature person whose childhood we were familiar with before we were told about them. The traits we observe in the adult are in fact the direct projection of childhood experiences.

When we listen to the most vivid recollections of patients' childhoods, and know how to interpret these recollections correctly, we can accurately reconstruct the pattern of their present character. In doing this we bear in mind the fact that it is extremely difficult for individuals to deviate from the patterns of behaviour they developed in their early life. Very few individuals have ever been able to change their childhood behaviour patterns, even though in adult life they may have found themselves in entirely different situations. Even a change of attitude in adult life need not necessarily lead to a change of behaviour pattern. The psyche does not change its foundation; individuals retain the same tendencies in childhood and in maturity, leading us to deduce that their goal in life is also unaltered.

There is another reason for concentrating on childhood experience if we wish to change an adult's behaviour pattern. It makes little difference whether we effect a change in the countless experiences and impressions of an individual in maturity; what is essential is to discover our patients' fundamental behaviour patterns. Once we have done so we can perceive their essential character and correctly diagnose their disorder.

Examination of the psychology of children thus became the linchpin of our science, and an enormous amount of research has been dedicated to the study of the first years of life. There is so much material in this field that has never been exploited that there is a good chance of discovering new and important data that may prove immensely valuable to the study of human nature.

At the same time, we investigated ways of preventing the development of bad character traits, in an effort to benefit humankind by our studies. Our researches led quite naturally into the field of education, to which psychologists have contributed for years. Education is a fascinating subject to researchers, for they can apply to it all they have learned from their studies of human nature. Our basic approach must be to identify ourselves closely with every manifestation of a person's psyche, project ourselves into it, and share the joys and sorrows of our fellow human beings, in much the same way that a good portrait painter paints the personality as well as the person.

Most human beings pride themselves on their mastery of the art of understanding human nature and would be offended if any one called their competence into question by demanding they put their knowledge to the test. However, those who genuinely wish to understand human nature have usually experienced the worth and value of others through their own empathy, either by living through their own crises or by observing, and identifying with, the crises of others. The study of human nature may be thought of as an art with many tools at its disposal, an art closely related to all the other arts, and relevant to them all. In literature and poetry, particularly, this is especially significant. Its primary aim must be to broaden our knowledge of human beings, that is to say, it must enable us all to become better, fuller and finer people.

With a knowledge of human nature comes the question of how best to apply that knowledge. Nothing is more likely to arouse resentment, and nothing will attract greater criticism, than brusquely presenting individuals with the stark facts we have discovered in the exploration of their psyche. Students of human nature must learn to tread warily in this minefield. An excellent way to acquire a bad reputation is carelessly to misuse one's knowledge, for example in the desire to show how much one has guessed about the character of one's neighbour at dinner. It is also dangerous to misrepresent the basic principles as iron laws, in order to edify someone who does not understand the science as a whole. Even those who do understand the science would feel insulted by such behaviour. We must repeat what we have already said: the science of human nature compels us to be modest. We must not announce the results of our experiments indiscriminately or hastily. To do so would be understandable in a child who is anxious to parade and show off all his or her accomplishments but this is hardly appropriate behaviour in an adult.

We would like to advise the explorers of the human psyche first to test themselves. They should never force the results of their experiments, won in the service of humankind, onto an unwilling victim. They would only be making fresh difficulties for a still-growing science, and actually defeat their purposes. Psychology would then have to bear the responsibility for the mistakes caused by the unthinking enthusiasm of young scientists. We must exercise wisdom, and always remember that we must have the complete picture in view before we can draw any conclusions about its parts. Such conclusions, furthermore, should be revealed only when we are quite certain that they are to someone's advantage. We can do a great deal of harm by asserting even a correct judgement about character in an inappropriate way, or at an improper moment.

Before going any further, we must examine a certain objection that will already have occurred to many readers. The assertion that an individual's life style remains permanently unchanged will be incomprehensible to many. Surely, they will say, individuals go through so many experiences in life that inevitably change their attitudes. Well, we have to remember that each experience may have many interpretations and that no two people will draw the same conclusion from the same event. This accounts for the fact that we do not always learn from our experiences. Older is not always wiser! We learn to avoid some difficulties, it is true, and develop a philosophical attitude towards others, but our *pattern* of behaviour does not usually change as a result of this. We shall see in the course of our further considerations that individual human beings use all their experiences to the same end. Closer examination reveals that they must all fit into their life style, into the mosaic of their life's pattern. It is proverbial that we actually fashion our own experiences; everyone determines how and what they will experience.

In our daily life we can observe people drawing whatever conclusions they wish from their own experiences. There is the man who makes the same mistake over and over again. If you succeed in convincing him of his mistake, he will react in one of several ways. He may say: 'You're right – I'll know better next time'. This is not a common reaction. He is more likely to protest that he has been making the same mistake for so long that it would be impossible to break the habit. Or he will blame his parents, or his education, for his mistake. He may complain that nobody ever cared for him, or that he was overindulged – or that he was abused as a child. Whatever excuse he makes, whichever alibi he uses, he reveals one thing, and that is a desire to be relieved of further responsibility. In this way he justifies his behaviour and puts himself above criticism. He himself is never to blame. It's always someone else's fault if he did not achieve what he set out to do.

What such individuals overlook is the fact that they themselves have made very few efforts to overcome their faults or avoid repeating their mistakes. They prefer to remain in error, fervently blaming their unsatisfactory upbringing for their shortcomings. They can carry on using the same excuse as long as they live. Any given experience can be interpreted in many ways, and widely varying conclusions can be drawn from it. So we can understand why people do not not change their behaviour pattern, but instead turn and twist and distort their experiences to fit into the pattern. The hardest thing for human beings to do is to know themselves and to change themselves.

Anyone who has not mastered the theory and technique of the science of human nature will experience great difficulty in attempting to re-educate people to be better human beings. They would be operating entirely on the surface, and would be drawn into the error of believing that because the external aspect of things had changed, they had accomplished something significant. Practical cases show us how little such 're-education' will change individuals, and how all the apparent changes are only a front, valueless so long as the basic motivation has not been modified.

The task of helping human beings to transform themselves is not a simple one. It demands a certain optimism and patience, and above all modesty, since the individual seeking help does not do so in order to feed someone else's personal vanity. The process of transformation, moreover, must be conducted in a way that seems justified to the subject. We know that if a tasty and nutritious dish is carelessly prepared and unattractively presented, it will often be rejected.

The science of human nature has yet another aspect, which we may call its social aspect. There is no doubt that people would get on better with each other, and would maintain closer relationships, if they could understand one another better. It would then be impossible for them to disappoint and deceive each other. An enormous danger to society lies in this possibility of deception. This danger must be clearly shown to our colleagues, whom we are introducing to this study. They must bring home to the subjects upon whom they are practising the importance of unknown and unconscious forces. In order to help them they must be aware of all the distortions, dissimulations and deceptions of human behaviour. Consequently we must learn the science of human nature and practise it consciously, always bearing its social implications in mind.

Who is best fitted to gather and make use of the material of this science? We have already noted that it is impossible to practise it on a purely theoretical basis. It is not enough simply to know all the rules and data. It is essential to put our studies into practice and correlate them if we are continuously to sharpen and deepen our insight. This is, of course, the real purpose of the theoretical side of the science of human nature. But we can bring this science to fruition only when we step out into life itself and put into practice the theories we have formed. In the course of our formal education we acquire very little knowledge of human nature, and much of what we learn is incorrect, because contemporary education is still unsuited to giving us a valid knowledge of the human mind. Children are left to evaluate their experiences for themselves, and to take care of their own personal development outside the classroom. There is no tradition for the acquisition of a true knowledge of the human psyche. The science of human nature thus finds itself today in the position that chemistry occupied in the days of alchemy.

In our experience, it is those who have not had their social relationship distorted by the complicated muddle of our educational system who are best adapted to pursue this research into human nature. They are men and women who are, in the last analysis, either optimists or struggling, would-be pessimists who have not yet given in to their pessimism. But social contact with humanity is not enough; there must also be experience.

In the face of our inadequate education, therefore, a real appreciation of human nature will only be gained by certain types of human beings. These include the reformed sinners: either those who have struggled in the whirlpool of the mind, almost drowning in all its mistakes and errors before dragging themselves clear, or those who have been close enough to it to feel its currents drawing them inwards. Others can learn it, of course, especially when they have the gift of identification, the gift of empathy, but the best way of understanding the human psyche is to live through its passions for oneself. Reformed sinners are therefore as valuable in our day and age as they were in the days when the great religions were first founded. They stand much higher than a thousand righteous people. How does this happen? Picture an individual who has lifted himself above the difficulties of life, extricated himself from the swamp, and learned to take bad experiences and make use of them. He truly understands the good and the bad sides of life. No one can compare with him in this understanding, certainly not the righteous ones who have seen only the good side.

When we come across individuals whose behaviour pattern has rendered them incapable of a happy life, we feel duty-bound because of our knowledge of human nature to help them to readjust their false perspectives. We must give them clearer perspectives, perspectives better adapted to the community, more appropriate for the achievement of happiness in this life. We must give them a new way of thinking, indicate another pattern for them in which social feeling and community spirit play a more prominent role. We do not propose to build an ideal emotional life for them. A new viewpoint in itself is of great value to the perplexed, since from this they learn where they have gone astray. According to our view, the strict determinists who consider all human activity to be a process of cause and effect are not so very wrong. But causes can change, and the results of experience acquire entirely new values, when the powers of self-knowledge and self-criticism are alive and functioning well. The ability to know ourselves increases with our ability to determine the origins of our actions and the dynamics of our minds. Once someone has understood this, they have become a different person and can no longer escape the inevitable consequences of their knowledge.

PART ONE

FUNDAMENTALS

OF

CHARACTER DEVELOPMENT

1

WHAT IS THE PSYCHE?

THE CONCEPT OF CONSCIOUSNESS
We attribute a consciousness only to moving, living organisms. The existence of consciousness presupposes free motion, since those organisms that are strongly rooted in one spot have no necessity for it. How unnatural it would be to attribute emotions and thoughts to an oak tree; to contend that the tree might consciously accept the destruction that it could in no way escape; to claim for it a presentiment of that destruction; to attribute reason and free will to it, knowing it could never make use of these qualities. Under such conditions the will and the reason of the oak tree would of necessity remain stillborn.

There is a strict corollary between movement and consciousness. This constitutes the difference between plant and animal. In the evolution of the psyche, therefore, we must consider everything that is connected with movement. All the questions connected with physical movement force the psyche to look ahead, to gather experiences and develop a memory, to equip itself more fully for the business of life. We can thus ascertain from the very beginning that the development of the psyche is connected with movement, and that the evolution and progress of all psychological phenomena are conditioned by the mobility of the organism. This mobility stimulates, promotes and requires an ever greater intensification of mental activity. Imagine individuals who have had every movement planned for them: their mental life will be at a standstill.

THE FUNCTION OF THE PSYCHE
If we regard the function of the psyche from this point of view, we will realize that we are considering the evolution of a heredi-

tary ability, an organ for attack and defence with which the living organism reacts to the situation in which it finds itself. Psychological activity is a complex of aggressive and defensive mechanisms whose final purpose is to guarantee the continued existence of the organism and to enable it to develop in safety. If we accept this premise, then further considerations grow out of it, which we deem necessary for a true conception of the psyche. We cannot imagine psychological activity in isolation. We can only imagine it in relation to its environment, receiving and responding to stimuli from outside.

This premise suggests many considerations about the peculiarities of human beings, their physical nature, their good and bad qualities. These are entirely relative concepts, since there are no objective criteria for judging whether an ability or a physical characteristic is an asset or a liability. These judgements are only relevant to the situation in which individuals find themselves. It is common knowledge that the human foot is, in a sense, a degenerate hand. In an animal that had to climb trees, a human foot would be a definite disadvantage, but for a human being who must walk on flat ground, a foot is so useful that no one would prefer to walk on a 'normal' hand rather than a 'degenerate' foot. It is a fact that in our personal lives, as in the lives of other people, apparent defects should not be considered the source of evil in themselves. Only the context can determine whether they are assets or liabilities.

OUR PURPOSE AND GOAL-DIRECTEDNESS

The first thing we can discover about ourselves is that we are always striving towards a goal. We cannot, therefore, imagine the human spirit as a single, static entity. We can best imagine it as a collection of moving parts, developed from a common origin, which strive to achieve a single goal. This teleology, this striving for a goal, is basic to the concept of adaptation, and the life of the psyche is inconceivable without a goal towards which all our efforts are directed.

Our mental life is determined by our goal. No human being can think, feel, wish or dream without all these activities being determined, continued, modified and directed towards an ever-present objective. This results from the necessity for the organism to adapt itself and respond to the environment. The physical and psychological phenomena of human life are based upon the fundamental principles we have demonstrated. It is impossible to conceive of psychological development except within a pattern depending on an ever-present objective, which is determined in turn by the dynamics of life. The goal itself we may conceive either as changing or as static. On this basis, all the phenomena of our psychological existence may be considered as preparations for some future situation. The soul, indeed, seems to consist chiefly of a force moving towards a goal, and Individual Psychology considers all the manifestations of the human spirit as though they were directed towards such a goal.

Knowing the goal of individuals and knowing also something of the world, enables us to understand the meaning of the ways they express themselves, and of the direction their life takes, and how these things function as a preparation for their goal. We also need to know what steps each individual must take to reach their goal – just as we can know the trajectory of a stone if we let it fall to earth – although people do not follow a fixed, natural law because the ever-present goal is always in flux. If, however, everyone has an ever-present goal, then every psychological tendency must move towards it, as though it were indeed obeying some natural law. A law governing our psychological life does exist, to be sure; but it is not a natural law like the law of gravity; it is a man-made law. To believe there is sufficient evidence to justify our speaking of a natural law of the psyche is to be deceived by appearances. Anyone who believes they have demonstrated the unchangeable and predetermining power of circumstances is playing with loaded dice. After all, if a painter sets out to paint a picture, the world attributes to him all the attitudes appropriate to an individual with that aim in mind. He will do all the usual things, with all the expected results, just as though there were a natural law at work. But is he under any necessity to paint the picture? Given his free will, we must deduce that it is his striving to attain his goal that keeps him putting the paint on the canvas.

There is a difference between physical movements and movements of the human psyche. All the questions about free will hinge upon this important point. Nowadays it is believed that human will is not free. It is true that human will becomes bound as soon as it commits itself to a particular goal. And since circumstances in the cosmic, physical and social relationships of humankind frequently determine this goal, it is not surprising that our psychological life should so often appear to be ruled by immutable natural laws. But if a man, for example, denies his relationships to society and rebels against them, or if he refuses to adapt himself to the realities of life, then all these seemingly immutable laws are abrogated and a new law appears that is determined by the new goal. In the same way, the law of communal life does not bind individuals who have become perplexed by life and attempt to deny their feelings for their fellow human beings. And so I repeat once again that movement in our mental life can only take place when an appropriate goal has been chosen.

On the other hand, it is possible to discover the goal of individuals from observing their present activities. This is particularly important because so few people know exactly what their goal is. On the practical level, this is the procedure we must follow if we are to gain some knowledge of humankind. Since actions may have many meanings, this is not always so simple. We can, however, take several examples of a person's known behaviour, compare them, and plot them on a graph. In this way we arrive at an understanding of a human being by connecting two points in which a definite psychological attitude was expressed, with the time difference indicated by a curve. This method is used to obtain a clear representation of a person's life. An example will serve to illustrate how we may discover a pattern of behaviour in an adult that reproduces with astonishing consistency the attitudes of childhood.

A thirty-year-old man of extraordinarily aggressive character, who has achieved success and acclaim despite a difficult childhood, comes to the therapist in a deep depression, complaining that he has no desire to work, or even to live. He explains that he is about to become engaged, but that he views the future with trepidation. He is tormented by jealousy and is close to breaking off his engagement. The facts that he cites to explain his jealousy are not very convincing, and since the young lady in question cannot be blamed, the obvious distrust he shows calls for investigation. He is one of those men who approach another individual, feel attracted, but immediately assume an aggressive attitude that destroys the very contact they wanted to establish.

Now let us plot the graph of this man's life style as described above, by taking one event in his life and seeking to link it with his present attitude. As is our usual practice, we ask for his first childhood memory, even though we know it is not always possible to test its objective truth. He tells us that he was in the market-place with his mother and his younger brother. The market-place was crowded and his mother picked him up, but then she realized she should carry the younger child, put him down again and picked up his younger brother, leaving our patient buffeted by the crowd and very perplexed. At that time he was four years old. In the recital of this memory, exactly the same points emerge that we heard in the description of his present complaint. He is not sure of his position as the favoured one, and he cannot bear to think that someone else might supplant him. Once the connection is made clear to him, our patient, quite astonished, sees the relationship immediately.

The psychological goal towards which every human being's actions are directed is determined by those influences and impressions that are imposed on children by their environment. The concept of the ideal state – that is, the goal – of each human being is probably formed in the first months of life. Even at this time certain sensations play a role in evoking a response of joy or sorrow in the child. Here the first traces of a philosophy of life come to the surface, expressed in the most primitive terms. The fundamental factors that influence the psyche are founded in infancy. Upon these foundations a superstructure is built that may be modified, influenced or transformed. A multiplicity of influences soon force children into a definite attitude towards life and condition their own particular response to the problems life poses.

Investigators who believe the characteristics of an adult to be discernible in infancy are not far wrong. This accounts for many people's belief that character is hereditary. But the idea that character and personality are inherited from one's parents is universally harmful. Among other things, it hinders educators in their task and erodes their confidence, and enables them to shirk their responsibilities simply by blaming heredity for their pupils' failures. This, of course, is quite contrary to the purpose of education.

Our civilization plays an important role in the development of a person's psychological goal. It sets up rules and boundaries against which children struggle until they discover how to fulfil their wishes in a way that promises both security and a successful adaptation to life. How much security children demand in relation to the everyday realities of our society may be learned early in their lives. By security we do not mean only security from danger, but that further element of safety that guarantees our continued existence under optimum circumstances. Children secure this by demanding a safety margin greater than is strictly necessary for the satisfaction of their basic needs, greater than would be necessary for a quiet life. Thus arises a new tendency in their psychological development, a tendency towards dominance and superiority.

Like adults, children want to surpass all their rivals. They strain for a superiority that will guarantee them the security and adaptation synonymous with the goal they have previously set for themselves. Thus a certain psychological uneasiness develops that becomes stronger as time goes on. Suppose now that the world begins to require a more powerful response. If in this time of need children do not believe in their own ability to overcome their difficulties, we will see strenuous evasions and complicated excuses, which serve only to emphasize their underlying thirst for glory.

In these circumstances the immediate goal frequently becomes the avoidance of all major difficulties. Children fight shy of difficulties or wriggle out of them in order to evade life's demands temporarily. We must understand that human psychological reactions are not fixed and absolute: every response is only a partial one, temporarily valid but not to be considered the final solution to a problem. In the development of the child's psyche especially, we are reminded that we are dealing with a purely temporary crystallization of the idea of a goal. We cannot apply to the juvenile psyche the same criteria we use to evaluate the adult psyche. In the case of children we must look further and guess at the final state to which their energies and activities will eventually lead them. If we could see into their mind, we could understand how all the expressions of their character are directed towards the ideal they have created for themselves as the crystallization of their desired final adaptation to life.

We must look at things from the children's point of view if we want to know why they act as they do. The basic attitude connected with their point of view directs children in various ways. First, there is an optimistic attitude to life in which children are confident that they can readily solve any problems they come across. Under these circumstances they will grow up with all the characteristics of individuals who consider the tasks of life easily within their power. In these cases we see the development of courage, openness, frankness, responsibility, hard work and so on. The opposite of this is the development of pessimism. Imagine the goal of children who are not confident of being able to solve their problems! How dismal the world must appear to such children! Here we find timidity, introspection, distrust and all those other characteristics and traits with which weaklings seek to defend themselves. Their goal will lie beyond their reach, but also far away from the front line where life's real battles are fought.

2

SOCIAL ASPECTS
OF MENTAL LIFE

In order to know how someone thinks, we have to examine their relationship to their fellow human beings. Person-to-person relationships are governed on the one hand by the very nature of the cosmos, and are thus subject to change. On the other hand, they are determined by human institutions such as political traditions in the community or nation. We cannot comprehend the workings of the human psyche without at the same time understanding these social relationships.

THE ABSOLUTE TRUTH
The psyche cannot act as an independent agent. Problems constantly crop up, and the need to solve them tends to govern the direction in which the psyche is able to develop. These problems are indivisibly bound up with the logic of our communal life; the demands of the community influence individuals, but seldom allow themselves to be influenced by them, and then only to a certain degree. The existing conditions of our communal life, however, cannot yet be considered final. They are too complex and too variable. Moreover, we are too enmeshed in our own relationships to be able to cast sufficient light on the problem of the psyche to understand it thoroughly.

Our sole recourse in this dilemma is to accept the logic of our communal life on earth as though it were an ultimate, absolute truth that can be approached step by step, after the correction of any mistakes and errors arising from our incomplete social organization and our limited capabilities as human beings. An important point in our considerations is the materialistic stratification of society described by Marx and Engels. According to their teachings, the economic basis of a community determines

the ideological thinking and behaviour of individuals. Our conception of the 'logic of human communal life', of the 'absolute
truth', is in part an acceptance of existing concepts. History, and
our insight into the life of the individual (that is, Individual
Psychology), have taught us, however, that it is occasionally convenient for individuals to give a mistaken response to the
demands of a socio-economic system. In attempting to evade the
system, they may become inextricably entangled in the convolu-
tions of their own mistaken reactions. Our way to the absolute
truth will lead us past countless errors.

THE NEED FOR COMMUNAL LIFE

The rules of communal life are just as self-explanatory as the laws
of the weather, which compel us to take certain measures: desire
for protection against the cold leads to house-building, and so
on. The human compulsion towards the community and
communal life is revealed in institutions whose forms we do not
need to understand fully; for example in religion, where group
worship creates a bond between members of the congregation.
Just as the conditions of our lives are determined in the first
place by the facts of the universe, further conditions arise
through the social and communal life of human beings and the
laws and regulations springing from it. The needs of the
community govern all human relationships. Communal life
predates the individual life of humanity. In the history of human
civilization no way of life has emerged of which the foundations
were not laid communally; human beings developed not singly
but in communities. This is very easily explained. The whole
animal kingdom demonstrates the fundamental law that species
whose members are individually incapable of facing the battle for
self-preservation gain additional strength through herd life.

Darwin long ago drew attention to the fact that weak
animals were never found living alone. We are forced to consider
human beings among these weaker animals, because they too are
not strong enough to live alone. Without tools they can only
offer the feeblest resistance to the depredations of nature. They
need all manner of artificial aids merely to stay alive on this
planet. Imagine being alone, without any tools except one's bare
hands, in a primitive forest! One would be more at risk than any

other living creature. Human beings are generalists, not specialists. They have neither speed nor power, not the teeth of the
carnivore, nor the sharp eyes or acute hearing that warn other
creatures of danger. Humanity needs a whole battery of tools to
guarantee its existence. Our diet, our physical characteristics and
our life style all demand these tools.

Now we can understand that human beings survive only in
particularly favourable conditions. These favourable conditions
have been created by communal living. Communal living
became a necessity because the community and the division of
labour through which all individuals subordinate themselves to
the group, ensured the continued existence of the species. Only
division of labour (which is another way of saying civilization) is
capable of ensuring that the tools of survival are available to
humankind. Only after they had learned about the division of
labour did humans learn how to assert themselves. Consider the
difficulties of childbirth and the extraordinary care necessary for
keeping a child alive during its infancy! This prolonged care and
attention could only be exercised where division of labour
existed. Think of the number of illnesses and disorders that
human flesh is heir to, particularly in infancy, and you have some
conception of the inordinate amount of care each human life
demands, and some understanding of the need for communal
living. The community is the best guarantor of the continued
existence of human beings!

SECURITY AND ADAPTATION

From the above we may conclude that the human being,
compared with other life forms, is an inferior organism. This
feeling of inferiority and insecurity is always present in the
human consciousness. It is a constant stimulus to the discovery
of better ways of adapting to life on earth. This stimulus forces
humans to seek situations in which they do not appear at a disadvantage in relation to the rest of the natural world.

The instinct for communal living has served humanity in
one particular way: it has fostered our most notable instrument
for protection against the rigours of the environment – the
human mind. It is the human intellect that has enabled such a
vulnerable creature to achieve successful adaptation and security.

It would have been much more difficult to take primitive humans and make them capable of subduing natural enemies by the addition of anatomical defence mechanisms such as horns, claws or teeth. The human mind could render immediate first aid and compensate for physical deficiencies. Constant feelings of inadequacy stimulated humanity's foresight and ability to avoid danger, and caused the mind to develop to its present condition as an organ of thinking, feeling and acting. Society has played an essential role in the process of adaptation, and the mind must interact from the very beginning with the conditions of communal life. All its faculties are developed upon one fundamental principle: the logic of communal life.

We should doubtless find the next stage in the development of humanity's mental capacities in human notions of logic, with its innate necessity for universal applicability. Only that which is universally useful is logical. Articulate and logical speech, that miracle which sets human beings apart from all other animals, is a vital instrument of communal life. The phenomenon of speech, whose form clearly indicates its social origins, cannot be divorced from this same concept of universal usefulness. Speech would be absolutely unnecessary for an individual living alone; it is of use only in a social setting. It is a product of communal life, a bond between the individuals of the community. The social origin of speech is attested in those individuals who have grown up under circumstances where contact with other human beings has been difficult or impossible. Some of these individuals have severed all connections with society deliberately; others are the victims of circumstance. In either case, they suffer from speech defects or impediments and never acquire the knack of learning foreign languages. It is as though this skill can be acquired and retained only when contact with humanity is well established.

Speech is enormously important in the development of the human spirit. Logical thinking is possible only through the use of language, which gives us the means to build concepts and to identify differences in values. Our very thoughts and emotions are understandable only when we accept that they are not unique to ourselves; our joy in beautiful things is based in the knowledge that recognition, understanding and feeling for beauty are universal. Thus it follows that thoughts and concepts, like reason, understanding, logic, ethics and aesthetics, are not a private matter but have their origin in the social life of humanity. They are bonds between individuals whose purpose is to preserve civilization.

SOCIAL FEELING

We may now understand that any rules that serve to secure the existence of humankind, such as legal codes, totem and taboo, superstition or education, must be governed by the concept of the community and be appropriate to it. We have already mentioned this idea in connection with religion. We find adaptation to the community is the most important psychological function, both in the individual and in society. What we call justice and righteousness and consider most valuable in the human character, is essentially nothing more than the fulfilment of the conditions that arise from the social needs of mankind. These conditions give shape to the spirit and direct its activity. Responsibility, loyalty, frankness, love of truth and the like are virtues that have been built up and maintained only by the universally valid principle of communal life. We can judge a character as bad or good only through the community's eyes. Good character, like achievement in science, politics or art, becomes noteworthy only when it has proved its universal value. The criteria by which we can measure individuals are determined by their value to humankind in general. We compare individuals with an ideal picture of a human being, with people who perform the tasks and conquer the difficulties that lie before them in a way that is useful to society in general, people who have developed their social feeling to a high degree. To quote one of our co-workers, Carl Furtmüller, these people 'play the game of life according to the laws of society'.

In the course of our investigations it will become increasingly evident that no well-adjusted person can grow up without cultivating a deep sense of fellowship with humanity and practising the art of being a complete human being.

3

THE CHILD AND SOCIETY

Society imposes certain obligations on us that influence the norms and forms of our lives, as well as the development of our minds. Society has an organic basis. The point where the individual and society meet may be found in the fact that the race consists of two sexes. In the community created by a male and female partnership, human beings satisfy the impulse towards life, achieve security and guarantee their happiness. When we consider the lengthy development of a child, we are reminded that human life cannot develop without the presence of a protecting community. The various obligations of life carry within themselves the necessity for a division of labour which, far from isolating human beings, strengthens their links with one another. Everyone must help their neighbour; everyone must feel connected to their fellows. That is how inter-personal relations began. We must now discuss in more detail some of the relationships that await children upon their birth.

INFANCY
All children, dependent as they are on the help of the community, finds themselves face to face with a world that gives and takes, that expects adaptation but satisfies their need for life. The fulfilment of their instincts is hindered by obstacles that are painful to confront. They realize at an early age that there are other human beings who are able to satisfy their needs more completely, and are better equipped for life. Their psyche is born, one might say, in those childhood situations that demand integration in order to make normal life possible. The psyche accomplishes this by evaluating each situation and negotiating it with the maximum satisfaction of instincts and the least possible discomfort.

In this way children learn to overvalue the size and strength required to open doors or move heavy objects, or the right of others to give commands and claim obedience. The desire to grow, to become as strong as or even stronger than others, arises within them. To dominate those around them becomes their chief purpose in life, since their elders, although they treat the younger children as inferior, are obligated to them because of their very weakness. Two possibilities of action lie open. On the one hand they can imitate the activities and methods they see the adults using, and on the other hand they can display their weakness, which is seen by these same adults as an inescapable demand for help. We shall continually find this branching of psychological tendencies in children.

The formation of character types begins at this early age. Whereas some children develop in the direction of the acquisition of power and choose to seek recognition through courage and self-assertiveness, others seem to trade on their own weaknesses and set out to demonstrate them in all manner of ways. One has only to observe the attitude, expression and bearing of individual children to discover which of the two groups they fit into. Each character type has meaning only if we understand its relationship to its environment, and children's environments are usually reflected in their behaviour.

At the very basis of children's development lies their struggle to compensate for their weaknesses; a thousand talents and capabilities arise from our feelings of inadequacy. The situations that life may present to children differ to an extraordinary degree between individuals. In some cases we are dealing with an environment that is threatening to children and gives them the impression that the whole world is hostile territory. The incomplete perspectives of children's thought processes create this dramatic impression. If their upbringing does not counteract this fallacy, the personality of such children may develop so that they always act as if the world really were hostile territory. Their impression of its hostility will grow with every difficulty they encounter. This often happens in the case of children born with physical disadvantages of some kind. Such children respond to their environment with an attitude entirely different from those who come into the world without such disadvantages. This so-called organ inferiority can express itself through difficulties with movement, inadequacies of individual organs, or in generally low resistance to infection resulting in frequent illnesses.

Physical inadequacies are not the only source of children's difficulties in facing the world. Any unreasonable demands made on children by a misguided family (or the unfortunate manner in which these demands are presented) are comparable to material obstacles in their environment. Children who are trying to adapt themselves suddenly find obstacles put in their way, especially when they grow up in a home that has itself lost heart and is governed by a pessimism only too quickly transferred to the children.

THE EFFECT OF OBSTACLES

When we consider the obstacles that confront children from every angle, it is hardly surprising that their response is not always appropriate. Their thought processes have only had a short time to develop, and children find it necessary to conform to the immutable laws of reality while their powers of adjustment are still immature. To them, life is one long experiment. Behind every example of an inappropriate response to the environment is a whole series of attempts by their psyche to respond correctly and to progress through life. Particularly interesting as an expression of a behaviour pattern is the adolescent response to a given situation. The manner of the response gives us an insight into the psyche. At the same time we must recognize the fact that the responses of any individual, like those of society, are not to be judged according to a fixed pattern.

The obstacles children encounter in their psychological development usually result in the stunting or distortion of their social feeling. These obstacles may be divided into two categories. There are those that stem from defects in children's material environment, such as abnormal relationships in their economic, social, racial or family circumstances, and those that arise out of physical disadvantage. Our culture is based on health and adequacy. Thus children with a major physical disadvantage are also at a disadvantage in solving the problems of life. Children who learn to walk late, or who have difficulties of any kind in locomotion, or those who are slow in learning to speak or are clumsy for a long time because their cerebral function is ing more slowly than normal, belong in this group. We all know children who are constantly bumping themselves, are clumsy and slow, and carry with them a burden of physical and mental distress. They receive scant sympathy from a world which was not created with their needs in mind. Many problems may arise from such development. Of course there is always the possibility that in the fullness of time such children will overcome their disabilities for themselves without any psychological ill-effects. This can happen, so long as the difficulties have not led to an entrenched sense of despair whose effects will be felt in later life. Such a state of affairs may be complicated, in addition, by economic disadvantage.

The laws of human society are a closed book to children inadequately equipped to take their place in it. They look with suspicion and mistrust on the opportunities they see developing around them, and tend to isolate themselves and avoid their tasks. They have a very keen sense of life's hostility, which they unconsciously exaggerate. Their interest in the bitter side of life is much greater than its brighter side. For the most part, they overrate both, so that theirs is a lifelong attitude of belligerency. They demand an extraordinary amount of attention, and of course they think far more of themselves than of others. They see the necessary obligations of life more as difficulties than as stimuli. Soon a gulf opens up between them and their environment, a gulf that is continually widened by their hostility to their fellows. Then they approach every experience with exaggerated caution, estranging themselves more and more from real life, and succeed only in creating fresh difficulties for themselves.

Similar difficulties may arise when the normal tenderness of parents towards their children is not adequately manifested. Whenever this occurs, the consequences for the development of children are serious. The children's attitude becomes so entrenched that they cannot recognize love or make proper use of it, because their instincts for tenderness have never been developed. It will be difficult to teach children who have grown up in a loveless or undemonstrative family to express any kind of tenderness. Their whole attitude to life will be escapist, an evasion of all love and affection. The same effect may also result from unthinking parents, teachers or other adults teaching children that love and tenderness are improper, ridiculous or unmanly. Many children are taught, for example, that gentleness is weakness. This escapist attitude is especially marked in those children who have often been ridiculed. Such children are genuinely afraid of showing emotions because they fear that their wish to show affection towards others is ridiculous. They fight against normal tenderness as though it were an instrument of enslavement or degradation.

In this way barriers to our capacity to love may be set up in early childhood. After a brutal education in which all tenderness is dammed up and repressed, children withdraw from the circle of their environment and lose, little by little, contacts that are of the utmost psychological and spiritual importance to them. Sometimes just one person they know offers an opportunity to be close; when this happens, children form a deep relationship with this friend. This accounts for the individual whose social relationships can never be stretched to include more than one other human being. The example of the boy who felt neglected when he noticed that his mother showed affection only to his younger brother, and therefore wandered through life searching for the warmth and affection he had missed in earliest childhood, demonstrates the problems such a person may experience in life. It goes without saying that the development of such individuals is fraught with difficulty.

An upbringing characterized by too much tenderness is as harmful as one without any. Pampered children, just as much as unloved ones, labour under great difficulties. Pampered children develop an inordinate and insatiable craving for affection, with the result that they bind themselves to someone and refuse to let go. The value of affection becomes so accentuated by various misunderstood experiences that the children conclude that their own love enforces certain responsibilities on the grown-ups around them. This is easily accomplished: a child says to his parents, 'Because I love you, you must do this or that'. This type of dogma is fairly common within the family circle. No sooner do such children recognize this tendency in others than they increase their own demonstrations of affection to intensify their dependence on the favour of others.

One must always watch out for such excessive attachment and tenderness towards one particular member of the family. There is no doubt that such an upbringing has a harmful influence on the future of children. Their life becomes bound up in a struggle to keep the affection of others by fair means or foul. To accomplish this they do not hesitate to use any means at their disposal. They may attempt to subjugate their rival, a brother or sister, or busy himself with tale-telling against them. Such children will actually incite their siblings to misdeeds so that they can sun themselves in the love and approval of their parents. They apply social pressures on their parents in order to focus their attention on them. To this end they will leave no stone unturned until they occupy the limelight and appear more important than anyone else. They may be lazy, or badly behaved, for the sole purpose of compelling their parents to give them more of their time. Or they may become model children so others will reward them with their attention.

Thus we may conclude that anything may become a means to an end, once the psychological pattern is fixed. The children may develop in an antisocial direction in order to achieve their goal, or they may become perfectly behaved and admirable, with the same goal in view. In any group of children there is usually one whose attention-seeking takes the form of unruly behaviour, while another, being more shrewd, attains the same goal through conspicuous virtue.

With spoilt children we may also group those who have had every difficulty removed form their path. These children's potential and capabilities have been belittled through kindness: they have never been allowed the opportunity of shouldering their responsibilities, and have been denied every chance to prepare themselves for adult life. No one teaches them to form relationships with people who actually want to get to know them, and they are certainly not capable of forming relationships with those who, as a result of difficulties and errors in their own childhood, shun human contact. Such children are utterly unprepared for life because they have never had the opportunity to practise overcoming difficulties. As soon as they step out of the hothouse atmosphere that makes their home into a tiny kingdom, they inevitably encounter bitter defeats and disappointments, simply because they cannot find anyone to give them the inordinate care, consideration and protection they have been brought up to expect as their due.

All problems of this type have one thing in common: to a greater or lesser degree, they tend to isolate the child. For example, children with digestive disorders assume a special attitude towards nutrition, and as a result go through an entirely different development process from children with normal digestion. Children with defective organs have a peculiar life style that may eventually drive them into isolation. There are other children who do not clearly understand how they fit into their environment, and actually try to avoid it. They cannot make friends, they stand apart from the games of their companions and, either envious of their peers or despising their games, busy themselves in their own private world.

Isolation also threatens children who grow up under the pressure of a too-strict upbringing. To them, the world is an unfriendly place, because they have come to expect bad experiences there. Either they assume that they must suffer in silence, or they feel like crusaders, ready to do battle with the environment they have always found so hostile. Such children feel that life and its tasks are inordinately difficult and, understandably, will be largely preoccupied with the defence of their personal space, desperately anxious to avoid any invasion of territory. Burdened by an exaggerated cautiousness, they develop a tendency to sidestep any major problem rather than to risk a possible defeat.

Another common characteristic of all such children, which is indicative of their inadequately developed social feeling, is that they think more about themselves than others. This trait clearly reflects their whole development towards a pessimistic view of the world. It is impossible for them to lead happy and fulfilled lives unless they can find a way of changing their false behaviour pattern.

THE INDIVIDUAL AS A SOCIAL BEING
We have explained in Chapter 2 how the personality of individuals can only be understood when we see them in their social environment, and assess them in their particular situation in the world. By situation we mean their place in the scheme of things

and their attitude towards their environment and the problems of life, such as the challenges of work, friendships and everyday dealings with their fellow human beings. In this way we have been able to determine that the impressions crowding in upon all individuals from their earliest infancy influence their attitude all through their lives. We can even determine how children stand in relation to life a few months after birth. It is impossible to confuse the behaviour of two infants of this age because they have already demonstrated well-defined behaviour patterns that become even clearer as they develop. Variations from the pattern simply do not occur.

Children's whole minds are increasingly permeated by their social relationships. The first evidence of inborn social feeling unfolds in an early search for affection, which leads children to seek the proximity of adults. Children's love is always directed towards others and not, as Freud would say, towards their own bodies. Depending on the individual, these erotic strivings vary in their intensity and the way they manifest themselves. In children over two years old these differences may be demonstrated in their speech. Only under the stress of the most severe psychopathological degeneration do children lose the social feeling that by this time has become firmly established within them. This social feeling remains throughout life, changed, coloured, circumscribed in some cases, enlarged and broadened in others, until it touches not only the members of the immediate family, but also the extended family, the nation and finally, the whole of humanity. It may also extend beyond these boundaries and express itself towards animals, plants, lifeless objects and finally towards the whole cosmos. According to our studies, it is essential to deal with the individual as a social being. Once we have grasped this, we have gained an important aid to our understanding of human behaviour.

4

THE WORLD WE LIVE IN

OUR MENTAL UNIVERSE

Because all human beings must adjust to their environment, their psyche is capable of taking in a multitude of impressions from the outer world. In addition, the psyche pursues a definite aim according to its own interpretation of the world, and along the lines of an ideal behaviour pattern dating from early childhood. Although we cannot define this cosmic interpretation and this goal in precise terms, we can nevertheless describe it as an ever-present aura, which always contrasts with the feeling of personal inadequacy. Psychological developments occur only where there is a personal goal. The construction of a goal, as we know, pre-supposes the capacity for change and a certain freedom of movement. The spiritual enrichment resulting from freedom of movement is not to be undervalued. When children stand up unaided for the first time, they enter an entirely new world, and in that second they somehow sense a hostile atmosphere. In their first attempts at movement, and particularly in getting to their feet and learning to walk, they experience various degrees of difficulty that may either strengthen their hope for the future or destroy it. Impressions that grown-ups might consider unimportant or commonplace may have an enormous influence on children's psyche and entirely shape their view of the world in which they live.

Thus children who have had difficulties in locomotion construct an ideal for themselves that is permeated by power and speed. We can discover this ideal by asking them what their favourite games are, or what they would like to do when they grow up. Usually such children answer that they want to be racing drivers, engine drivers and so on – signifying clearly their desire to overcome every difficulty that hinders their freedom of movement. Their life's goal is to reach a stage where their feeling of inferiority and their sense of handicap are replaced by perfect freedom of motion. It is clear that such a sense of handicap can easily arise in the psyche of children who have developed slowly or have suffered frequent illness. Similarly, children who have come into the world with defective vision attempt to translate the entire world into more intense visual images. Children with hearing defects show a keen interest in certain sounds that they find pleasing: in short, they become 'musical'.

Of all the tools with which children attempt to conquer the world, the sense organs play the most important part in determining their essential relationships with the world in which they live. It is through the sense organs that they construct their own cosmic picture. Above all, it is the eye that confronts the environment, since it is primarily the visual world that forces itself upon the attention of every human being and feeds them the main data in their experience. The visual picture of the world in which we live is uniquely significant in that it deals with unchanging images, in contrast with the other sense organs, the ear, the nose, the tongue and the skin, which are sensitive only to temporary stimuli. There are individuals, however, in whom the ear is the predominant organ. Here a fund of information is built up based upon acoustic data. In this case the psyche might be said to have a predominantly auditory pattern.

Less frequently we find individuals in whom motor activity is predominant. Another type is characterized by a keen interest in the stimuli of smell or taste, of which the first group, those more sensitive to smell, is at a relative disadvantage in our civilization. Then there are a number of children in whom the musculature plays the leading role. This group comes into the world characterized by great restlessness, which forces them to constant movement in childhood, and to greater activity in maturity. Such individuals are interested only in activities in which the muscles play the chief role. They exhibit their activity even during sleep, as anyone can verify by observing them restlessly tossing about in their beds. We must class 'fidgety' children, whose restlessness is often considered a bad thing, in this category.

In general we can say that virtually every child approaches the world with heightened interest in one particular organ or group of organs, whether these are their sense organs or their musculature. All children construct a picture of the world in which they live from the impressions that their most sensitive organ gathers from their surroundings. Consequently we can only understand human beings when we know what sense organs or groups of organs they approach the world with, because all their relationships are coloured by this fact. We can only interpret their actions and reactions if we first understand the influence their organic defects have had on their attitude to the world – on their cosmic picture – in childhood, and thus on their later development.

THE WAY WE SEE THE WORLD

The ever-present psychological goal that determines all our activity also influences the choice, intensity and activity of those particular psychological faculties that give shape and meaning to our picture of the world. This explains the fact that each of us experiences a very specific segment of life, or of a particular event, or indeed of the entire world in which we live. We all ignore the whole and value only that which is appropriate to our goal. Thus we cannot fully understand the behaviour of any human beings without a clear comprehension of the secret goal they are pursuing; nor can we evaluate every aspect of their behaviour until we know how their whole activity has been influenced by this goal.

Perception

Impressions and stimuli from the outer world are transmitted by the sense organs to the brain, where certain traces of them may be retained. These traces form the foundations of the world of imagination and the world of memory. But a perception can never be compared with a photographic image because in the case of a perception something of the peculiar and individual quality of the person who perceives is inextricably bound up with it. One does not *perceive* everything that one sees. No two human beings react to the same picture in quite the same way. If you ask them what they have seen they will give very different answers.

Children perceive only those elements in their environment that fit into a behaviour pattern previously determined by a variety of causes. The perceptions of children whose visual sense is especially well developed have a predominantly visual character. The majority of humankind is probably visually biased. Others fill in the mosaic picture of the world they have created for themselves with predominantly auditory perceptions. These perceptions need not be strictly identical with actuality. Everyone is capable of reconfiguring and rearranging their contacts with the outer world to fit their own life pattern. The individuality and uniqueness of human beings consists in what they perceive and how they perceive. Perception is more than a simple physical phenomenon; it is a psychological function from which we may draw the most far-reaching conclusions concerning the inner life.

Memory

As we saw in Chapter 1, the development of the psyche is intimately related to the mobility of the human organism, and its activities are determined by the goal and purpose of this mobility. It is necessary for individuals to collect and arrange their relationships with the world in which they live, and their psyche, as an organ of adaptation, must develop all those faculties that play a role in their defence and are otherwise active in maintaining their existence. One such faculty is the memory, whose functions are dominated by the necessity for adaptation. Without memories it would be impossible to take any precautions for the future. We may deduce that all recollections have an unconscious purpose within themselves. They are not fortuitous phenomena, but convey clear messages of encouragement or of warning. There is no such thing as a random or meaningless recollection. Memory is selective. We can evaluate a recollection only when we are certain about the goal and purpose that it serves. It is not necessary to wonder why we remember certain things and forget others. We remember those events whose recollection is important for a specific psychological reason, because those recollections further an important underlying movement. Likewise we forget all those events that detract from the fulfilment of a plan. Thus we find that memory, too, is subordinated to the business of purposive adaptation, and that every memory is dominated by the unifying theme or goal that directs the personality as a whole. A lasting recollection, even though it is a distorted one (as is often the case in children, whose memories are frequently 'loaded' or one-sided), may move out of our conscious minds and appear as an attitude, an emotional tone or even a philosophical point of view, if this is what is needed for the attainment of the desired goal.

Imagination

Nowhere does the uniqueness of individuals show more clearly than in the products of their imagination. By imagination we mean the power of perception independent of the presence of an object giving rise to it. In other words, the imagination reproduces perception, another example of the creative power of the psyche. The product of imagination is not only the repetition of a past perception (which in itself is a product of the creative power of the mind), but is an entirely new and unique product built upon it, just as the original perception was created on the basis of physical sensations.

There are fantasies that far exceed the general run of imaginings in their sharpness of focus. Such visions seem so vivid and real that they transcend mere fantasy and actually influence the behaviour of individuals as though an objective stimulus were present. When fantasies assume this air of reality we call them hallucinations.

The conditions for the production of hallucinations are in no way different from those that determine day-dreams. Every hallucination is an artistic creation of the psyche, designed and fashioned according to the goals and purposes of the particular individual who creates it. Let us illustrate this with an example.

An intelligent young woman married against the advice of her parents. Her parents were so angry at her decision that they broke off all contact with her. In the course of time the young woman became convinced that her parents had treated her badly, but many attempts at reconciliation failed because of pride and obstinacy on both sides. As a result of her marriage this young woman, who belonged to a wealthy and aristocratic family, had fallen into rather impoverished circumstances. Yet

throughout all this no one could observe any signs of unhappiness in her marriage. Anyone would have been convinced that
she had adjusted very well, except for the appearance in her life
of a very strange phenomenon.

This girl had grown up pampered by her father. They had
been so close that their present estrangement was even more
remarkable. Her marriage, however, caused her father to treat
her very badly and the rift between them was very deep. Even
when her baby was born, her parents could not be persuaded to
visit their daughter or to see their grandchild. The young woman
resented her parents' harsh treatment all the more because she
was greatly motivated by ambition, and she was cut to the quick
by their attitude towards her at a time when she might well have
been treated with consideration. We must note that the
behaviour of this young woman was completely dominated by
ambition; it is this character trait that gives us an insight into
the reasons why the breach with her parents affected her so
deeply.

Her mother was a stern, self-righteous person who had many
good qualities, although she had ruled her daughter with a heavy
hand. She knew how to submit to her husband, at least so far as
outward appearances were concerned, without really relinquish-
ing her own status; indeed, she drew attention to her submission
with a certain pride, and considered it an honour. There was also
a son who was considered a chip off the old block and was the
heir to the family name. The fact that his parents valued him
rather more than his sister served only to increase her ambition.
The difficulties and poverty that this young woman, brought up
in a comparatively sheltered atmosphere, was experiencing in
her marriage, now caused her to think constantly and with ever-
increasing resentment about the ill-treatment she had received
at the hands of her parents.

One night, before she had fallen asleep, it seemed to her that
a door opened and the Virgin Mary stepped over to her bed and
said: 'Because I love you so dearly, I must tell you that you will
die in the middle of December. I do not want you to be unprepared.'

The young woman was not frightened by this apparition, but
she woke her husband and told him everything. The next day

she went to the doctor and told him about the hallucination. The young woman maintained that she had seen and heard everything quite clearly. At first glance this seems impossible, yet when we use our knowledge of the psyche it becomes quite clear. Here is the situation: a young woman who is very ambitious and, as the case history shows, has the tendency to want to dominate everyone else, breaks with her parents and finds herself in poverty. It is quite understandable that a human being, in an effort to master everything in the physical sphere in which she lives, should attempt to approach and converse with God. If the contact with the Virgin Mary had taken place only in prayer, no one would have found it particularly noteworthy. But this young woman needed something stronger.

The phenomenon loses all its mystery when we understand the tricks the psyche is capable of playing on us. Is not every human being who dreams in a similar position? There is really only one difference: this young woman can dream while she is awake. We must add, too, that her feeling of depression has placed a great strain upon her. In her hallucination, the woman rejected by her mother sees another mother coming to her, indeed that Mother who in popular conception is the greatest Mother of all. These two mothers must stand in a certain contrast to one another. The Mother of God appeared to her because her own mother did not. The apparition is an accusation against her own mother's inadequate love for her child.

The young woman was trying to find some way of proving her parents wrong. The middle of December is a deeply significant time. In many cultures it is the time of year when people are likely to consider their deeper relationships, when they approach each other more warmly, exchange presents and so on. It is at this time too that the possibility of reconciliation comes closer, so we can understand that this particular time has a deep significance for the young woman in the quandary in which she found herself.

The only strange thing in this hallucination seems to be that the friendly approach of the Mother of God was accompanied by the sad news of the young woman's approaching death. The fact that she told her husband about this vision in an almost happy tone of voice is also significant. This prophecy quickly spread beyond the narrow circle of her family and it was a simple way of ensuring that her own mother actually visited her.

A few days later the Virgin Mary appeared again and spoke the same words. When the young woman was asked how her meeting with her own mother had turned out, she answered that her mother could not admit that she had done wrong. Thus we see the old theme cropping up again. Her desire to dominate her mother had not yet been gratified.

At this time an attempt was made to help the parents understand what was actually going on in the life of their daughter. As a result, a very satisfactory meeting took place between the young woman and her father. A touching scene occurred, but the young woman was still not satisfied, because she said there was something insincere in her father's behaviour. She complained that he had kept her waiting too long! Even in victory she could not rid herself of the desire to prove everyone else wrong and cast herself in the role of a triumphant victor.

We may conclude from our discussion that hallucinations appear at that moment when psychic tension is at its greatest and in circumstances in which one fears that the attainment of one's goal is impossible. There is no question that in days gone by hallucinations exerted a considerable influence in areas where the population was somewhat backward in its development.

Descriptions of hallucinations in the writings of travellers and explorers are well known. It is clear that the tension that arises when life is in danger stimulates the imagination of sufferers, enabling them to escape from the oppressive realities of their present condition. On the other hand, a hallucination may act as a drug that can soothe away their fears.

Hallucination is nothing new to us, since we have already seen similar phenomena in the mechanism of memory and in imagination. We shall observe these same processes again when we consider dreams. By accentuating our imagination and excluding our critical faculties it is easy to produce the phenomena of hallucination. In necessity or danger, and under the pressure of a situation in which our power is threatened, we may strive to get rid of the feeling of weakness and overcome it by this mechanism. The greater the stress, the less use will be made of the critical faculties. Under such circumstances, with

the motto 'Sauve qui peut!', anyone can, using every ounce of
their mental energy, force their imagination to project itself into
hallucination.

Illusion is closely related to hallucination. The only difference is that some point of external contact remains, but is
misinterpreted; the underlying situation, the feeling of stress, is
the same. Here is another case history that will show how the
creative power of the mind can produce either an illusion or a
hallucination as the need arises.

A man of excellent family who had never achieved anything
because of a poor education, held an unimportant post as a clerk.
He had given up all hope of ever making his mark. His hopelessness weighed heavily upon him, and in addition his stress was
increased by the reproaches of his friends. In these circumstances
he took to alcohol, which provided both a way to forget his
worries and an excuse for his failure. After some time he was
brought to the hospital in a state of delirium tremens. Delirium is
closely related to hallucination. In the delirium of alcoholic
intoxication, small animals such as mice, insects or snakes frequently appear. Other hallucinations related to the patient's
occupation may also occur.

Our patient came into the hands of doctors who were
strongly opposed to the abuse of alcohol. They put him through
a strict course of treatment and he seemed to be completely
cured of his alcoholism. After he left the hospital he did not
touch alcohol for three years. Then he returned to the hospital
with a new complaint. He said he constantly saw a leering,
grinning man who watched him at his work; he was now a casual
labourer. Once when he was particularly angry because this man
was laughing at him, he took his pick and threw it at him to see
whether he was real or only an apparition. The apparition
dodged the missile, but promptly attacked him and beat him
badly. In this case we are not dealing with a simple apparition,
because the hallucination had very real fists. But the explanation
is not hard to find. The man was in the habit of hallucinating,
but he threw his pick at a real person.

Although he had been freed of his desire to drink, he had in
reality sunk further since his discharge from hospital. He had lost
his job, been evicted from his house and now had to earn his

living as a casual labourer, which he and his friends considered the most menial kind of work. The mental stress under which he had lived was undiminished. In being freed from alcohol he had actually lost an important consolation. He could do his previous job with the help of drink, for when he was reproached too loudly at home for not accomplishing anything, the excuse that he was an alcoholic seemed less shameful to him than his inability to hold down a better job. After his treatment he was again face to face with reality and in a situation no better than before. Should he now fail, he had nothing to console himself with and nothing to blame his failure on, not even alcohol.

In this stressful situation, the hallucinations reappeared. He identified himself with his previous situation and viewed the world as if he were still an alcoholic. This behaviour announced to the world, 'I have ruined my whole life with my drinking and nothing can be done about it now.' By being ill he hoped to be freed from his undervalued, and therefore very unpleasant, occupation as a ditch digger, without having to make a decision about it himself. The hallucination described above lasted for a long time, until he was finally admitted to hospital again. Now he could console himself with the thought that he could have accomplished a great deal more if his alcoholism had not ruined his life. This strategy enabled him to maintain his sense of self-worth. It was more important for him not to lose his self-esteem than it was for him to work. All his efforts were directed towards maintaining the conviction that he might have accomplished great things if he had not been visited by misfortune. This was the state of affairs that enabled him to feel he was as good as anyone else, but that an insurmountable obstacle lay in his way. The desperate search for a consoling excuse produced the hallucination of the leering man; this apparition was the saviour of his self-esteem.

5

ASPECTS OF UNREALITY

FANTASY

Fantasy is just another creative faculty of the psyche. Traces of this activity may be found in the various phenomena we have already described. Like the projection of certain memories into the sharp focus of consciousness, or the erection of the bizarre superstructures of the imagination, fantasy and day-dreaming are part of the creative activity of the psyche. The ability to predict and prejudge, an essential faculty in any organism capable of movement, is also an important factor in fantasy. Fantasy is bound up with the mobility of the human organism and is indeed nothing more than a method of foresight.

The fantasies of children and grown-ups, sometimes called day-dreams, are always concerned with the future. These 'castles in the air' are the goal of their activity, built up in fictional form as models for real activity. Studies of childhood fantasies show clearly that the striving for power plays the predominant role. Children express their ambition in their day-dreams. Most of their fantasies begin with the words 'when I grow up', and so on. There are many adults who live as though they too were not yet grown up. The clear emphasis on the striving for power indicates again that the psyche can develop only when a certain goal has been set; in our civilization, this goal involves social recognition and significance. An individual never stays long with any neutral goal, for the communal life of humankind is accompanied by constant self-evaluation giving rise to the desire for superiority and the hope of success in competition. The fantasies of children almost always involve situations in which the child exercises power.

We must not generalize because it is impossible to lay down rules for the degree of fantasy or the extent of imagination. What we have said is valid in many cases, but may not be applicable to others. Children with a belligerent approach to life will develop their powers of fantasy to a greater extent because their need to protect themselves is strongly developed as a result of their attitude to others. And very weak children for whom life is not always pleasant develop great powers of fantasy and have the tendency to become particularly engrossed in a world of their own. At a certain stage in their development their powers of fantasy may become a way of avoiding the realities of life. Fantasy may be misused as a rejection of reality, and in such cases it becomes a kind of magic carpet for individuals who raise themselves above the meanness of living by the power of their imagination.

Social feeling, together with the striving for power, also plays a major role in our fantasy life. In childhood fantasies, power strivings almost always include some application of this power to social ends. We see this trait clearly in those fantasies in which the dreamer becomes a saviour or crusader, triumphing over the powers of evil and oppression. The fantasy that the child does not belong to his or her own family is also a frequent one. Many children believe that they actually came from a different family and that some day their real parents, people of some eminence, will come and fetch them. This happens most frequently in children with a deep feeling of inferiority. They feel deprived of love and affection, or forced into the background within their family circle, so they invent a new family for themselves. Ideas of grandeur betray themselves in another very common attitude: that of children who act as though they were already grown up. Sometimes one finds almost pathological expressions of this fantasy, as for instance in boys who want to use their father's shaving foam; or in the case of young girls who adopt more masculine attitudes, and behave and dress in a boy-like manner.

There are children who are said to have no imagination. This is surely an error. Either such children cannot express themselves, or there are other reasons that compel them to fight off their fantasies. Children may gain a feeling of power by suppressing their own imagination. In their desperate striving to adjust to adult reality, such children believe that fantasy is childish and refuse to indulge in it; and there are cases in which this dislike goes so far that a child seems to be totally lacking in imagination.

DREAMS: GENERAL CONSIDERATIONS

In addition to the day-dreams previously described, we must deal with that important and significant activity that occurs during our sleep, the 'night' dream. In general it may be said that night dreaming is a repetition of the same process that goes on in day-dreams. Experienced psychologists have pointed to the fact that the character of human beings may easily be read from their dreams. Actually dreams have preoccupied mankind to an enormous degree since the dawn of history. In the sleep dream, as in the day-dream, we are dealing with an attempt to map, plan and direct the future life towards a goal of security. The most obvious difference is that day-dreams are comparatively easily understood, whereas sleep dreams are only seldom comprehended. It is not surprising that dreams are not readily understandable, and we might easily be tempted to see in this an indication that dreams are superfluous and insignificant. For the time being let it be said that the striving for power of individuals who are seeking to overcome difficulties and maintain their position in the future is echoed in their dreams. Dreams offer us important insights into the problems of someone's emotional life.

EMPATHY AND IDENTIFICATION

The psyche has the ability not only to perceive what actually exists, but also to feel or guess what will happen in the future. This is an important contribution to the function of foresight, which is necessary to any organism capable of movement, since such an organism is constantly faced with the problem of how to make adjustments. This faculty is also linked with the power of identification, or empathy, which is extraordinarily well developed in human beings. Its extent is so great that one finds it in every corner of every psyche, and the necessity for foresight is the prime condition for its existence. If we must pre-judge and predict how we should act if a certain situation were to occur, we must learn to gain a sound judgement of a situation by correlating our thinking, feeling and perceiving. It is essential to find a viewpoint that enables us either to tackle the new situation with more strenuous efforts, or to avoid it with greater caution.

Empathy occurs in the moment when one human being speaks with another. It is impossible to understand another individual if one cannot at the same time identify oneself with him or her. Drama is the clearest artistic expression of empathy, since through the playwright's skill we readily identify with the characters on stage and act the most varied roles within ourselves. Examples of empathy in everyday life are those cases in which we have a strange feeling of uneasiness when we notice another person in danger. This empathy may be so strong that we make involuntary movements in self-defence, even though there is no actual danger to us; for example, we all know the involuntary movements people make when someone drops a glass! At a bowling alley one may see certain players following the course of the ball with movements of their body as though they wanted to influence its progress by these gestures. Similarly, during football games whole sections of the crowd in the grandstand will push in the direction of their favourite team. Another common example is the involuntary application of imaginary brakes by the passengers in a car whenever they feel they are in danger. Few people can watch a window cleaner at work on a tall building without a shudder of fear, and when public speakers lose their thread and cannot proceed, the audience feels uncomfortable and embarrassed. Our entire life is very much dependent upon this faculty of identification. If we look for the origin of this ability to act and feel as if we were someone else, we can find it in each human being's inborn empathy with others. This is a universal feeling and a reflection of the oneness of the whole cosmos of which we are each a part; it is an inescapable characteristic of being human. It gives us the ability to identify ourselves with things outside our own direct experience.

Just as there are various degrees of social feeling or community spirit, so there are various degrees of empathy. These may be observed even in childhood. There are children who play with dolls just as though they were human beings, whereas others are more interested in seeing how they were made. The development of individuals may be entirely arrested if they transfer communal relationships away from human beings onto animals or inanimate objects.

Instances of cruelty to animals by children are only possible with an almost total absence of social feeling and of the ability to empathize with other living creatures. The consequence of such a defect is that children develop an interest in things that are of very little value or significance for their development into social human beings. They think only of themselves and lose all interest in the joys or woes of others. This inability to put oneself in the other person's place, to empathize with them, may go so far that individuals may completely refuse to co-operate with their fellow human beings.

INFLUENCE, SUGGESTION AND HYPNOSIS

Individual Psychology answers the question, 'How is it possible for one individual to influence the behaviour of another?' by saying that susceptibility to influence is one of the major manifestations of our psychological life. Our communal way of life would not be possible unless one individual could influence another. This pattern of influence becomes markedly accentuated in some cases, such as the relationship between teacher and pupil or parent and child. Because of natural social feeling, human beings show a certain degree of willingness to be influenced by each other. The extent of this willingness is dependent upon the degree to which the person exercising the influence considers the rights of the person on whom the influence is to be exerted. It is impossible to have a lasting claim upon the respect of individuals to whom we are doing harm. We can influence other individuals best when they feel their own rights are safeguarded. This is a very important point in education. Perhaps it is possible to conceive or even to carry out some other form of education, but a system of education that takes this point into consideration will be effective because it appeals to people's most primitive instinct, their feeling of relatedness to humanity and the cosmos.

This approach will fail only when it is dealing with human beings who have deliberately withdrawn from the influence of society. Such withdrawals do not occur by accident. A long

battle must have been waged in which they dissolved their connections with the world little by little, until they stand in open
opposition to the community. Influencing such people's
behaviour is now difficult or impossible, and we see the dramatic
spectacle of human beings responding with fierce opposition to
every attempt to influence them.

We may expect children who feel oppressed by their environment to show a lack of response to their educators. Cases occur,
however, in which external pressure is so strong that it removes
all obstacles, with the result that the authoritative influence is
retained and obeyed. But it is easy to demonstrate that such
obedience is devoid of social good. It sometimes shows itself in
such a grotesque fashion that the obedient individuals are
rendered unfit for life, because their habits of slavish obedience
have left them incapable of any independent action or thought.
The danger of developing this submissive tendency can be seen
in obedient children who, when they develop into adults, readily
submit to any authoritative commands, even to the point of
breaking the law.

Gangs are an interesting example of the way submission and
dominance work. Those who carry out the gang's commands are
submissive, whereas the dominant leader usually keeps well away
from the action. In almost every important criminal case dealing
with a gang crime, some such servile person has been the
scapegoat. This far-reaching, blind obedience plumbs such unbelievable depths that we occasionally find people who are actually
proud of their slavishness and find in it a means of satisfying
their self-esteem.

If we limit ourselves to normal cases of mutual influence, we
find that the people most susceptible to influence are those most
amenable to reason and logic, those whose social feeling has
been least distorted. On the other hand, those who thirst for
superiority and desire domination are very difficult to influence.
We see examples of this every day.

When parents complain about children it is rarely because
they are blindly obedient. The most common complaint is
about disobedience. If we examine such children we find that
they feel restricted and are protesting about it, trying to
overcome the limitations of their environment. The way they

have been treated at home has made it impossible to educate them in a normal way.

The intensity of our striving for power is inversely proportional to the degree to which we can be educated. In spite of this, family upbringing is concerned, for the most part, in spurring on the ambition of children and awakening ideas of grandeur. This does not happen because of thoughtlessness, but because our whole culture is permeated with similar grandiose delusions. In the family, as in the whole of society, the greatest attention is paid to whoever is biggest, best, or most glorious. In the chapter on vanity we shall have occasion to show how unsuited this method of ambition-oriented education is to the life of the community, and how the development of the mind can be stunted by the obstacles ambition places in its way.

Individuals who are easily influenced by every slight shift in their circumstances because of their habit of unconditional obedience are like the subjects of a hypnotist. Imagine obeying, for several minutes, every whim that anyone cares to express! Hypnosis is based upon this idea of submission. One person may say, and believe, that he is willing to be hypnotized, but the psychological readiness to submit may not be present. A second individual may consciously resist but still be subconsciously willing to submit. In hypnosis only the psychological attitude of the subject determines their behaviour. What they say or think is of no consequence. Confusion over this fact has allowed the spread of much misinformation concerning hypnosis. We are usually concerned with individuals who appear to be struggling against hypnosis, but are fundamentally willing to submit to the demands of the hypnotist. This readiness to submit may vary from one subject to another, so that the effects of hypnosis will differ in every individual. In no case does the degree of readiness to be hypnotized depend upon the will of the hypnotist. It is conditioned entirely by the attitude of the subject.

In its essence, hypnosis is similar to sleep. It is mysterious only because this sleep may be produced at the command of another person, and the command is effective solely when it is given to someone who is willing to submit to it. The determining factors are, as usual, the nature and character of the subject. Only someone who is willing to go along with the demands of another without the exercise of their critical faculties can be hypnotized. Hypnosis differs from ordinary sleep in that it subjugates the faculty of movement to such a degree that even the motor centres are mobilized at the command of the hypnotist. A certain twilight slumber is all that is left of normal sleep in this state, and subjects can remember only those things the hypnotist allows them to remember. The most important fact about hypnosis is that our critical faculties, those finest expressions of the soul, are completely paralysed during the hypnotic trance. The hypnotized subject becomes, so to speak, the tool of the hypnotist, an organ functioning at his or her command.

Most people who have a particular ability to influence the behaviour of others ascribe this faculty to some mysterious power peculiar to them. This causes an enormous amount of harm, not least in the pernicious activities of stage hypnotists. These charlatans commit such arrant crimes against humankind that they are quite capable of utilizing any instrument appropriate to their nefarious purposes. This does not mean that everything they do is a swindle. The human animal, unfortunately is capable of such submission that it can fall victim to anyone who poses as the possessor of special powers. Only too many human beings have acquired the habit of accepting authority without testing it. The public wants to be fooled. It wants to swallow every tall story whole without subjecting it to rational examination. Such activity will never bring any order into the communal life of humankind but will only lead, again and again, to the revolt of those who have been deceived. No stage hypnotist has been successful for very long. Very frequently they have come in contact with someone, some so-called subject, who has taken them for a ride. This has sometimes also been the experience of important scientists attempting to demonstrate their powers. There are other cases in which there is a curious mixture of truth and falsehood: the subjects are, so to speak, deceived deceivers; they fool the hypnotist in part, but also subordinate themselves to the hypnotist's will. The power that is apparently at work here is never the power of the hypnotist, but always the readiness of the subjects to submit to the hypnotist's influence. There is no magic power influencing the subjects unless it is the hypnotist's ability to bluff. Anyone who is accustomed to living rationally, who makes their own decisions, who does not accept anyone's say-so uncritically, cannot be hypnotized, and will therefore never be able to show any telepathic powers. Hypnosis and telepathy are only the manifestations of servile obedience.

At this point we must also consider suggestion. Suggestion can best be understood when we include it in the category of impressions and stimuli. It is self-evident that no human being is stimulated only occasionally. All of us are constantly under the influence of countless stimuli from the outside world. Stimuli, moreover, are never merely perceived: every stimulus has some effect. Once felt, an impression continues to have an effect on us. When an impression takes the form of the demands and entreaties of other human beings, their arguments and attempts to convince us, we call it suggestion. It is a case either of the transformation or of the reinforcement of a point of view already present in the person to whom the suggestions are made. The more difficult problem really arises from the fact that all human beings react in differing ways to stimuli from the outside world. The degree to which individuals can be influenced is intimately connected with their degree of independence.

There are two types of human beings whom we must bear in mind in this connection. One type always overvalues the other person's opinions and therefore undervalues their own, whether they are right or wrong. Such individuals are exceptionally susceptible to suggestion or hypnosis. A second type sees every stimulus or suggestion as an insult. These are the individuals who consider that only their own opinion is right. They are really not concerned about its actual correctness or incorrectness. They disregard any opinion that comes from another human being. Both types carry with them a sense of weakness. The first expresses this weakness through compliance. The second type expresses it in an inability to listen to the views of others. People in this category are usually very belligerent, although they may pride themselves on their openness to suggestions. They talk about this openness and reasonableness, however, purely to reinforce their isolated position; they are in fact thoroughly bigoted, and it is very difficult to have any influence on them.

6

THE INFERIORITY COMPLEX

EARLY CHILDHOOD

We are now able to understand that the attitude of disadvantaged children towards life and towards their fellow human beings differs from the outlook of those for whom the joys of existence were present at an early age. We can state as a fundamental law that children who come into the world with disabilities become involved at an early age in a bitter struggle that results only too often in the strangulation of their social feelings. Instead of trying to adjust to others, they are preoccupied with themselves and with the impression they make on other people. What holds good for a physical disability is equally valid for any social or economic burden that might become a handicap, capable of producing a hostile attitude towards the world.

The decisive trend is determined at an early age. Such children are frequently aware as early as two years old that they are somehow less adequately equipped for the struggle than their playmates. They sense that they dare not take part in their peers' games and pastimes. As a result of past privations they have acquired a sense of being neglected, which is expressed in an attitude of anxious expectation. We must remember that all children occupy an inferior and dependent position in life. Without a certain amount of social feeling on the part of their family they would be incapable of independent existence. We realize that the beginning of every life is fraught with a fairly deep-seated sense of inferiority when we see the weakness and helplessness of all children. Sooner or later all children become conscious of their inability to cope alone with the challenges of existence. This feeling of inferiority is the driving force, the starting point from which every childish striving originates. It determines how individual children acquire peace and security in life, it determines the very goal of their existence and it prepares the path along which this goal may be approached.

The basis of children's potential for education is closely bound up with their physical potential. Educational receptivity may be shattered by two factors. One of these factors is an exaggerated, intensified, unresolved feeling of inferiority and the other is a goal that demands not only security, peace and social equilibrium, but also a struggle to gain power over the environment, a goal of dominance over one's peers. Such children are easy to spot. They become 'problem' children because they interpret every experience as a defeat, and because they consider themselves always neglected and discriminated against both by nature and by humanity. We have only to consider these factors to see with what inevitability a crooked, inadequate, error-ridden development may unfold in the life of a child. All children run the risk of a mistaken development. All children find themselves in a precarious situation at some time or another.

Since all children must grow up surrounded by adults, they are predisposed to consider themselves small, weak and incapable of living alone. They do not trust themselves even to do those simple tasks of which adults believe they are capable without mistakes or clumsiness. Most of our errors in child-rearing begin at this point. When we demand more than children can do, the idea of their own helplessness is thrown into their faces. Some adults even consciously make children feel their smallness and helplessness. Others treat children as animated dolls to be played with. Others again treat children as valuable property that must be carefully watched, while still others make them feel they are so much useless human freight. A combination of these attitudes on the part of parents and other adults often leads children to believe they have control over only two things: the pleasure and displeasure of her elders.

The type of inferiority feeling produced by the parents may be further intensified by certain peculiar characteristics of our civilization. The habit of not taking children seriously belongs in this category. Children get the impression that they are nobodyies, people without rights; that they are to be seen and not heard; that they must always be courteous, quiet, and so on. Many children grow up in the constant dread of being laughed at. Ridicule of children is well-nigh criminal. It leaves a permanent mark on the psyche of children which resurfaces in the habits and actions of their adult lives. It is easy to spot adults who were continually laughed at as children. They cannot rid themselves of the fear of appearing ridiculous again. Another manifestation of not taking children seriously is the custom of telling children palpable lies, with the result that they begin not only to doubt their immediate environment but also to question the seriousness and reality of life. Cases have been recorded of children who laughed continually at school, with no apparent reason. When questioned, they admitted that they thought school was one of their parents' jokes and not worth taking seriously.

COMPENSATION: THE STRIVING FOR RECOGNITION AND SUPERIORITY

Feelings of inferiority, inadequacy and insecurity determine the goal of an individual's existence. The tendency to push oneself into the limelight, to demand parents' attention, makes itself apparent in the first days of life. Here are found the first indications that the awakening desire for recognition is developing alongside the sense of inferiority. Its purpose is the attainment of a state in which individuals are seemingly superior to their environment.

The degree and quality of a person's social feeling helps to determine their goal of superiority. We cannot judge individuals, whether children or adults, without comparing their goal of personal superiority with the extent of their social feeling. Their goal is so constructed that its achievement promises the possibility either of a feeling of superiority or an elevation of the personality to a level that makes life seem worth living. It is this goal that gives value to our experiences. It links and co-ordinates our feelings, shapes our imagination, directs our creative powers and determines what we will remember and what we must forget. We can see how relative the values of sensations, sentiments, emotions and imagination are; these elements of our psychological activity are influenced by our striving for a definite goal. Our very perceptions are prejudiced by it and are chosen, so to speak, with a hidden reference to the final goal towards which the personality is striving.

We orient ourselves according to an artificially created fixed point, a point that has no actual basis in reality: in other words, a fiction. This assumption of a fiction is necessary because of our psychological inadequacy. It is very similar to the fictions we use in science, such as the division of the earth by non-existent but highly useful meridians. With psychological fictions we assume a fixed point even though closer observation forces us to admit that, like the meridian, it does not exist. The purpose of this assumption is simply to orient ourselves in the chaos of existence, so that we can arrive at some appreciation of relative values. The advantage is that once we have assumed this fixed point we can categorize every sensation and every sentiment according to it.

Individual Psychology, therefore, creates for itself a heuristic system and method: to regard human behaviour and understand it as a final pattern of relationships produced by the effect of the pursuit of a definite goal upon the organism's basic inherited potentialities. Our experience, moreover, has shown that this assumption about striving for a goal is more than simply a convenient fiction. It has shown itself to be largely consistent with the actual facts, whether these facts are to be found in the conscious or the unconscious life. The striving for a goal, the purposiveness of the psyche, is not only a philosophical assumption, but a fundamental fact.

When we ask ourselves how we can best oppose the development of striving for power and superiority, this most prominent evil of our civilization, we are faced with a difficulty, for this striving begins at an age when we cannot easily communicate with children. We can begin to make attempts at improvement and clarification only much later in life. But living with children at this time does offer an opportunity to develop their social feeling to an extent where the striving for personal power becomes a negligible factor.

A further difficulty lies in the fact that children do not express their striving for power openly, but hide it under the guise of concern and affection and carry on their work behind a façade. They expect to escape discovery in this way. An uninhibited striving for power and security can damage the psychological development of the child, and may change courage to impudence, obedience to cowardice, tenderness to a subtle strategy for total domination. Eventually, every natural feeling or expression of the child carries with it a hypocritical element with the final aim of the subjugation of their environment.

Education influences children by virtue of its conscious or unconscious aim of compensating them for their insecurity, by schooling them in life skills, by educating their understanding and by encouraging in them a social feeling for their fellow human beings. All these measures, whatever their source, are ways of helping growing children to rid themselves of their insecurity and feeling of inferiority. What happens in the psyche of children during this process we must judge by the character traits they develop, since these are the mirror of their psychological activity. Children's actual degree of inferiority, important as it is for their psychology, is no criterion by which we can measure their feelings of insecurity and inferiority, since these depend largely upon their interpretation.

One cannot expect children to have an accurate estimation of themselves in any particular situation; we do not even expect that of adults. But it is precisely here that difficulties proliferate. One child will grow up in a situation so complicated that she is bound to make mistakes about the degree of her inferiority. Another child will be better able to interpret his situation. But by and large the way children interpret their feeling of inferiority varies from day to day until it finally becomes consolidated and is expressed as a definite self-estimation. This becomes a 'constant' of self-evaluation that stays with children in all their dealings with the world. The compensatory devices children create to guide them out of their inferiority will be directed towards some goal appropriate to this crystallized norm or constant of self-estimation.

The mechanism of the striving for compensation with which the psyche attempts to neutralize the tortured feeling of inferiority has its analogy in the organic world. We have seen that those organs of our body that are essential for life seem to become over productive when their normal function is impaired by illness or injury. Thus in circulatory disorders the heart, seeming to draw new strength from the whole body, may enlarge until it is more powerful than a normal heart. In the same way the psyche, under pressure from feelings of inferiority or helplessness, tries with all its might to overcome this 'inferiority complex'.

When the feeling of inferiority is intensified to the degree that children fear they will never be able to overcome their weakness, the danger arises that in striving for compensation they will not be satisfied with a simple restoration of the balance of power. They will seek to tip the scales in the opposite direction. In such cases the striving for power and dominance may become so exaggerated and intensified that it must be called pathological, and the ordinary relationships of life will never be satisfactory. The urges in these cases are apt to have a certain grandiose quality about them and are well adapted to their goal. Individuals with a pathological power-drive seek to secure their position in life with extraordinary efforts, with exceptional haste and impatience, with violent impulses, and all without the slightest consideration for others. These are the children whose behaviour is characterized by their frantic strivings towards an exaggerated goal of dominance. Their attacks on the rights of others in turn put their own rights at risk; they are against the world and the world is therefore against them.

This does not necessarily happen openly. Some children strive for power in a manner that is not calculated to bring them into immediate conflict with society, and their ambition at first seems perfectly normal. Yet when we carefully investigate their activities and achievements we find that society at large does not benefit from their triumphs, because their ambition is antisocial, always casting them as obstacles in the path of other human beings. Little by little, too, other characteristics will appear that, if we take a wider view of their human relationships, will take on an increasingly anti-social aspect. In the forefront of these are pride, vanity and the desire to get the better of everyone at any price. The last may be subtly accomplished. The relative elevation of individuals may be achieved by belittling all those with whom they come into contact. In this case the important thing is the 'distance' that separates them from their fellows. Such an attitude is not only uncomfortable for society, but also for the individuals who hold it, because it continually brings them into contact with the dark side of life and prevents them from experiencing any joy in living.

The exaggerated drive for power with which some children wish to assert their mastery over their environment soon forces them into an attitude of resistance to the ordinary tasks and duties of everyday life. If we compare such power-hungry individuals to the ideal social being we can, with a little experience, specify their social index: that is, the degree to which they have removed themselves from their fellow creatures. A keen judge of human nature, remembering the importance of physical defects and inferiorities, knows nevertheless that such character traits could not arise without previous difficulties in psychological development.

When we have gained a true knowledge of human nature, built upon a recognition of the importance of difficulties occurring in the proper development of the psyche, it can never be an instrument of harm so long as we have thoroughly developed our own social feeling. We can only help our fellow human beings with it. We must not blame bearers of a physical disability or a disagreeable character trait for their indignation. They are not responsible for it. We must uphold to the end their right to their indignation, and we must not forget that we are partly to blame for their situation. The blame belongs to us because we have not done enough to prevent the social misery that produced it. If we stick to this point of view we can eventually improve the situation.

We approach such individuals not as a degraded, worthless outcasts, but as fellow human beings; we create an atmosphere in which they can feel just as valuable as anyone else. Be honest, and admit how uncomfortable the sight of a severely disabled person can make you. That is a good indication of the amount of social education you yourself need, and helps you to judge how much our civilization owes to such a suffering individual.

It is self-evident that those who are born with physical disabilities feel an added burden from their earliest days, and as a result can become thoroughly pessimistic about life in general. Children in whom the feeling of inferiority has become intensified for one reason or another, although their organ inferiorities may be negligible, find themselves in a similar situation. The feeling of inferiority may be so artificially intensified that the result is exactly the same as if the child had come into the world severely disabled. A very strict upbringing during the critical period, for instance, may have this unfortunate result. The thorn that pierced a child's side in the early days of her existence is never removed, and the coldness she has experienced makes her shrink from approaching other human beings. Thus she believes she is in a world devoid of love and affection, a world with which she has no point of contact.

Here is an illustrative case: a patient, notable for continually telling us about his great sense of duty and the importance of all his actions, has a miserable life with his wife. Here are two individuals who each measure with pinpoint accuracy the value any event holds as a means of subjugating their spouse. Arguments, reproaches, insults, in the course of which the two become entirely estranged from one another, are the inevitable result. What little social feeling for his fellow human beings the husband retains, at least so far as his wife and friends are concerned, is choked by his thirst for superiority.

We learn the following facts from the story of his life. He was physically underdeveloped until his seventeenth year. His voice was the voice of a young boy, he had no body or facial hair, and he was one of the smallest boys in his school. Today he is thirty-six and is a normal, fully developed man. Nature has apparently caught up with itself and completed the work it was so late starting. But for eight years he suffered from this failure to develop, and at that time he had no guarantee that Nature would ever compensate for his deficiencies. During this entire period he was tortured with the thought that he must always remain a 'child'.

At that age the beginnings of his present character traits could be noted. He acted as though he were very important, as if his every action carried the utmost weight. Everything he did was calculated to make him the centre of attention. In the course of time he acquired the characteristics we see in him today. After he married he was continually preoccupied with impressing his wife with the fact that he was really bigger and more important than she thought, while she spent her time showing him that his assertions concerning his value were untrue! Under these circumstances their relationship, which showed signs of disruption even during their engagement, could hardly be a success, and it finally broke down completely. The patient came to the therapist at this time, since the break-up of his marriage served only to accentuate the dilapidation of his already battered self-esteem. To be helped, he had first to learn from the therapist to understand human nature, then he had to learn how to come to terms with the error he had made early in life. This error, this wrong evaluation of his inferiority, had coloured his entire life up to the time of his treatment.

THE GRAPH OF LIFE AND THE COSMIC PICTURE

When we cite cases like these it is frequently convenient to show relationships between childhood experience and the actual complaint as presented by the patient; this is best done by a graph. The relationship is shown by a line connecting two points. In many cases, when we plot such a graph, the psychological curve that charts an individual's development, the curve shows the behaviour pattern this individual has followed since earliest childhood. Perhaps some readers will feel that we are attempting to belittle human fate by over-simplifying it. Others will say that we are trying to deny that all human beings are masters of their fate and that we are therefore denying free will and human judgement. So far as free will is concerned, this accusation is true. Here we are dealing with a definite behaviour pattern. Its final configuration is subject to a few changes, but its essential content, its momentum and meaning, remain unchanged from earliest childhood. This behaviour pattern is the determining factor, although, as subjects grow up, their changing relations with the adult environment may tend to modify the problem slightly in some respects. In our examination we must ferret out the subject's earliest childhood experiences, because the impressions of early infancy indicate the direction in which children have developed as well as the way in which they will respond in the future to the challenges of life. In their responses to these challenges children will make use of all the physical and mental equipment they were born with; the particular pressures they felt in the days of earliest infancy will colour their attitude towards life and determine in a rudimentary way their view of the world, their cosmic philosophy. We should not be surprised to learn that people do not change their attitude towards life after their infancy, though their expressions of that attitude in later life are quite different from those of their earliest days.

It is important therefore not to subject small children to relationships that are likely to give them a wrong impression of life. The strength and resistance of their body are an important factor in this process. Their social position, and the characteristics of those who educate them, are almost equally important. Even though the response to life is at first merely automatic and reflexive, in later life reactions are modified according to a certain sense of purpose. In the beginning it is physical necessity that conditions children's pain and happiness, but later they acquire the ability to evade and circumvent the pressures of these primitive needs. This phenomenon occurs at the time of self-discovery, about the time when children begin to refer to themselves as 'I'. It is at this time too that children are already conscious that they stand in a fixed relationship to their environment. This relationship is by no means neutral, since it forces children to assume a different attitude and to adjust their relationships according to the demands that their view of the world, and their conception of happiness and completeness, give them.

If we recall what has been said concerning the teleology (goal-directedness) of the human mind, it will become increasingly obvious that an indestructible unity must be a special feature of this behaviour pattern. The necessity of dealing with a human being as an indivisible personality becomes more and more apparent in those cases where seemingly contrasting expressions of psychological goals are to be found.

Just as there are children who behave quite differently at school and at home, there are adults whose character traits appear so contradictory that their true character is a mystery to us. In the same way the movements and expressions of two human beings may be outwardly identical, yet when they are examined for their underlying behaviour patterns, they prove to be entirely different. When two individuals appear to be doing the same thing, each one is really doing something distinct and different, yet when two individuals are doing seemingly different things they may actually be doing the same thing!

Because of this ambiguity we can never judge the expressions of the psyche as isolated phenomena; on the contrary, we must evaluate them according to the common goal towards which they are directed. The essential meaning of a phenomenon can be learned only when we know what importance that phenomenon has in the context of a person's whole life. We can understand how their mind works only when we have reaffirmed the law that every expression of a person's life is an aspect of their total behaviour pattern.

When we have finally grasped that all human behaviour is based upon the striving for a goal, that it is conditioned by its end as well as by its beginning, then we can also indicate the areas where the greatest mistakes are likely to be made. The source of these errors lies in the fact that all of us utilize our triumphs and satisfactions according to our own psychological makeup, in such a way as to reinforce our individual life pattern. This is possible only because we do not analyse anything objectively, but receive, transform and assimilate all our perceptions in the light of our own conscious mind, or the depths of our unconscious mind. Science alone can illuminate the process and make it comprehensible; science alone is finally able to modify it. We shall conclude our exposition at this point with an example in which we will analyse and explain every phenomenon by means of those aspects of Individual Psychology we have already learned.

A young woman comes as a patient and complains of her unbearable dissatisfaction with life. She is dissatisfied, she says, because her whole day is taken up with a great number of duties of all kinds. Externally we can see in her a hasty person, with restless eyes, who complains of the great anxiety she feels whenever she must perform some simple task. From her family and friends we learn that she takes everything to heart and seems to be breaking down under the burden of her work. The general impression that we get is that of a person who takes everything very seriously, a characteristic common to many people. One member of her family gives us the clue by saying, 'She always makes such a big fuss over everything!'

Let us take this tendency to consider every simple task a particularly hard and important one and test it by attempting to imagine what kind of impression this behaviour would make upon a group of people or on a marriage partner. We cannot help feeling that such a tendency is an appeal to the world not to pile any more work upon her for she is no longer able to take on any more. We do not, however, yet know enough about this woman's personality. We must get her to tell us more about herself. We must proceed by cautious hints and with proper delicacy. There must be no attempt to dominate the patient, as this would only antagonize her. Once her confidence is gained and she is talking to us freely, we come to the conclusion that her whole life is concerned with just a single goal. Her behaviour shows that she is trying to show someone, probably her husband, that she cannot take on any further obligations or responsibilities, that she must be treated with tenderness and consideration. We further guess that all this must have begun at some time in the past when demands must have been made on her. We succeed in eliciting from her the admission that many years ago she had to live through a time when she lacked affection more than anything else. Now we can understand her behaviour better; it is a reinforcement of her desire for consideration, and an attempt to prevent the recurrence of a situation in which her hunger for warmth and affection might somehow remain unsatisfied.

Our findings are confirmed by a further explanation on her part. She tells of a friend who is completely different from her in many ways, who would like to escape from an unhappy marriage. Once, she found her friend standing, book in hand, telling her husband in a bored voice that she really did not know whether she would be able to prepare dinner that day. This so irritated the husband that he started criticizing her in harsh terms. Our patient's comment on this incident was: 'When I think about what happened, I think that my method is much better. No one can reproach me in this way because I am overburdened with work from morning till night. If lunch is late at my house no one can say anything to me because I always have so many calls on my time. Should I give up this method now?'

We can understand what is going on in this person's mind. In a relatively innocuous way she attempts to attain a certain superiority, but remain at the same time beyond reproach by pleading constantly for consideration. Since this strategy is successful it seems hardly reasonable to ask her to discontinue it, but there is more to her behaviour than just this. Her appeal for consideration (which at the same time is an attempt to dominate others) can never be made strongly enough. This results in all kinds of problems. If anything is mislaid in the house there is 'much ado about nothing'. She has so much to do that she is constantly suffering from headaches. She can never sleep soundly because she is always worrying about her past, present and future activities. An invitation to dinner is in itself an important occasion. Enormous preparations are necessary for its acceptance. Since the least activity appears to her inordinately important, going to a dinner party is a difficult task that demands hours and days to complete. We can predict with some certainty that she will either send her regrets or, at the very least, come late. The social feeling in the life of such a person can never go beyond certain limits.

In married life there are a number of situations that assume a particular significance because of this appeal for consideration. It is conceivable, for instance, that one partner must sometimes be away from home on business, have evening appointments, or attend meetings of clubs to which he or she belongs. If the other partner is left at home at these times, would this not be a breach of tenderness and consideration? At first we might say that marriage entails both partners staying at home as much as possible. Pleasant as this obligation might seem in part, if taken to extremes it creates insurmountable difficulties for anyone who has a profession. Trouble would appear unavoidable in such cases, and it occurred quickly in this one. The husband tried occasionally to slip into bed late at night without disturbing his wife, only to be surprised to find her still awake and full of reproaches.

We need not go into details here – the problem is well known. We must emphasize, too, that it is not only women who play these games. There are just as many men whose attitude is similar. We are simply concerned with showing that the demand for care and consideration may occasionally take a somewhat different course. In the case of our patient the pattern would be as follows: Suppose the husband has to go out in the evening.

'Don't worry about coming home early, dear,' says his wife. 'You so seldom socialize – make an evening of it.' Although she says this in a jocular tone her words have a very serious meaning. They appear contrary to what we know about her, but when we observe more closely we can see the connection: she does not want to seem too demanding. Outwardly she is convincing, and her character seems sincere. Yet the real significance of her words to her husband lies in the fact that it is she who has given the ultimatum. Now, since *she* has decreed it, he may stay out late, whereas she would be dreadfully hurt and slighted if he had stayed away for reasons of his own. Her words cast a veil over the whole situation. She has become the directing partner; and her husband, even in socializing, is made dependent upon the wish and will of his wife.

Now let us link this hunger for tenderness and consideration with our new idea that this woman can handle only those situations in which she herself is in command. We suddenly become aware that throughout her life she has been actuated by a determination never to play second fiddle, always to maintain her dominance, never to be toppled from her secure position by any reproach, and always to remain in the centre of her little universe. We shall find this determination in every situation of her life; for instance, when she has to get a new cleaning woman, she becomes highly excited. Clearly she is concerned about maintaining the same dominance over the new employee that she had over the old. In the same way, when she has to go out of the house, she leaves a sphere where her dominance is assured and goes out into a world where suddenly nothing is under the shadow of her dominance, where she has to dodge every car, indeed where she plays a very subordinate role. The cause and meaning of her stress become perfectly clear when we understand the tyranny she exercises at home.

These characteristics often appear in such a pleasant guise that at first glance no one would ever think that the person in question was suffering. This suffering can, however, reach a great intensity. Just imagine this stress exaggerated and enlarged. There are human beings who are afraid of taking a bus, because in a bus they are not masters of their own fate; this fear may go so far that they are finally unable to leave their homes at all.

A further development in this case illustrates the influence that childhood impressions exercise on the life of an individual. We cannot deny the fact that this woman, from her standpoint, is perfectly right. If one's attitude and one's whole life are intensely directed towards the acquisition of warmth, respect, honour and tenderness, then to act as though she were constantly overloaded and constantly exhausted is not a bad means to this end. Indeed, it is an excellent way of warding off criticism, and simultaneously compelling everyone to be gentle with her, while avoiding everything likely to disturb her wavering psychological equilibrium.

If we go back a long way in the life of our patient we learn that even in school, whenever she could not do her homework, she became extremely upset, in this way forcing her teacher to be very gentle with her. She was also the oldest of three children, with a younger brother and sister. She was constantly at war with her brother, who always seemed to be the favourite. It particularly annoyed her that people paid such attention to his school work, whereas her work (and she had originally been a good pupil) was met with a certain indifference. Finally she could bear it no longer, and was forever nagging to know why her accomplishments were not equally valued.

Thus we can understand that this young girl was striving for equality, and that from earliest childhood she had had a feeling of inferiority that she strove to overcome. Her way of compensating in school was to become a bad pupil. She attempted to outdo her brother by means of bad school reports! This was not very admirable in her, but according to her childish interpretation she acted rationally, for it seemed an excellent way of gaining the attention of her parents. Some of her tricks seemed to be consciously motivated because she declared quite clearly that she wanted to be a bad pupil!

Her parents, however, did not trouble themselves in the least about her failures in school. And then something interesting happened. She suddenly showed marked success in her studies, for now her younger sister had come upon the scene in a new role. This younger sister had failed in school too, but her mother paid almost as much attention to her sister's failures as she had to the brother's successes. This was because the younger sister's failures took a different direction. Whereas our patient had had bad reports only for academic work, her sister got bad reports for conduct and behaviour. She was thus able to gain her mother's attention more easily, since bad behaviour has an entirely different social effect than bad academic reports. These bad reports all involved 'emergencies' that forced the parents to drop everything and deal with their child.

The battle for equality was temporarily lost. Now the loss of a battle for equality never leads to permanent peace. No human being can bear such a situation. And so our patient found other ways of attracting attention, which left permanent effects on her character. We can now understand more fully the meaning of the great fuss she made, her constant haste, her frantic desire to appear extremely busy. They were meant originally for her mother and were intended to attract her parents' attention and divert it from her brother and sister. At the same time they were a reproach to her parents for treating her less favourably than her siblings. The fundamental attitude created at that time is still with her today.

We can go back even further in her life. She has a particularly vivid childhood memory of wanting to hit her newborn brother with a piece of wood. Only her mother's intervention had prevented her from injuring him severely. At this time she was three years old. Even at that early age, the little girl had discovered that she was less highly regarded because she was only a girl. She remembers quite vividly that her wish to be a boy was expressed on countless occasions. The arrival of her brother not only forced her out of the warmth of a cosy nest but also insulted her deeply, because as a boy he was treated much better than she had ever been. In her striving to compensate for this lack of consideration she hit on the ploy of always appearing overloaded with work.

Let us now interpret one of her dreams to show how deeply this behaviour pattern is rooted in her soul. This woman dreamt that she was at home conversing with her husband; but her husband did not look like a man, he looked like a woman. This is symbolic of the attitude with which she approaches all her experiences and all her relationships. The dream means that she has found equality with her husband. He is no longer the dominant male as her brother once was, he is like a woman. There is no difference in status between them. In her dream she has achieved the thing she has always wished for since her childhood.

In this way we have succeeded in linking two points in the psychological development of a human being. We have discovered her life style, her life curve, her behaviour pattern, and from these we can acquire a unified picture that we might sum up as follows: we are dealing here with a person who strives to play the dominant role by amiable means – an iron hand in a velvet glove.

7

PSYCHOLOGICAL
CHARACTERISTICS

PREPARATION FOR LIFE

One of the fundamental tenets of Individual Psychology is that all psychological phenomena are appropriate to a specific goal. In the development of the psyche as previously described we can see a constant preparation for a future in which the wishes of individuals appear to have been fulfilled. This is a universal human experience and all of us must go through this process. All the myths, legends and sagas that speak of an ideal future state are concerned with it. The belief that there was once a paradise, and the echo of this in the desire for a paradise regained, may be found in all religions. The widespread belief in the immortality of the soul, or reincarnation, is firm evidence of a conviction that the soul can achieve a totally new state. Every fairy tale with a happy ending is a witness to the fact that humanity's hope of a happy future has never faltered.

In child development there is an important phenomenon that shows very clearly the process of preparation for the future: play. Games must not be considered as the haphazard creations of parents or educators. They should be seen as educational aids and as stimuli for the child's psyche, imagination and life skills. Every game is a preparation for the future. The manner in which children approach a game, their choice of game and the importance they place upon it, show their attitude and relationship to their environment and how they relate to their fellow human beings. Whether they are hostile or whether they are friendly, and particularly whether they show leadership qualities, are evident in their play. In observing children at play we can see their whole attitude towards life; play is of the utmost importance to every child.

But play is more than a preparation for life. Games are above all communal exercises that enable children to develop their social feeling. Children who avoid games and play are always open to the suspicion that they have not adjusted satisfactorily to life. These children gladly withdraw from all games, or when they are sent to the playground with other children usually spoil the pleasure of the others. Pride, lack of self-esteem and the consequent fear of 'getting it wrong' are the three main reasons for this behaviour. In general, by watching children at play, we can determine with great certainty the extent and quality of their social feeling.

The goal of superiority, also revealed in play, betrays itself in the child's tendency to be the leader and organizer. We can discover this tendency by watching how children push themselves forward and to what degree they prefer those games that give them an opportunity to satisfy their desire to play the leading role. There are very few games that do not incorporate at least one of these factors: preparation for life, social feeling, or the striving for dominance.

There is, however, one other factor that is present in play: the opportunity for children to express themselves. Children are more or less left to their own devices in play, and their performance is stimulated by their interaction with other children. There are a number of games that especially emphasize this creative bent. In the preparation for a future profession, those games providing the opportunity for children to exercise their creative spirit are especially important. In the life stories of many people, it is not uncommon that some who made dresses for dolls in their childhood went on to make dresses for adults in later life.

Play is indivisibly bound up with the psyche. It is, so to speak, a kind of profession and must be considered as such. Therefore it is not a trivial matter to disturb children in their play. Play should never be considered merely as a way of passing the time. With regard to the goal of preparing for the future, all children have in them something of the adult they will become. Thus in the appraisal of individuals we can reach more accurate conclusions when we have a knowledge of their childhood.

ATTENTION AND DISTRACTION

Attention is one of the characteristics of the psyche that is in the very forefront of human accomplishments. When we focus on some particular event outside or inside our person, we have a feeling of particular tension, not spread over our entire body, but confined to a single sense organ such as the eye. We have the feeling that somehow, somewhere, information is being processed. In the case of the eye, the focusing of our gaze gives us this particular feeling of tension.

If an effort to attend to something calls forth a particular tension in any part of the psyche or in our musculature, then other tensions are at the same time excluded. Thus, as soon as we wish to be attentive to any one thing we try to exclude all other disturbances. Attention, so far as the psyche is concerned, means an attitude of willingness to relate to a definite fact or situation, perhaps as a preparation against an attack, certainly as a focusing of all our senses on to one particular subject.

Every human being, if we disregard mental illness, possesses the ability to pay attention; why then are there so many inattentive people? There are a number of reasons for this. In the first place, fatigue and sickness influence our ability to pay attention. Further, there are individuals whose lack of attention is due to the fact that they do not *want* to pay attention, because the object to which they should be attentive does not fit into their behaviour pattern. On the other hand their attention immediately awakens when they are considering some matter of importance to themselves. A further reason for lack of attentiveness is found in the tendency towards opposition. Children are often obstructive by nature, and answer 'No' to every suggestion offered to them. They feel the need to express opposition openly. It is the duty of the tactful educator to reconcile such children to the task in hand by relating their learning material to their behaviour pattern and making it applicable to their life style.

Some people see and hear and perceive every stimulus. Most people have a dominant sense, however. Some experience life exclusively through their eyes. Others depend entirely on their ears: they see nothing, take notice of nothing and are not interested in visual things, yet are on the alert to the slightest sound.

We may find individuals inattentive when their situation would warrant their utmost interest because their more dominant sense is not stimulated.

The most important factor in the awakening of attention is a genuine and deep-rooted interest in the world. Interest goes a lot deeper than attention. If we are interested, then it is obvious that we also pay attention; and where interest exists, educators need not concern themselves with attention. It becomes a simple instrument with which we conquer a field of knowledge for a definite purpose. No one has ever grown up without making mistakes in the process. It follows that attention is likewise involved when some mistaken attitude has become fixed in individuals; this happens when attention is directed towards things not relevant to the preparation for life. When interest is directed towards our own bodies, or towards our own power, we are attentive wherever these matters are involved, wherever there is something to be gained or wherever our power is threatened. Attention can never be given to anything extraneous unless some new interest is substituted for the power interest. We can see how children immediately jump to attention when their status and importance are in question. Their attention, on the other hand, is easily distracted when they have the feeling there is 'nothing in it' for them.

Lack of attention actually means nothing more than that individuals prefer to withdraw from a situation to which they are being asked to pay attention. It is therefore incorrect to say that someone cannot concentrate. It can easily be proved that they concentrate very well, but always on something else. Alleged lack of willpower and lack of energy are similar phenomena to the so-called inability to concentrate. In such cases we usually find an obdurate will and an indomitable energy pulling in a different direction. Treatment is not a simple matter. It can be attempted only by changing the entire life style of the individual. In every case we can be sure that we are dealing with a defect caused only by the pursuit of a different goal.

Inattention often becomes a permanent trait. We often meet individuals who have been given a definite task that they have declined to do, have only partially accomplished or have avoided altogether, with the result that they are always a burden to someone else. Their constant inattention is a fixed character trait that appears as soon as someone asks them to do anything.

CRIMINAL NEGLIGENCE AND FORGETFULNESS

We usually speak of criminal negligence when health or safety is threatened by the neglect of necessary precautions. Criminal negligence is a phenomenon that demonstrates the utmost degree of inattention. Such lack of attention is based on a lack of concern for one's fellow human beings. We can determine whether children think only of themselves, or whether they take into consideration the rights of others, by watching for signs of negligence in their games. Such phenomena are accurate indications of the community consciousness and social feeling of a human being. People whose community spirit is insufficiently developed take an interest in their fellows only with the greatest difficulty, even under threat of punishment; whereas in the presence of a well-developed community consciousness, this interest is self-evident.

Criminal neglect, therefore, amounts to a defective social feeling. We must not condemn, however, before we have tried to find out why individuals are less interested in their fellow human beings than we might expect.

We can induce forgetfulness, just as we can arrange the loss of valuables, by limiting our attention. The possibility for greater attention and interest may be so restricted by antagonistic attitudes that a memory lapse becomes inevitable, or at least more likely. This is the case, for instance, when children lose their school books. It is always evident that they have not yet become accustomed to their school surroundings. People who are constantly losing or misplacing their keys usually have never become resigned to the responsibility of their role. Forgetful people are usually those who prefer not to revolt openly, but their forgetfulness reveals a certain lack of interest in their tasks.

THE UNCONSCIOUS

Our case histories often describe individuals who do not understand the workings of their own minds. Only rarely will attentive people be able to tell you why they think as they do. Certain mental processes are not to be found in the realm of consciousness; although we can consciously force our attention to a certain degree, the stimulus for that attention lies not in our consciousness but in our interest. These again lie for the most part in the sphere of the unconscious. In its widest application, this is an important aspect of the life of the psyche.

We may seek and find the behaviour pattern of individuals in their unconscious. In their conscious life we have only a reflection, like a photographic negative, to deal with. A vain woman is usually unconscious of most of the instances in which she exhibits her vanity; she will behave in such a way as to present a charmingly modest picture to the world. It is not necessary, in order to be vain, actually to know that one is vain. Indeed, for the purposes of such a woman, it would be quite counterproductive for her to know that she was vain, for she could not then continue to be so. We can gain a certain security in failing to see our own vanity through directing our attention to something extraneous or irrelevant. The whole process takes place under cover. If you try to talk to a vain man about his vanity you will find it very difficult to carry on a conversation on the subject. He may show a tendency to evade the issue, to beat about the bush. This bears out our opinion; he wants to play his little game and immediately assumes a defensive attitude when someone attempts to reveal his little deception.

Human beings may be divided into two types: those who know more than average about their unconscious life and those who know less. In a great many cases we will also find that an individual of the second type concentrates upon a small sphere of activity, whereas individuals of the first type inhabit a much broader mental universe and have wide-ranging interests in people, things, events and ideas. Those individuals who feel pushed aside will naturally satisfy themselves with a small section of life, since they feel like strangers in a strange land and cannot see life's problems with as much clarity as those who are playing the game of life according to the rules. They make bad teammates. They will be less capable of understanding the finer points of life. Because of their very limited interest in living, they perceive only an insignificant segment of life's problems. This is because they are afraid that a broader view would be synonymous with a loss of personal power.

Individuals are often unaware of their own life skills because they undervalue themselves, we will find also that many individuals are not sufficiently aware of their own shortcomings. They may consider themselves to be good people, whereas in reality they do everything out of selfishness. Conversely, individuals will consider themselves selfish in circumstances where closer analysis shows them to be very good indeed. It really does not matter what you think of yourself, or what other people think of you. The important thing is your general attitude towards society, since this determines every wish, every interest and every activity of each individual.

We are dealing again with two types of human beings. In the first group are those who live a more conscious life, who approach the problems of life objectively and unblinkered. Those in the second group tend to approach life with a prejudiced attitude, and thus see only a small part of it. The behaviour and speech of individuals of this type always express unconscious attitudes. Two human beings living with one another may encounter difficulties in life because one of them is always obstructive. This is not an uncommon occurrence, but it is perhaps even more common to find both parties at loggerheads. Each party is unconscious of his or her obstructiveness. One is sure he is in the right, and argues that all he wants is a quiet life. The facts nevertheless prove him wrong; it is impossible for him to say a single word without sniping at his partner, even if his attack is not obvious to outsiders. On closer inspection we find that he has given himself up to a lifelong belligerence.

Human beings develop powers in themselves that are constantly at work, though they have no conscious knowledge of them. These faculties lie hidden in the unconscious, influence our lives and unless revealed and treated may have bitter consequences. In his novel *The Idiot*, Dostoevsky describes this so beautifully that psychologists have been marvelling at it ever since. At a social gathering a lady tauntingly cautions the hero of the novel not to upset an expensive Chinese vase that stands near him. The hero assures her that he will take care, but a few minutes later the vase lies shattered on the ground. No one in the group sees this occurrence as a mere accident; everyone feels it to be deliberate and in keeping with the whole character of the man, who felt insulted by the lady's teasing words.

In judging human beings we must not be guided solely by their conscious actions and expressions. Often little details of their thought and behaviour, of which they themselves are not aware, will give us a better insight into their real nature.

For example, people who practise such unpleasant habits as nail-biting or nose-picking do not know that in doing so, they betray their stubborn nature, because they do not understand what has led them to adopt these habits. We can assume that children must have been scolded repeatedly because of them. If, then, they persist despite the scoldings, they must be stubborn. With more expert observation, we would be able to draw very far-reaching conclusions about anyone, by watching for such significant details that mirror their whole being.

The two following cases will show how important it is to our psychological well-being that events experienced unconsciously remain in the unconscious. The human psyche has the capability of controlling consciousness. That is, it can make conscious something that our psyche wants brought to the surface, and conversely it can allow something to remain in the unconscious or even relegate it from conscious to unconscious, when the individual's comfort and peace of mind necessitate it.

The first case is that of a young man, an eldest child, who grew up with a sister younger than himself. His mother died when he was ten years old and from that time he was brought up by his father, who was a very intelligent, well-meaning, upright man. The father devoted most of his efforts to developing his son's ambition and spurring him on to greater efforts. The boy strove to be top of his class, did extraordinarily well academically, especially in science, and was also of extremely upright character and a born leader. All this was much to the joy of his father, who expected him to be a big success from the very first.

The boy's sister grew up to be his obdurate rival. She also developed very well, although she resorted to using weakness to achieve attention for herself at the expense of her brother. She had acquired considerable housekeeping skills, which her brother could not easily compete with. He found it very difficult to achieve the recognition and eminence in home life that he had so easily won in other fields of endeavour. The father soon noticed that his son was acquiring a bizarre attitude towards social life, which became more evident as he approached puberty. As a matter of fact he had no social life at all. He was wary of all new relationships and where these relationships concerned girls he simply ran away. At first his father saw nothing extraordinary in this, but as time went on the boy's social inhibitions acquired such dimensions that he hardly went out of the house. He would not even go out for walks except after dark. He became so shut in that he finally refused even to greet his old acquaintances, although his attitude in school and towards his father remained beyond criticism.

When matters had gone so far that no one could do anything with him, the father brought this boy to the doctor. A few consultations were enough to discover an explanation for the difficulty. This boy believed that his ears were small and that therefore everyone considered him very ugly. His ears were in fact perfectly normal. When he was told that his ears were no different from anyone else's, and when it was demonstrated to him that he was using this as an excuse to withdraw from society, he added that his teeth and his hair were ugly too. This also was untrue.

On the other hand it was obvious that he was inordinately ambitious. He was well aware of his ambition and believed that his father, who had constantly pushed him on to greater and greater efforts, had produced this trait in him. His plans for the future included a desire to become a great scientist. This would not be so remarkable if it had not been combined with a tendency to avoid all the obligations of humanity and fellowship. Why did this boy make use of such very childish arguments? If he had been right about his appearance, he might have been justified in approaching life with a certain caution and anxiety, because it is undoubtedly true that our civilization is unsympathetic to unattractive people.

Further examination showed that this boy's ambition was directed towards a particular goal. Previously, he had always been top of his class and he wanted to stay there. To achieve such a goal we have certain tools at our disposal, such as concentration, industry and so on. These were not enough for him. He attempted to exclude from his life everything that seemed an unnecessary distraction. He might have expressed himself like this: 'Since I am going to become famous and to dedicate myself entirely to science, I must exclude all social relationships as unnecessary.'

But he neither said nor thought this – at least, not consciously. On the contrary, he took his alleged unattractiveness as an excuse and made use of it to achieve his goal. The exaggeration of this insignificant fact gave him a good reason for doing what he really wanted to do. All he needed to do now was to have the courage to use his appearance as an excuse for pursuing his secret purpose. If he had said that he wished to live like a hermit in order to shun everything that could distract him from attaining his goal, his ambition would have been transparent to everyone. Although unconsciously he was dedicated to the idea of playing this heroic role, he was consciously unaware of his purpose.

It had never occurred to him that he wished to risk everything else in life to gain this one point. If he had consciously decided to stake everything in life on becoming a great scientist, he could not have been so secure as he was in his attempt to accomplish this by saying that he was ugly and dared not mix in society. In addition, anyone prepared to state openly that he wanted so much to be first and best that he was prepared to sacrifice all human relationships for the sake of his goal, would make himself ridiculous in the eyes of the world. It would be a fearful, unthinkable idea. There are certain things we cannot express too openly, both for our own sakes and for the sake of others. For this reason the guiding principle of this boy's life had to remain an unconscious one.

If we expose the motives of someone like this and show him the secret workings of his mind, we shall naturally disturb the balance of his entire psyche. What this individual has been trying at all costs to prevent, now happens! His unconscious thought processes are revealed for all to see. Unthinkable thoughts, untenable ideas, tendencies that, if conscious, would disturb our entire behaviour, are laid bare. It is a universal human phenomenon that everyone seizes upon those thoughts that justify their attitudes and rejects every idea that might prevent them from carrying on. Human beings dare to do only those things that, in their interpretation of the world, are valuable to them. We acknowledge whatever is helpful to us; whatever does not suit us is consigned to our unconscious.

The second case concerns another very young boy whose father, a teacher, also constantly spurred him on to be top of the class. In this case, too, the early days of the child were a series of victories. Wherever he appeared he was always the successful one. He was one of the most charming members of his community and he had several close friends.

A great change occurred in his eighteenth year. He lost all pleasure in life, was depressed and distracted and went to great lengths to withdraw from the world. No sooner did he make a friendship than he broke it off. Nobody understood his behaviour. His father, however, had hoped that his isolated life would enable him to dedicate himself more intensely to his studies.

During his treatment, this boy complained constantly that his father had robbed him of all joy in life, that he could find no self-confidence or courage to go on with life, and that there was nothing left for him to do but to live out the rest of his days in bitter solitude. His progress in his studies had already slowed down and he was failing in college. He explained that the change in his life had begun at a social gathering when his ignorance of modern literature had made him an object of ridicule among his friends. This and several similar experiences drove him into isolation and made him shun society. He was obsessed by the idea that his father was to blame for his misfortune, and their relationship became worse day by day.

These two cases are similar to each other in many respects. In the first case our patient was damaged by the rivalry of his sister, whereas in the second it was his belligerent attitude towards his father that was at fault. Both patients were led on by an idea we have been accustomed to call the heroic ideal. Both of them had become so intoxicated with their heroic ideal that they had lost all contact with life, had become discouraged and would have liked nothing better than to withdraw entirely from the struggle. But can we believe that the second boy would ever have declared openly to himself: 'Since I cannot be a great hero,

I shall withdraw from life and live out the rest of my days in bitter solitude'?

To be sure, his father had been wrong and his upbringing was at fault. It was quite evident that the boy had eyes for nothing but the bad upbringing of which he constantly complained, and that he wanted to justify his withdrawal by assuming that his upbringing had been so bad only withdrawal from society offered a solution to his problems. In this way he created a situation in which he could suffer no more defeats and could lay all the blame for his misfortune at his father's door. Only in this way was he able to salvage a fraction of his self-esteem and satisfy his striving for significance. He had a glorious past, and his future triumphs had been prevented only by the fact that his father, because of misguided ideas, had hindered him from going on to even more brilliant accomplishments.

We might say that something like this train of thought remained unconsciously in his mind: 'As I grow up, I'm getting nearer the sharp end of life. I realize that it will no longer be so easy for me always to be the first. I shall therefore withdraw from the race rather than compete unsuccessfully.' Such an idea is clearly unthinkable. No one would actually voice this attitude, but an individual can nevertheless act as if he had deliberately taken such a decision. This can be done by finding other arguments to use. By busying himself entirely with his father's mistakes, he manages to bow out of society and duck all life's decisions. Had this train of thought become conscious, the secret springs of his behaviour would of necessity have been disturbed. Therefore it remained unconscious, to great effect. How could anyone say that he was lacking in talent, when he had such a glorious past? To be sure no one could blame him now if he did not notch up any new triumphs! His father's guilt was never to be laid aside. The son was judge, plaintiff and defendant all rolled into one. Should he now give up such a favourable position? He knew too well that his father was to blame only so long as he, the son, continued to believe it was so.

DREAMS

It has long been maintained that we can draw conclusions about the personality as a whole from dreams. G. C. Lichtenberg, a contemporary of Goethe, once said that the character of a human being could be deduced more accurately from his dreams than from his actions and words. This is going a little too far. In our view, psychological phenomena must be considered with the greatest care and only in connection with other phenomena. Therefore we can only draw conclusions concerning the character of individuals from their dreams when we can find additional supporting evidence in other characteristics to substantiate our interpretations.

Attempts to interpret dreams date from prehistoric times. From historical research and the evidence of myths and sagas, we conclude that in times gone by people were far more concerned with the interpretation of dreams than we are today. We also find a much better understanding of dreams on the part of average people of those days than is the case today. We have only to recall the enormous role of dreams in the lives of the ancient Greeks, or remind ourselves of the many dreams described in the Bible, to make this point. Moreover, dreams in the Bible are either cleverly interpreted, or described as though it were understood that everyone would be able to interpret them correctly. This is so in the case of Joseph's dream of the sheaves of wheat, which he told to his brothers. In the case of the Nibelungen sagas, which originated in an entirely different culture, we can also conclude that dreams were accepted as evidence of facts.

If we study dreams as a means of approaching and learning something of the human psyche, we are hardly likely to view the problem from the standpoint of those investigators who seek fantastic and supernatural influences in dreams and in dream interpretation. We should rely upon the evidence of dreams only when we can be justified and supported in our assertions by other detailed observations.

The tendency to believe that dreams have a particular meaning for the future persists even today. There are idealists who go so far as to allow themselves to be influenced by their dreams. In this way, one of our patients tricked himself into avoiding every honourable occupation and devoted himself to gambling on the Stock Exchange. He always gambled according to the dreams he had. He had collected 'evidence' to prove he had always had bad luck whenever he failed to follow one of his dreams. To be sure, his dreams simply echoed all his daytime preoccupations. He patted himself on the back, so to speak, in his dream, and was able for a considerable time to say that he had prospered under the influence of his dream. Some time later he explained that he no longer attached any value to his dreams. Apparently by then he had lost all his money. Since this frequently happens to stock market speculators, even without dreams, we see no miracle at work here.

Individuals who are intensely interested in some particular task are preoccupied with the problem even at night. Some people do not sleep at all and constantly go over their problem while awake; others sleep but busy themselves with their plans in their dreams.

This peculiar phenomenon occupying our thoughts during our sleep is nothing more than the bridge from yesterday to tomorrow. If we know the attitude of individuals towards life in general, how they link the present and the future, we can usually understand the peculiarities of the bridge structure in their dreams and be able to draw valid conclusions from it. In other words our general attitude to life is the basis of all our dreams.

A young woman has the following dream: she dreams that her husband has forgotten their wedding anniversary and she reproaches him for it. This dream may mean several things. It immediately shows us that this marriage may be in trouble and the wife feels neglected. She explains, however, that in the dream she too forgot about the wedding anniversary at first, but finally remembered it, whereas her husband had to be reminded of it by her. She is the 'better half'. To a further question she replied that nothing like this had ever happened in real life and that her husband had always remembered their wedding anniversary. Therefore in the dream we see her tendency to be concerned about the future: something like this *might* happen. We can further conclude that she tends to make reproaches, to employ hypothetical arguments, and to nag her husband about possible rather than actual misdeeds.

Still, we could not be sure of our interpretation if we did not have other evidence available to reinforce our conclusions. Asked about her earliest childhood memories, this woman described an event that had always remained in her memory. When she was three years old, her aunt presented her with a carved wooden spoon of which she was very proud, but once as she was playing with it, it fell into a brook and floated away. For many days she cried so bitterly about her lost spoon that everyone at home was distressed too. The dream might lead us to believe that she was now thinking of the possibility that her marriage also might float away from her. What if her husband should forget their wedding anniversary?

Another time she dreamt that her husband had led her up into a high building. The stairs grew steeper and steeper. Thinking that she had perhaps climbed too high, she became terribly dizzy, had an attack of anxiety, and fainted. We may experience a similar sensation while awake, especially if we suffer from dizziness at a height. If we connect the second dream with the first one and blend them together, the thought, feeling, and content of these dreams give a clear impression that this is a woman who is afraid of falling, who is afraid of danger or calamity. We can imagine that the waning of her husband's affection would be such a calamity. What would happen if she and her husband were in some way incompatible? What if their marriage broke down? Scenes might occur and fights might take place, which might end with the wife's fainting away. This actually occurred once during a family argument!

Now we come closer to the meaning of the dream. It does not matter what forms the thought and emotional content of the dreams take, or what images are used for expressing them, so long as they *are* expressed. In dreams the waking problems of an individual are expressed in a metaphor. It is as though our patient said, 'Do not climb too high so that you will not fall too far!'

It may be worth recalling the reproduction of a dream in the 'Marriage Song' of Goethe. A knight comes home and finds his castle deserted. Tired out, he falls into his bed. In his dream he sees little figures coming out from under his bed and watches them going through a marriage ceremony. He is pleased by this dream. It is as though he wanted to confirm his need for a wife. What he saw here in miniature occurred later in reality as he celebrated his own marriage.

We find many well-known elements in this dream. In the first place the preoccupation of the poet with his own marriage is hidden behind it. We can see further how the dreamer relates the dream to his present situation. He feels a need to be married. In his dream he addresses the problem of marriage and on the following day decides that it would be better if he were to get married.

Now let us consider a dream of a 28-year-old patient. The pattern of the dream, going up and down like a temperature chart, indicates very clearly the preoccupations that fill the life of this man. It is easy to recognize the feeling of inferiority that gives rise to strivings for power and dominance. He says:

I am on a boat trip with a large group of people. We get out *en route* because the ship on which we are to take this trip is too small, and we must stay in a town overnight. During the night, a report comes that the ship is sinking, and all the travellers are called to work the pumps to keep the ship afloat. I remember that I have some valuables in my baggage on board and rush to the ship, where everyone else is already working at the pumps. I try to avoid this work and look for the baggage room. I succeed in fishing my knapsack through the window and at the same time I see a penknife that I like very much lying next to my knapsack. I put it in the knapsack. With an acquaintance I jump off as the ship sinks deeper and deeper. We jump off into the sea and get to dry land. Since the pier is too high for us to climb, we wander further along and come to a precipitous cliff that I must go down. I slide down. I have not seen my companion since leaving the ship. I slide faster and faster and fear that I will be killed. Finally I land at the bottom and fall just in front of another acquaintance. It is a young man who I do not know well, who once took part in a strike and walked very quietly among the strikers. I liked him. He greets me with reproachful words, as though he knew that I had abandoned the others on the ship. 'What are you doing here?' he asks. I try to escape from this abyss, which is surrounded by precipitous cliffs from which ropes hang down. I dare not use the ropes because they are too thin. I keep trying to climb out of the abyss, but I always slide back again. Finally I am on top, but I don't know how I got there. It seems to me that I purposely did not want to dream this part of the dream, as if I wanted to skip over it impatiently. On the edge of the abyss, on top, there is a road which is separated from it by a fence. People are going past, and greet me in a friendly fashion.

If we look back into the life of this dreamer the first thing that we learn is that he constantly suffered from severe illness up to the fifth year of his life, and that even after this time he was often ill. As a result of his bad health he was carefully and anxiously protected by his parents. His contact with other children was very slight. When he wanted to make contact with grown-ups he was always told by his parents that children should be seen and not heard and that children do not belong with adults. He thus failed at a very early age to make those relationships that are necessary for social life, and he had contact only with his parents. A further consequence of this was that his development lagged considerably behind that of his companions of the same age. It is not surprising that they considered him stupid and soon made him the butt of all their jokes. This circumstance, again, prevented him from making friends.

An already strong feeling of inferiority was made much worse by these circumstances. He was brought up by his well-intentioned, but very irascible, military father, and by his weak, uncomprehending, very domineering mother. Although his parents did what they believed to be their best, his upbringing must have been very strict. Discouragement played a considerable role in his development. An early and very significant childhood memory was that when he was only three years old his mother made him kneel on peas for half an hour because he had disobeyed her, although she knew the reason for it. He had been frightened by a man on a horse and had therefore refused to run an errand for his mother. As a matter of fact he was beaten very seldom, but when he was, he was always beaten with a multiple-thonged dog whip. Afterwards he always had to say why he had been beaten and beg for forgiveness. 'The child should know', said the father, 'how he has misbehaved.' Once he was beaten unjustly. As he could not say afterwards why he had been beaten, he was beaten again and again until he invented some misdeed or other and confessed to that.

A feeling of hostility towards his parents was present from his earliest days. His feeling of inferiority had acquired such dimensions that he could not even imagine being superior. His life at school as well as at home was an almost unbroken chain of greater or lesser defeats. He felt that even the smallest victory was denied him. At school, up to the time when he was eighteen years old, he was always a laughing-stock. Once he was laughed at even by his teacher, who read his work aloud to the class and accompanied the reading with mocking remarks.

Every one of these occurrences forced him further and further into isolation. Eventually he began to withdraw from the world of his own accord. In his battle with his parents he discovered a very effective though costly method of attack. He refused to speak. With this gesture, he cut the main link between himself and the outer world. Since he was unable to speak to anyone, he became entirely solitary. Misunderstood by everybody, he spoke to no one, particularly not his parents; and finally no one spoke to him. Every attempt to get him to socialize foundered, as every attempt to establish intimate relationships later in his life also failed, much to his sorrow. This is the story of his life until his twenty-eighth year. The deep inferiority complex that had permeated his whole spirit had given rise to an ambition beyond all reason, an uncontrolled striving for significance and superiority that ceaselessly distorted his attitude to the world. The less he spoke, the more his mind was filled, day and night, with dreams of triumphs and victories.

And thus he dreamt one night the dream we have described above, in which we see clearly the workings of his psyche. In conclusion let us recall a dream the Latin orator Cicero related. It is one of the most famous prophetic dreams in literature.

Once the poet Simonides found the corpse of an unidentified man lying in the street and gave it a decent burial. Later he was about to attempt a sea journey, but was warned by the ghost of this dead man in a dream that if he made the journey, he would be shipwrecked. Simonides did not go. The ship was indeed lost with all hands.

According to Cicero, this occurrence made a profound impression on all who heard of it for hundreds of years. If we want to interpret this occurrence we need to bear in mind that in those days shipwrecks were common. We also need to remember that because of this, many people dreamt of shipwrecks on the eve of a sea journey. Among these many dreams, this one particular dream was so close to real-life events that it was handed down to posterity. Lovers of mysterious happenings have a special weakness for just such stories. Our more down-to-earth interpretation of this dream is as follows: our poet, for reasons of self-preservation, was probably less than enthusiastic about this trip. As the date of departure approached, he needed to justify his hesitation. For this reason he allowed the dead man, who was under an obligation to him for his decent burial, to appear in a prophetic role. Of course he did not take the trip. If the ship had not sunk, the world would never have heard anything about the dream. We take notice only of those things that disturb us, that remind us there are more things in heaven and earth than we can comprehend. The prophetic nature of dreams is understandable as far as we know that both dream and reality are experienced in a way that reflects an individual's attitude to life.

Another thing we must consider is the fact that not all dreams are so easily understood; as a matter of fact, only a few are. We forget the dream immediately after it has left its peculiar impression on us and do not understand what lies behind it, unless we have been instructed in the interpretation of dreams. Yet these dreams, too, are only a symbolic and metaphorical expression of an individual's activity and behaviour pattern. The main significance of such a simile or comparison is that it gives access to a solution. If we are struggling to solve a problem and our personality points us in a specific direction, then we have only to find something to give us a final push in that direction. The dream is extraordinarily well suited to intensify an emotion, or produce the impetus needed to resolve a particular problem in a particular way. The fact that dreamers do not understand the connection does not matter. It is enough that they get the necessary material and boost from somewhere. The dream itself will give evidence of the manner in which dreamers' thought processes express themselves, just as it will indicate their behaviour pattern. The dream is like a column of smoke that shows a fire is burning somewhere; the experienced woodsman can observe the smoke and tell what kind of wood is burning, just as the psychiatrist can draw conclusions about the nature of individuals by interpreting their dreams.

To sum up, we can say that dreams show not only that dreamers are searching for a solution to one of their problems, but also how they approach these problems. In particular, social feeling and the striving for power, those two factors that influence dreamers in their relationship with the world and reality, will be especially evident in their dreams.

INTELLIGENCE

In considering those psychological characteristics that enable us to understand individuals, we have not yet looked at intellectual abilities. We have placed little value upon what individuals say or think about themselves, because we know that each of us can go astray and each of us feels obliged to retouch the psychological image we present to the world, using various subtle ploys. One thing we can safely do, however, is to draw certain limited conclusions from specific processes and their expression in speech. We cannot exclude thought and speech from our examination if we wish to judge individuals accurately.

What we are pleased to call intelligence – that is the special ability to make judgements – has been the subject of numerous observations, analyses and tests, including so-called intelligence tests, in children and adults. Up to the present time these tests have been unsuccessful. Whenever a group of pupils are tested, the results usually show what the teacher could easily have determined without tests. At first, experimental psychologists were very proud of this, although it must have been evident at the same time that the tests were, to a certain degree, superfluous. Another objection to intelligence tests is the fact that children's abilities and their thought and judgement processes do not develop uniformly, so that many children who previously scored poorly may do extremely well a few years later. Another point that must be considered is that city children, and those from well-educated backgrounds, are better prepared for the tests by virtue of their broader life experiences and thus obtain artificially high scores that overshadow other less well-prepared children. It is well known that eight- to ten-year-old children of well-to-do families score much more highly than poor children of the same age. This does not mean that the children of the wealthy are more intelligent; the reason for the difference lies entirely in their environment.

Up to the present time we have not progressed far with intelligence tests, as is obvious when we examine the sorry results obtained in Berlin and Hamburg, where a large proportion of those children who scored highest in intelligence tests failed dismally later on in their education. This phenomenon would seem to prove that good intelligence-test results are no certain guarantee of a child's future healthy development. The experiments of Individual Psychology, on the other hand, have stood up far better, because they have not been directed towards the measurement of a particular degree of development, but have been designed rather to further the understanding of the positive factors underlying this development. These same observations have, when necessary, given children the chance to improve their situation for themselves. It has been the principle of Individual Psychology never to consider children's powers of thought and judgement in isolation, but to look at them only in the context of their whole psyche.

8

MALE AND FEMALE

MEN, WOMEN AND THE DIVISION OF LABOUR

From our previous considerations we have learned that two great tendencies dominate all psychological activities. These two tendencies, social feeling and the individual striving for power and domination, influence every human activity and colour the attitude of all individuals both in their striving for security and in their fulfilment of the three great challenges of life: love, work and social relationships. In examining the workings of the psyche, we shall have to become skilled in investigating the quantitative and qualitative relationships of these two factors if we want to understand the human psyche. The relationship of these factors to one another conditions the degree to which individuals are capable of comprehending the logic of communal life, and therefore the degree to which they are capable of subordinating themselves to the division of labour that grows out of the requirements of that communal life.

Division of labour is a vital factor in the maintenance of human society. Everyone at some time, or in some place, must do their share. Anyone who does not do their share, who denies the value of communal life, is by definition anti-social and opts out of human fellowship. In simple cases of this sort we speak of egotism, of malice, of self-centredness, of trouble-making. In more complicated cases we see the eccentrics, the layabouts and the criminals. Public condemnation of these characteristics grows out of an understanding of their origins, a feeling that they are incompatible with the demands of social life.

Any person's value, therefore, is determined by their attitude towards their fellow human beings and by the extent to which they take part in the division of labour that communal life demands. Their acceptance of this communal life makes them important to other human beings, makes them a link in the great chain binding society together. The place of individuals in society is determined by their capabilities. Much confusion has clouded this simple truth, because the striving for power and the desire for dominance have introduced false values into the normal division of labour. This striving for power and dominance has distorted the overall pattern and has given us a false basis for the judgement of human values.

Individuals have disturbed this division of labour by refusing to adapt to their role in the community. Further difficulties have arisen out of the selfish ambition and power-hungriness of individuals who have interfered with communal life and communal work for their own selfish interests. Similarly, complications have been caused by class differences in our society. Personal power and economic interest have influenced the division of labour by reserving all the better positions – that is, those affording the greatest power – for members of certain groups, while other individuals from other groups have been excluded from them. The recognition of these numerous influences on the structure of society enables us to understand why the division of labour has never worked smoothly. Forces are continually at work disturbing this division of labour and attempting to create privilege for one group, and slavery for another.

The fact that the human race consists of both men and women leads to another kind of division of labour. For purely physical reasons, women have been excluded from some activities, while certain tasks have not been given to men on the grounds that they may be better employed doing other things. This division of labour ought to have been instituted quite impartially. Movements for the emancipation of women, when able to view the matter dispassionately, have accepted the logic of this point of view. The aim of division of labour is not to rob women of their femininity, or disturb the natural relationships between men and women. Ideally, we are all given the opportunity to do the things we are best suited for. In the course of human civilization this division of labour has developed in such a way that women have taken over certain tasks to enable men to function more effectively elsewhere. We cannot condemn this division of labour so long as it is operated fairly and without misuse of abilities or resources.

MALE DOMINANCE
As a result of the development of our culture in the direction of personal power, especially through the efforts of certain individuals and certain classes of society who wish to secure privileges for themselves, this division of labour has fallen into characteristic patterns that have affected our entire civilization. Consequently, the importance of the male is greatly emphasized in today's culture. The division of labour is such that the privileged group – men – are guaranteed certain advantages, and this results in their domination over women in the division of labour. Thus the dominant male directs the activity of women in such a way that men always seem to get the good things of life, whereas women are given the tasks that men prefer to avoid. As things stand now there is a constant striving on the part of men to dominate women, and a corresponding dissatisfaction with masculine domination on the part of women. Since the two sexes are so interdependent it is easy to understand how this constant tension leads to discord and friction, which must of necessity be extraordinarily painful to both sexes.

All our institutions, our traditional attitudes, our laws, our morals, our customs, bear witness to the fact that they are determined and maintained by privileged males for the glory of male domination. These institutions reach out even into the nursery and have a far-reaching influence upon the child's psyche. Children need not fully understand these influences for their emotional life to be deeply affected by them. Such attitudes are worth considering when, for example, we see a little boy flying into a rage when asked to put on 'girlish' clothes. If you let a boy's craving for power reach a certain level, you will surely find him showing a preference for the masculine privileges which, he realizes, guarantee his superiority everywhere.

We have already mentioned that child-rearing in our families nowadays is only too likely to overvalue the striving for power. The consequent tendency to maintain and exaggerate masculine privileges follows naturally, for it is usually the father who is the family symbol of power. His mysterious comings and goings interest children much more than the constant presence of a mother. Children quickly recognize the prominent role their father plays. They notice if Father sets the pace, makes all the arrangements and appears everywhere as the leader. They see how everyone obeys him and sees how the mother may ask him for advice. From every angle, the father seems to be the strong, powerful one. There are children who look up to their fathers to such an extent that they believe everything the father says must be right; they prove the rightness of their own views simply by asserting that their father once said so. Even in those cases in which the father's influence seems less marked, children will still get the impression of the dominance of the father if he seems to bear the whole load of family responsibility, whereas in fact it is only the division of labour that may enable him to use his powers to better advantage.

As far as the history of the origin of masculine dominance is concerned, we must point out that this phenomenon does not occur naturally. This fact is borne out by the large body of legislation that is necessary to guarantee male domination. It is also an indication that before masculine domination was legally enforced, there must have been other times in which masculine privilege was not nearly so assured. History bears this out. In the days of the matriarchy it was the mother – the woman – who played the dominant role, particularly so far as the children were concerned. At that time every man in the clan was duty bound to respect the honoured position of the mother. Certain customs are still coloured by this ancient institution, for example in some cultures, all strange men are introduced to children with the title of 'uncle' or 'cousin'. A terrific battle must have preceded the transition from matriarchy to masculine domination. Men who like to believe that their privileges and prerogatives evolved naturally will be surprised to learn that men did not possess these prerogatives from the beginning, but had to fight for them. The triumph of men was simultaneous with the subjugation of women, and it is most clearly seen in the development of the law, which bears witness to this long process of subjugation.

Masculine dominance, therefore, is not a natural thing. There is evidence to prove that it developed chiefly as a result of constant battles between primitive peoples, in the course of which man assumed the more prominent role as warrior and finally used his newly won superiority to retain the leadership for himself and for his own ends. Hand in hand with this process was the development of property rights and inheritance rights that became a tool of masculine domination, in that man was usually the acquirer and owner of property.

Growing children need not, however, read books on this subject. Although they know nothing of ancient history, they sense that the male is the privileged member of the family. This occurs even when fathers and mothers, with considerable insight, reject those privileges inherited from former days in favour of a greater equality. It is very difficult to convince children that a mother engaged in household duties is as important as a father holding down a responsible job outside the home.

Think what it means to a young boy who witnesses the prevailing masculine privilege from his earliest days. From the day of his birth he may be received with greater enthusiasm than a girl child, for all too often parents prefer male children. A boy senses at every step that, as the son and heir, he has greater privileges and higher social value. Chance remarks and incidents constantly call his attention to the greater importance of the masculine role. Male domination is also made clear to him when he sees female workers doing menial tasks, and his impressions are reinforced by the fact that the women around him are not at all convinced of their equality with men.

The vital question all women should ask their prospective husbands before marriage is: 'What is your attitude towards male domination, particularly in family life?' This question, however, is seldom asked and even more seldom answered. Sometimes we find women striving for equality and sometimes we find varying degrees of resignation. In contrast we see men convinced from boyhood that they have a more important role to play. They interpret this conviction as an implicit duty and concentrate on responding to the challenges of life and society in a privileged, masculine manner.

Every situation that arises out of this relationship is absorbed by children. What they get out of it is a number of pictures concerning the nature of woman, in which for the most part the woman presents a sorry figure. In this way the development of the boy has a distinct masculine influence. What he believes to be the worthwhile goals in his striving for power are exclusively masculine qualities and a masculine outlook. A typical male attitude grows out of this and clearly reveals its origins. Certain character traits are labelled as masculine, others as feminine, although there is no objective basis for these evaluations. If we compare the psychology of boys and girls and find evidence that seems to support this classification, we are dealing not with natural phenomena but with individuals who have been directed along a very narrow channel, whose life style and behaviour patterns have been narrowed down by specific conceptions of power. These conceptions of power have indicated to them with compelling force their places in the scheme of things.

There is no justification for the differentiation between 'manly' and 'womanly' character traits. We shall see how both groups of traits are liable to be used to gratify the striving for power. In other words, we shall see that a person can pursue power with so-called 'feminine' traits such as obedience and submissiveness, just as the advantages obedient children enjoy sometimes bring them much more into the limelight than disobedient children, though the striving for power is present in both cases. Our psychological investigations are often made more difficult by this fact that the striving for power can express itself in the most complex fashion.

As a boy grows older, masculinity becomes an important duty. His ambition, his desire for power and superiority, are indisputably connected and identified with the duty to be masculine. For many boys who desire power it is not sufficient simply to be aware of their masculinity; they must prove that they are men, and therefore they must have privileges. They may accomplish this on the one hand by efforts to excel; on the other hand, they may succeed by lording it over all the females around them in every possible way. According to the degree of resistance they meet, these boys make use of either stubbornness and rebellion or craft and cunning to gain their ends.

Since every human being is judged according to the criteria of the privileged male, it is no wonder that we always hold this standard up in front of a boy. Inevitably he measures himself according to it, observing himself in action and wondering whether his activities are sufficiently 'masculine', whether he is 'fully a man'. What we consider 'masculine' nowadays is, above all, something purely egotistical, something that satisfies self-love and brings a feeling of superiority and domination over others. It accomplishes all this with the aid of seemingly positive characteristics such as courage, strength, devotion to duty, the winning of all manner of victories (especially over women), the acquisition of positions, honours and titles, resistance against so-called 'feminine' tendencies, and so on. There is a constant battle for personal superiority because dominance counts as a 'masculine' virtue.

In this way every boy imitates the characteristics he sees in adult men, especially his father. We can see the ramifications of this artificially induced delusion of grandeur throughout our society. At an early age a boy is urged to secure for himself a reserve of power and privilege. This is what is called 'manliness'. In bad cases it degenerates into arrogance and brutality.

The advantages of being a man are, under present conditions, very inviting. We must not be astonished, therefore, when we see many girls who maintain a masculine ideal either as an unattainable desire or as a standard for the judgement of their own behaviour. This ideal may manifest itself as a pattern for both behaviour and appearance. It seems that in our culture many women want to be like men! In this group, particularly, we find those girls who have an uncontrollable desire to distinguish themselves in games and activities that for reasons of physique are more appropriate to boys. They climb trees, prefer to play with boys and avoid every 'womanly' activity as a shameful thing. They gain satisfaction only through masculine activities. We can understand their preference for manliness when we realize that the striving for superiority is more concerned with the meaning we attach to activities than with the activities themselves.

THE ALLEGED INFERIORITY OF WOMEN
Man has habitually justified his domination not only by claiming that this position is a natural one, but also that his dominance arises inevitably from the inferiority of woman. This conception

of the inferiority of woman is so widespread that it affects all races. Linked with this prejudice is a certain uneasiness on the part of men, which may well have originated in the time of the war against the matriarchy when female power was a source of real anxiety. We are constantly coming across indications of this in literature and history. A Latin author writes: 'Mulier est hominis confusio', 'Woman is the confusion of man'. A popular theme of theological debates was whether women had souls, and learned theses were written on the question of whether women were actually human. The centuries of witch-hunting bear sorry witness to the errors, the fears and the confusion over such questions, all through that shameful era.

Women were often regarded as the source of all evil, as in the biblical conception of original sin, or as in the *Iliad* of Homer. The story of Helen demonstrated how one woman could throw whole nations into confusion and disaster. Legends and fairy tales from all ages are concerned with the moral inferiority of women, their wickedness and duplicity, their treachery and fickleness. A concept of 'womanly folly' has even been used as an argument in legal cases. Along with these prejudices goes the denigration of women's ability, work and intelligence. Proverbs, anecdotes, mottoes and jokes, in all literatures and among all peoples, are full of degrading references to women. Women have been accused of spitefulness, pettiness, stupidity and so on.

Men can go to extraordinary lengths to bear witness to the inferiority of women. The ranks of men like Strindberg and Schopenhauer who have upheld this thesis have been swelled by a not inconsiderable number of women who have been resigned to a belief in their own inferiority. These are the champions of woman's duty of submission. The degradation of women and of their work continues to be demonstrated by the fact that women are frequently paid less than men, regardless of whether their work is of equal value.

In the comparison of results of intelligence and aptitude tests it was found that in some subjects, such as mathematics, boys showed more talent, whereas girls showed greater aptitude for other subjects, such as languages. Boys do actually show greater talent than girls for studies that can prepare them for traditionally masculine occupations; but this talent is more apparent than real. If we investigate the situation of the girls more closely we learn that the story of women's inferior abilities is a palpable lie.

Girls are daily subjected to the argument that they are less able than boys and are capable only of trivial activities. It is not surprising, then, that sooner or later they become convinced that a bitter and immutable fate is reserved for women and actually believe in their own inferiority. Discouraged in this manner, a girl will approach 'masculine' occupations, if she ever gets the opportunity to approach them at all, with a closed mind. She assumes, first, that she will not be sufficiently interested in them. And if she does become interested, she soon loses heart through lack of encouragement and belief in herself.

Under such circumstances, so-called proof of the lesser capability of women can appear convincing. There are two reasons for this. In the first place, the error is accentuated by the fact that the value of a human being is frequently judged from purely commercial angles, or on one-sided and purely egotistical grounds. With such prejudices we can hardly be expected to understand how far performance and capability coincide with psychological development. And this leads us to the second main point that is responsible for the fallacy of women's lesser capability. It is frequently overlooked that girls come into the world with a prejudice sounding in their ears calculated solely to rob them of their belief in their own value, to shatter their self-confidence and destroy their hope of ever doing anything worthwhile. If this prejudice is constantly reinforced, if girls see again and again how women are assigned to servile roles, it is not difficult to understand how they lose courage, fail to face their obligations and shrink from tackling life's problems. After all that, no wonder girls can appear useless and incapable!

Yet if we were to approach any human being, undermine their self-respect so far as their relationship to society is concerned, create in them a sense of hopelessness about accomplishing anything, and destroy their courage, and then we were to find that they never amounted to anything, we would not dare to maintain that we were right all along. We would surely have to admit that we ourselves had caused all his distress!

It is easy enough in our civilization for a girl to lose courage and self-confidence. And yet, certain intelligence tests revealed the interesting fact that a particular group of girls, aged from fourteen to eighteen, demonstrated greater talent and intelligence than any other group, boys included. Further researches showed that these were all girls from families in which the mother was either the sole breadwinner or contributed largely to the family budget. These girls were in a home background in which the prejudice about the lesser capability of women was either absent or slight. They could see with their own eyes the rewards of their mothers' hard work, and as a result they developed much more freely and much more independently, entirely uninfluenced by those inhibitions inevitably associated with a belief in the lesser powers of women.

A further argument against there being any truth in this prejudice is the not inconsiderable number of women who have achieved equal eminence with men in a wide range of fields, particularly in literature, art, crafts and medicine. As well as these outstanding women there are, of course, equal numbers of men who not only do not achieve anything but are so thoroughly ineffectual that we could easily cite them as proof (spurious, of course) that men were the inferior sex.

One of the bitter consequences of the prejudice concerning the inferiority of women is the clear-cut division and pigeon-holing of concepts: thus 'masculine' denotes worthwhile, powerful, victorious, capable; whereas 'feminine' is synonymous with obedient, servile, subordinate. This thinking has become so deeply embedded in human thought processes that in our civilization everything laudable has a 'masculine' connotation, whereas everything less valuable or actually derogatory is designated 'feminine'. We all know men who would feel deeply insulted if we told them they had feminine qualities, whereas it is no insult if we say to a woman that she has masculine ones. The emphasis is always such that everything characteristic of woman appears inferior.

Character traits that are alleged to prove the fallacious contention of woman's inferiority reveal themselves on closer observation to be nothing more than the manifestations of inhibited psychological development. We do not claim to be able to make all children into what are called 'talented' individuals, but we can always make 'untalented' adults out of them. We ourselves have never done this, fortunately. We know others, however, who have succeeded only too well. That such a fate overtakes girls more frequently than boys, in our day and age, can easily be recognized. Moreover, we have often seen these apparently 'untalented' children suddenly become so talented that it seemed nothing short of a miracle!

REJECTING THE WOMAN'S ROLE

The obvious advantages of being a man have caused such severe disturbances in the psychological development of women that there is an almost universal dissatisfaction with the feminine role. The mental development of women moves in much the same way, and according to much the same set of rules, as that of men who have a strong sense of inferiority because of their position in life. An additional, aggravating complication awaits a girl because of the prejudice about her alleged inferiority as a woman.

If a considerable number of girls achieve some sort of compensation, they owe it to their own character and intelligence, but sometimes also to certain acquired privileges. This shows clearly how one mistake may lead to others. Such privileges are the special dispensations, the exemptions from obligations and the luxuries that give a semblance of advantage in that they appear to show a high degree of respect for women. There may be a certain degree of idealism in this, but it is, basically, always an ideal that has been fashioned by men for their own advantage. George Sand once described this very tellingly when she said: 'The virtue of woman is a fine invention of man.'

In general we can distinguish three kinds of reactions by women faced with the feminine stereotype. One kind has already been indicated: the girl who develops in an active, 'masculine' direction. She becomes extraordinarily energetic and ambitious and is constantly fighting for the prizes of life. She strives to outdo her brothers and male comrades, chooses activities usually chosen by men, is interested in male-dominated sports and so on. Very often she evades all the relationships of love and marriage. If she enters into such a relationship she may threaten it by striving to be superior to her husband. She may show a strong disinclination for housewifery of any kind. She may voice her disinclination directly, or show it indirectly by claiming to be hopeless at it. If so, she will prove her point every day with displays of domestic ineptitude.

This is the type that seeks to compensate for the evil of the masculine attitude with a 'masculine' response. She is forever on the defensive. She is called a tomboy, a hoyden, a 'mannish' woman, and so on. These labels, however, are based upon a misconception. There are many people who believe that there is a congenital factor in the makeup of such girls, a certain 'masculine' secretion of the glands that causes their 'masculine' attitude. The whole history of civilization, however, shows us that the pressure exerted upon women, and the restrictions to which they must submit even today, cannot be borne by any human being; they always give rise to revolt. If this revolt now manifests itself in the direction we call 'masculine', the reason for it is simply that there are only two sex roles possible. We must pattern ourselves on one of two models, either the ideal woman or the ideal man. Rejection of the woman's role must therefore appear 'masculine', and vice versa. This does not happen because of some mysterious glandular secretion, but because there *is* no other possible role. We must never lose sight of the difficulties under which the psychological development of a girl takes place. Until we can guarantee each woman absolute equality with men we cannot ask her to subscribe to all the expected patterns of behaviour that make up our society.

The second type of reaction comes from the woman who goes through life with an attitude of resignation, who exhibits an almost unbelievable degree of adjustment, obedience and humility. To all outward appearances she stays put and does as she is told, but she demonstrates such a high degree of clumsiness and helplessness that she never gets anything done. She may display nervous symptoms, which show the world how weak and in need of protection she is. In this way she shows clearly how ill-prepared she is for her role in life. She is a martyr to her 'nerves'. 'Look at me', she seems to say, 'I try so hard. It isn't my fault that I'm sick and can't cope.' And because she is 'sick', she cannot take up any of life's challenges satisfactorily. This woman's submission, her humility, her self-denial, emanate from the same spirit of revolt as that expressed by the type of woman previously described, a revolt that says clearly enough: 'This is no life for me!'

The woman who does not rebel in any way against the womanly role, but carries within her the torturing consciousness that she is condemned to a life of inferiority and subordination, makes up the third type. She is fully convinced of the inferiority of women, just as she is convinced that only men are called on to do the worthwhile things in life. In consequence, she accepts men's privileged position. She swells the chorus of voices singing the praises of man as the doer and the achiever, and demands a special position for him. She shows her feeling of weakness as clearly as if she sought recompense and demanded additional support because of it. But this attitude is the beginning of a long-prepared revenge. She will shift her responsibilities onto her husband with a light-hearted aside such as : 'It takes a man to do that!'

Although there are those who consider women inferior, the business of child-rearing is largely delegated to them. Let us now picture these three types of women in relation to this most important and difficult task. At this juncture we can differentiate the types even more clearly. Women of the first type, those with the 'masculine' attitude, may be excessively strict and preoccupied with punishment, and thus impose tremendous pressures on their children – pressures that the children will, of course, attempt to escape. This type of upbringing results at best in a sort of military training, which is quite valueless. Children usually think that mothers of this kind are very bad parents. Any shouting and fuss always have a bad effect, and there is always the danger that girls will be encouraged to imitate their mothers, whereas boys may be permanently frightened away from women. Among men who have suffered the tyranny of such mothers we find a number who avoid women like the plague, as if incapable of trusting any woman. The result is a clear-cut division between the sexes, which we can readily understand despite the fact that there are still some researchers who speak of a 'faulty apportionment of the masculine and feminine elements'.

Individuals of the other two types are equally ineffective as parents. They may be so hesitant that the children soon discover their lack of self-confidence and become out of control.

In this case the mother renews her efforts, nags and scolds and threatens to tell the father. The fact that she calls upon a man to enforce discipline betrays her again, and shows her lack of faith in her child-rearing skills. She abrogates her child-rearing responsibilities as if to justify her view that only men are capable of everything, including bringing up children. Such women may simply avoid all efforts at child-rearing and shift the responsibility for it onto husbands and teachers without any remorse, since they feel they are incapable of doing it successfully themselves.

Dissatisfaction with the womanly role is even more evident among girls who escape from life for some so-called 'higher' reason. Nuns, and anyone else who takes up an occupation demanding celibacy, are a case in point. Their lack of acceptance of their role as women is clearly demonstrated in this gesture. Similarly, many girls go into employment at an early age because the independence they achieve at work seems to offer them a protection against the threat of marriage. Here again the driving force is the disinclination to assume the womanly role.

What of those cases in which marriage takes place, in which we could believe that the feminine role had been voluntarily assumed? We find that marriage need not necessarily indicate that a girl has reconciled herself with her womanly role. The example of a thirty-six-year-old woman is typical of this. She came to the doctor complaining of various nervous symptoms. She was the eldest child of a marriage between an ageing man and a very domineering woman. The fact that her mother, a very beautiful young girl, had married an old man leads us to suspect that in her parents' marriage the disinclination for the feminine role played some part. This marriage did not turn out happily. The mother ruled the house like a virago, insisted upon having her own way at all costs, and disregarded everyone else's feelings. The old man was pushed into a corner at every opportunity. The daughter described how her mother would not even allow her father to lie down on the sofa to rest. All her mother's activity concentrated on maintaining certain 'principles of domestic economy' that she felt had to be enforced. These were absolute laws within the family.

Our patient grew up a very capable child who was made much of by her father. On the other hand, her mother was never satisfied and seemed to be always against her. Later, when a son was born, towards whom the mother was far more understanding and affectionate, the atmosphere became unbearable. The little girl was conscious that she had an ally in her father who, no matter how modest and retiring he was in other things, could take up the cudgels when his daughter's interests were at stake. Thus she began to hate her mother deeply.

In this stubborn conflict the obsessive cleanliness of the mother became the daughter's favourite point of attack. The mother was so fastidious in her cleanliness that she did not even allow the servant girl to touch a door knob without wiping it afterwards. The child took a special pleasure in going about as dirty and ill-clad as possible, and in making the house dirty whenever she had the opportunity.

She developed all those characteristics that were the exact opposite of what her mother expected of her. This fact speaks very clearly against the theory of inherited characteristics. If a child develops only those characteristics that annoy and frustrate her mother almost beyond endurance, there must be either a conscious or an unconscious plan underlying them. The enmity between mother and child continued, and it would be impossible to imagine a more bitter hostility.

When this little girl was eight years old, the situation was as follows. The father was permanently on his daughter's side; her mother went about with a face like thunder, making pointed remarks, enforcing her 'rules' and reproaching the girl. She, embittered and belligerent, used her sarcastic tongue to hurt her mother. An additional complicating factor was the congenital heart disease of the younger brother, who was his mother's favourite and a very pampered child who used his illness to hold the attention of his mother to an even greater degree. It was clear that neither parent got on with both children. These were the circumstances in which this little girl grew up.

The girl then fell ill with a nervous complaint that no one could explain. The main symptom of her sickness was that she was tortured by evil thoughts about her mother, to such an extent that they interfered with everything she tried to do.

Finally she became very suddenly, deeply and fruitlessly interested in religion. After some time her evil thoughts disappeared.
Some medicine or other was given the credit for their disappear-
ance, although it is more probable that her mother was forced
onto the defensive. But vestiges of her evil thoughts remained,
which expressed themselves in an intense fear of thunder and
lightning.

The little girl believed that thunder and lightning were the
resultof her bad conscience, and would some day cause her death
because she harboured such evil thoughts. It is easy to see how at
this time the child was struggling to free herself from her hatred
for her mother. The child made good progress and her future
seemed bright. The statement of a teacher who said: 'This girl
could do anything she set her mind to!' had a profound effect on
her. These words are unimportant in themselves, but for this girl
they truly meant, 'I can accomplish anything if I really try.' This
realization was followed by an escalation of the conflict with her
mother.

Adolescence came, and she grew up into a beautiful young
woman with many admirers; yet all her relationships with the
other sex were broken off because of the sharpness of her tongue.
She felt herself drawn only to one man, an elderly man who
lived in her neighbourhood, and everyone feared that some day
she would marry him. But this man moved away after some time
and the girl remained without a boyfriend until she was twenty-
six years old. In the circles in which she moved this was very
remarkable, and no one could explain it because no one understood her history. Because of the bitter war that she had been
waging against her mother ever since her childhood, she had
become unbearably quarrelsome. Fighting was her only pleasure.
The behaviour of her mother had constantly irritated the child
and made her long for victories over her. A bitter battle of words
was her greatest happiness; in this she showed her vanity. Her
'masculine' attitude also expressed itself in that she sought out
such battles only when she could defeat her opponent.

When she was twenty-six she made the acquaintance of a
very honourable man who was not repulsed by her belligerent
character and courted her very earnestly. He was very humble
and submissive in his approach. Pressure from her relatives to

marry this man led her to explain repeatedly that he was so very uncongenial to her that she could not possibly consider marrying him. As we know her character, this is not hard to understand, yet after two years of resistance she finally accepted him in the deep conviction that she had enslaved him, and that she could do whatever she wished with him. She had hoped secretly that she would find him to be a second edition of her father, who would give in to her whenever she wanted.

She soon found her mistake. Within days of her marriage, her husband was very much at home, smoking his pipe and comfortably reading his paper. He went to the office, came home punctually for his meals, and grumbled a little if his meals were not ready. He demanded cleanliness, affection, punctuality and all manner of things that she considered unreasonable and was not prepared to provide. Their relationship was not even remotely similar to the one between her and her father.

She came down to earth with a bump. The more she demanded, the less her husband acceded to her wishes. The more he pointed out her domestic responsibilities, the less he saw any domestic activity from her. She lost no opportunity to remind him that he really had no right to make these requests, as she had expressly told him she did not like him. This made absolutely no impression upon him. He continued his demands with a stubbornness that caused her to view the future with alarm. It was in an intoxication of self-effacement that this righteous, dutiful man had wooed her, but no sooner did he have her in his possession, than this self-effacement had disappeared.

The situation did not improve when she became a mother. New responsibilities were forced upon her. Meanwhile her relationship with her own mother, who was energetically taking up the cudgels on behalf of her son-in-law, became worse and worse. The constant warfare in her house was carried on with such heavy artillery that, as is no surprise to us, her husband occasionally acted wrongly and inconsiderately, so sometimes the wife was justified in her complaints. The behaviour of her husband was the direct consequence of her unapproachability. This, again, was the result of her failure to accept her womanliness. She had believed originally that she could play the spoilt princess for ever, that she could go through life accompanied by a slave who would carry out all her wishes. Life seemed, to her, to be possible only under such conditions.

What could she do now? Should she divorce her husband, return to her mother and declare herself beaten? She was incapable of earning her own living, for she had never been prepared for it. A divorce would have been a blow to her pride and vanity. Her life was a misery; on the one hand she faced her husband's criticisms, and on the other her mother with her heavy artillery, preaching cleanliness and tidiness.

Then suddenly she too became clean and tidy! She spent the whole day polishing and cleaning. It seemed as though she had finally seen the light and had at last taken to heart the teachings her mother had drummed into her for so many years. In the beginning both her mother and her husband must have been pleased at this sudden change of heart, at the sight of this young woman spring-cleaning the house. But you can have too much of a good thing. She kept washing and scouring every inch of the house until it shone; everyone else got in her way and she got in everyone else's. If she washed something and someone else touched it, then she would have to wash it again, and only she could do so.

The disorder that manifests itself in continual washing and cleaning is extremely common in women who rebel against their womanliness and attempt in this way to elevate themselves by their conspicuous cleanliness over those who are less fastidious. Unconsciously, all these efforts are aimed solely at disrupting the entire household. Few households were ever more disrupted than this woman's. Her goal was not cleanliness, but the discomfort of her entire family.

We could cite many cases in which a reconciliation with the role of being a woman was only apparent. The fact that our patient had no woman friends, could not get along with anyone and had no consideration for others, fits very well into the pattern we might have expected in her life.

It will be necessary for us to develop better methods of rearing girls in the future, so that they will be better prepared to reconcile themselves with life. Even under the most favourable circumstances it is not always possible to effect this reconciliation, as in the above case. The fiction of women's inferiority is maintained in our age by law and tradition, though it is denied by anyone with any real psychological insight. We must therefore be on the alert for examples of this fiction, and correct the mistaken attitudes that give rise to it. We must do so not because of some pathologically exaggerated and thus insincere respect for women, but because the present fallacious attitude negates the logic of our whole social life.

Let us take this opportunity to discuss another matter that is often used in order to degrade women: the so-called 'dangerous age', that period that occurs about the fiftieth year, accompanied by the accentuation of certain character traits. To every menopausal woman, the bodily changes she is going through seem to signal the loss of whatever claim to significance she ever had. Under these circumstances she searches with redoubled efforts for any means of securing her position, which has now become more precarious than ever before. Our civilization is dominated by the principle that only present performance is valued; all ageing individuals, but especially ageing women, experience difficulties at this time.

The kind of damage done to an ageing woman by devaluing her in this way is suffered by every human being, in that every human life has its unproductive times. What people have accomplished at the height of their powers must be credited to them during their declining years. It is wrong to cut people off from the spiritual and material comforts of society simply because they are growing old. In the case of a woman, such treatment virtually amounts to degradation and enslavement. Imagine the anxiety of an adolescent girl who looks ahead to this stage in her life. Womanliness does not end with the menopause. The honour and worth of a human being extend beyond this age and suitable respect must be guaranteed.

TENSION BETWEEN THE SEXES

All these unhappy situations are the result of the mistakes of our civilization. If a civilization is marked by prejudice, then this prejudice reaches out and touches every aspect of that civilization, and evidence of it is found everywhere. The fallacy of the inferiority of women, and its corollary, the alleged superiority of men, constantly disturb the harmony of the sexes. As a result, an

entirely inappropriate tension is introduced into all sexual relationships, thereby threatening and even destroying every chance
for happiness between the sexes. Our whole existence in relationships is poisoned, distorted and corroded by this tension.
This explains why harmonious marriages are so rare; this
explains too why so many children grow up with the idea that
marriage is an extremely difficult and dangerous business.

Prejudices such as we have described here may to a large
extent prevent children from understanding what life is all
about. Think how many young girls consider marriage only as a
sort of emergency exit from life, and think of those men and
women who see marriage only as a necessary evil! The difficulties that originally grew out of this tension between the sexes
have assumed gigantic proportions today. The less inclined
women are to play the part of the submissive female, and the
more men strive to keep their privileged status, however
spurious, the greater this tension becomes.

Companionship and friendship are hallmarks of a true reconciliation with the sexual role and true equilibrium between the
sexes. The subordination of one individual by another is just as
unbearable in sexual relationships as it is in relationships between
nations. Everyone should consider this problem very carefully
since a mistaken attitude may give rise to considerable difficulties
for both partners. This aspect of human life is so important that
every one of us is involved in it. It becomes even more complicated nowadays, when children are forced into behaviour patterns
that involve a depreciation and rejection of other people.

A calm upbringing could certainly overcome these difficulties, but we live in hasty times, with a shortage of really tried and
tested educational methods. A particular problem is the competitive nature of our whole lives, which reaches even into the
nursery. All these things determine only too harshly the pattern
for later life. The fear that makes so many human beings shrink
from forming loving relationships is caused largely by the
pointless pressure that compels every man to prove his masculinity under all circumstances even if he has to do so by treachery
and malice or by force.

Obviously, these factors work together to destroy all candour
and trust in relationships. The Don Juan type is a man who is

unsure of his own manliness and constantly seeks reassurance in his conquests. The distrust between the sexes that is so universal prevents people from being frank with one another, and all humanity suffers in consequence. The exaggerated masculine ideal signifies a constant challenge, a constant spur, a constant restlessness that leads only to vanity, self-glorification and maintenance of the 'privileged' attitude. All these, of course, are contrary to healthy communal life.

We have no reason to oppose the purposes of the women's emancipation movements. It is our duty to support them in their struggle for freedom and equality, because in the end the happiness of the whole of humanity depends upon creating conditions where women can live fully according to their capabilities and men can achieve happy relaxed relationships with them.

WHAT CAN WE DO?

Of all the institutions that have been developed to improve the relationship between the sexes, co-education is the most important. This institution is not universally accepted; it has its opponents and its advocates. Its supporters' chief argument is that through co-education the two sexes have the chance to get to know one another at an early age and that this early familiarity can to some extent break down prejudice and save a lot of anxiety later. The opponents of co-education usually argue that boys and girls are already so different by the time they enter school that educating them together only accentuates these differences since the boys feel pressured. This is because during the school years girls develop more quickly than boys intellectually. The boys, who feel obliged to assert their importance and appear superior, suddenly recognize that their superiority is an illusion. Other investigators have maintained that in co-education boys become anxious in the company of girls and lose their self-esteem.

There is, no doubt, some measure of truth in these arguments, but they apply only when we consider co-education in the sense of competition between the sexes, for the prize of greater talent and ability. If that is what co-education means to teachers and pupils, it is a damaging doctrine. If co-education is to succeed, we need teachers with a better understanding of it. Co-education represents a training and preparation for future co-operation between the sexes in shared tasks. Without such teachers, co-education will fail – and its opponents will feel amply justified in their opposition to it.

Only a poet could capture all the nuances of the whole situation between the sexes. We must be content merely to indicate the main points. An adolescent girl acts very much as though she were inferior, and everything we have said concerning the compensation for physical disadvantages applies equally well to her. The difference is this: the belief in her inferiority is forced upon a girl by her environment. She is so irrevocably channelled into this behaviour that even investigators with a great deal of insight have from time to time fallen into the fallacy of believing in her inferiority. The result of this is that both sexes have finally fallen into the midden of prestige politics, and each sex tries to play a role for which it is not suited. What happens? Their lives become complicated, their relationships are robbed of all candour, and they are stuffed with fallacies and prejudices that destroy any hope of happiness.

9

The Family
Constellation

We have often drawn attention to the fact that before we can judge human beings we must know the situation in which they grew up. An important influence is the position of children in their family constellation. After we have gained sufficient expertise, we can often categorize human beings accordingly and can recognize whether they are firstborn, only children, the youngest in the family, and so on.

People seem to have known for a long time that youngest child are usually a special case. This is evidenced by the countless fairy tales, legends, Bible stories, and so on in which the youngest always appears in the same light. As a matter of fact they do grow up in a unique situation, for to parents they are special children, and as the youngest they receive special, solicitous treatment. They are not only the youngest, but also usually the smallest and in consequence the most helpless. Their brothers and sisters have already acquired some degree of growth and independence and for this reason youngest children usually grow up in a warmer atmosphere than their siblings experienced. Hence there arise a number of characteristics that influence their personality and attitude to life in a remarkable way. One seemingly paradoxical circumstance must be noted. No child likes to be the smallest, the least capable, all the time. Such a position stimulates children to prove that they can do everything. Their striving for power becomes markedly accentuated, so the youngest often grows up into a person desperate to excel, determined to be the very best at everything. It is not uncommon for the youngest child to outstrip every other member of the family and become its most capable member.

There is another less fortunate group of youngest children; they too have the desire to excel, but they lack the necessary

energy and self-confidence because of the nature of their relationships with their older brothers and sisters. If they cannot
outshine the older children, youngest children frequently shy
from their tasks, become cowardly, chronic complainers forever
seeking an excuse to dodge their duties. They do not become any
less ambitious, but they adopt the type of ambition that forces
them to wriggle out of situations and busy themselves in activity
outside the necessary problems of life, in order to avoid, as far as
possible, the danger of an actual test of their ability.

It will doubtless have occurred to many readers that youngest
child behave as though they felt neglected and inferior. In our
investigations we have always been able to detect this feeling of
inferiority and also to analyse their psychological development
given the presence of this tortured feeling. In this sense youngest
children are like children who have come into the world with
physical disabilities. What the child feels need not actually be
true. It does not matter what has really happened, whether an
individual is or is not inferior. What is important is *their* interpretation of their situation. We know very well that children easily
get hold of the wrong end of the stick. Childhood is a time of a
great number of questions, possibilities and consequences.

What should educators do? Should they supply additional
stimuli and spur on the vanity of these children? Should they
constantly push them into the limelight so that they are always
first? This would be a feeble response to the challenge.
Experience teaches us that it makes very little difference whether
we are first or not; it would be better to exaggerate in the other
direction, and maintain that being first or best is unimportant.
We can get tired of hearing about 'first and best' people all the
time. History as well as experience demonstrates that there is far
more to life than being first or best. To insist on it makes
children one-sided; above all it robs them of their chance to
develop as good human beings.

The main consequence of the 'first and best' doctrine is that
children think only of themselves and waste their time worrying
in case someone overtakes them. Their soul is filled with envy
and hate for their fellows and anxiety for their own position.
Their place in the family makes the youngest child into a com-
petitor, straining to beat the others. This competitive element is

betrayed by their whole behaviour, especially by little gestures that are obvious to anyone who has learned to examine the psychological aspects of relationships. These are the children, for instance, who always march at the head of the procession and cannot bear to have anyone in front of them. Such a racecourse attitude is characteristic of a large number of children.

This type of youngest child is occasionally to be found as a clear-cut example, although variations are common. Among the youngest we find active and capable individuals who have gone so far that they have become the saviours of their whole family. Consider the Bible story of Joseph! Here is a wonderful exposition of the situation of the youngest son. It sets it out more clearly and informatively than modern researchers, in possession of all the evidence, could ever hope to do. Much valuable material has been lost through the centuries, material we must try to rediscover.

There is another type of youngest child, who are like athletes running a marathon who suddenly come to an obstacle they are not sure they can jump over. They attempt to avoid the difficulty by going around it. When youngest children of this type lose their courage they become the most total cowards imaginable. They always lag behind, every task seems too much for them; they become masters at making excuses. In the end they never attempt anything useful, but spend all their energy wasting time. In any actual conflict they always fail. Usually they are to be found carefully seeking a field of activity in which every chance of competition has been excluded. They will always find excuses for their failures. They may contend that they were always too weak or too spoilt, or that their brothers and sisters did not let them grow up. Their fate becomes more bitter if they actually have a physical handicap, in which case they are certain to capitalize on their weakness to justify their failure.

Neither of these types ever develops into a useful member of society. The first type, the one who always seeks to be the best, fares better in a world where competition is valued for its own sake. People like this will maintain their spiritual equilibrium only at the cost of others. Individuals of the second type remain crushed by their feelings of inferiority and suffer from their lack or reconciliation with life as long as they live.

Eldest children in a family also have well-defined character-istics. For one thing, they have the advantage of an excellent position for psychological development. History recognizes that eldest sons occupy a particularly favourable position. Among many peoples, in many classes, this advantageous status has become fixed as an institution. There is no question, for instance, that among European farmers the firstborn son knows his position from his early childhood and realizes that some day he will take over the farm, and therefore is in a much more favourable position than the other children who must eventually leave their father's farm. In the aristocracy it is the eldest son who will some day inherit the family title. Even in humbler families, eldest children are usually the ones who are credited with enough ability and common sense to be of great assistance to their parents. We can see how valuable it is to children to be constantly entrusted with responsibilities by those around them. We can imagine that their thought processes go something like this: 'I am older, bigger, stronger than the others, and therefore I must also be cleverer than they are.' If their development in this direction goes on without disturbance then we shall find them with all the characteristics of a guardian of law and order. Such people value power very highly indeed. This does not only apply to their own personal power; it also affects their evaluation of power in general. Power is a concept that comes quite naturally to eldest children, something that is important and must be respected. It is not surprising that such individuals are markedly conservative.

The striving for power in the case of second children also has its special nuance. Second-born children are constantly under pressure, striving for superiority; the racecourse attitude that determines their aim in life is very evident in their actions. The fact that there is always someone ahead of them who has already gained power is a strong stimulus for second children. If they are able to develop their potential and take on the firstborn, they will usually make rapid strides, while firstborn children, already possessing power, feel relatively secure until the second child threatens to surpass them. This situation has also been described in a very lively fashion in the biblical legend of Esau and Jacob. In this story the battle goes on relentlessly, not so much for actual power, but for the semblance of power. In cases like this the second child's struggle continues inexorably until either the goal is reached and the firstborn is overcome, or the battle is lost, and the retreat, which is often characterized by nervous disorders, sets in. The attitude of second children is similar to the envy of the poor classes. There is a dominant note in it of being despised and neglected. Second children may aim so high that they suffer all their life and destroy their peace of mind by striving after an insubstantial and unattainable goal.

Only children are of course in a very special situation. They are at the utter mercy of their education. Their parents, so to speak, have no choice; they focus all their attention on their only child. Only children may become extremely dependent, always waiting for someone to show them the way, and searching for support at all times. Indulged throughout their lives, they are quite unused to difficulties, because someone has always smoothed their path for them. Being constantly the centre of attention they very easily acquire the feeling that they are very valuable people indeed. Their position is so difficult that they are almost certain to pick up misconceptions about life. If the parents understand the dangers of this situation, to be sure, they can prevent many of them, but at best it remains a difficult problem.

Parents of 'only' children may frequently be exceptionally devoted people to whom life seems full of dangers and temptations. They therefore treat their children in an exaggeratedly concerned and caring manner. The children in turn interpret their concern and warnings as a source of additional pressure. Finally, their constant attention to only children's health and security cause them to see the world as a very hostile place. They may become habitually fearful of difficulties, which they approach awkwardly, having only experienced the pleasant things in life. Such children have problems with every independent activity, and sooner or later they become unfitted for life. They are sure to meet with disasters along life's way. They are like parasites who do nothing, but enjoy life while everyone else cares for their wants.

Various combinations are possible in which several brothers and sisters compete with each other; the evaluation of any one case therefore becomes exceedingly difficult. The situation of an only boy among several girls is a case where the feminine influence may dominate the household so that the boy is pushed into the background, particularly if he is the youngest, and sees himself opposed by a phalanx of women. His striving for recognition encounters great difficulties. Threatened on all sides, he never experiences with any certainty the privilege that our unenlightened masculine civilization accords to every male. Lasting insecurity and an inability to evaluate himself as a human being are his most characteristic traits. He may become so intimidated by his womenfolk that he feels men are only second-best. On the one hand his courage and self-confidence may easily be eclipsed; but on the other, the stimulus may be so violent that the young boy forces himself on to great achievements. Both responses arise from the same situation, and what becomes of such boys in the end is determined by other closely related phenomena.

We can therefore see what an effect the position of children in the family can have on all the psychological and intellectual equipment they are born with. This fact robs all the theories of heredity, so harmful to educational effort, of their cogency. There are doubtless cases in which the effect of hereditary influences can be shown, such as in children who grow up far away from their parents, yet develop certain similar 'family' traits. This becomes much more understandable if we remember how closely certain types of faulty development in children are related to inherited physical defects. Take a given child who is born with a physical weakness that makes him anxious and tense. If his father came into the world similarly handicapped and approached the world in a similar way, it is not surprising that similar mistakes and character traits would result. Looked at from this point of view, it would seem to us that the theory of inheritance of acquired characteristics is based upon very weak evidence.

From our previous descriptions, we may assume that whatever errors children are exposed to in their development, the most serious consequences arise from their desire to dominate all their peers, to seek personal power that will give them advantages over them. In our culture they are practically compelled to develop according to a fixed pattern. If we wish to prevent such a pernicious development we must know and understand the difficulties they have to face. There is one single and essential point of view that helps us to overcome all these difficulties; it is the viewpoint of the development of social feeling. If children acquire this community spirit, the obstacles they meet are unlikely to harm their development. However, since the opportunities for the development of social feeling are relatively rare in our culture, the obstacles children encounter play an important and probably harmful role. Once we recognize this, we should not be surprised to find many people who spend their whole lives fighting and others to whom life is a vale of tears. We must understand that these people are victims whose psychological development has taken a wrong turning with the unfortunate result that their very attitude towards life is misguided.

We must be very modest, then, in our assessment of our fellow human beings, and above all we must never allow ourselves to make any moral judgements, judgements concerning the moral worth of human beings. On the contrary, we must use our knowledge for the good of society. We must approach mistaken and misguided people sympathetically, because we are in a much better position than they are to understand what is going on inside them. Our insight gives rise to important new points of view in the matter of education. The very recognition of the source of error puts into our hands a great many influential instruments for improvement. By analysing the psychological structure and development of human beings we may not only understand their past, but also make an informed guess concerning their future. Thus our science gives us some conception of what human beings really are. They become living beings for us, not just cardboard cut-outs. In consequence we can have a richer and more meaningful sense of their worth as human beings than is usual nowadays.

PART TWO

THE

SCIENCE OF CHARACTER

10

GENERAL CONSIDERATIONS

HOW DO WE BECOME WHO WE ARE?
What we call a character trait is the expression of some aspect of people's attempt to adjust to the world they live in. Character is a social concept. We can speak of a character trait only when we consider individuals in relation to their environment. It would make very little difference what kind of character Robinson Crusoe had – at least until he met Friday. Character is a psychological attitude, it is the quality and nature of individuals' approaches to the environment in which they live. It is the behaviour pattern according to which their striving for significance is elaborated in line with their social feeling.

We have already seen how the goal of superiority, of power, of the conquest of others, is the goal that directs the activity of many human beings. This goal modifies an individual's view of the world. It shapes their behaviour pattern and directs their various thoughts and feelings into specific channels. Traits of character are only the external manifestations of an individual's life style and behaviour pattern. As such they enable us to understand their attitude towards their environment, towards their fellow human beings, towards the society in which they live and towards the challenge of existence in general. Character traits are instruments, the tools used by the total personality in acquiring recognition and significance; the use of such tools in the personality amounts to a 'technique' for living.

Character traits are not inherited, as many would have it, nor are they present at birth. They are like a blueprint for existence that enables every human being to live their life and express their personality in any situation without the need to think about it consciously. Character traits are not the expressions of inherited powers or tendencies. We acquire them to help us go through life in a particular way. No child, for instance, is born lazy. Children become lazy because laziness seems to them the best way of making life easier, while at the same time enabling them to keep their feeling of significance. The striving for power can to some extent be expressed in the pattern of laziness. An individual may draw attention to a congenital handicap and thus save face before a defeat. The end result of such introspection is always something like this: 'If I did not have this disadvantage, my talents would develop brilliantly. But unfortunately I *am* handicapped!' A second individual, involved in a long-standing war with her environment because of her undisciplined striving for power, will develop whatever weapons of power can help her war effort: weapons like ambition, envy, mistrust and so on. We believe that such traits of character are indistinguishable from the personality, but are neither inherited nor unchangeable. Closer observation shows us that the person has found them necessary and suitable for her behaviour pattern, and has acquired them for this purpose, sometimes very early in life. They are not primary factors, but secondary ones, and have been forced into being by the secret goal of the personality. They must be judged from the standpoint of teleology.

Let us recall our previous explanations in which we have shown how the style of the life of individuals, their actions, their behaviour, their position in the world, are all closely connected with their goal. We cannot think anything, nor set anything into motion, without having some distinct purpose in mind. In the murky depths of the psyche of children this goal is already present, directing their psychological development from their earliest days. This goal gives form and character to their life. Because of it, every individual is a particular and discrete unity, different from all other personalities. All their actions and all the expressions of their life are directed towards the same private goal. Knowing the goal enables us to know the person.

So far as a person's psyche and character are concerned, heredity plays a relatively unimportant role. There is no concrete proof to support the theory of inherited character traits. Our characters begin to be formed very early in life: so early in fact that they appear to be inherited. They are, however, at best learned through observation and mimicry. The reason why there are character traits common to a whole family, nation or race, lies simply in the fact that one individual acquires them from another by imitation or sharing in the other's activity. Children and adolescents are great imitators.

The thirst for knowledge, which is sometimes expressed as a desire to see, can lead to curiosity as a character trait in children with eye defects, but if the behaviour patterns of this child demands it, the same thirst for knowledge might develop into quite a different character trait. The same child might satisfy himself by investigating things and taking them apart or breaking them up. Or such a child might, under other circumstances, become studious and fond of books.

We may examine tendencies for mistrust in people with hearing defects in much the same way. In our civilization they are exposed to great danger and they sense that danger keenly. They are also exposed to ridicule and degradation and are frequently treated as feeble-minded. These are factors of the utmost importance in the development of a mistrustful character. Since the deaf are excluded from many pleasures, it is not surprising that they should be hostile to those pleasures. But it would be wrong to assume that they were born with a mistrustful character.

The theory that criminal character traits are congenital is equally fallacious. We can counter the argument that many families produce several criminals by pointing out that older family members pass on their antisocial attitudes to younger members, who learn by example. Children in these families are taught from early childhood that theft is a lucrative way of making a living, and so the family tradition continues.

The striving for recognition may be considered in much the same way. All children face so many obstacles in life that no children ever grow up without striving for some kind of significance. This striving may take many different forms, and every human being approaches the problem of their personal significance in an individual way. The observation that children are similar in character to their parents is easily explained by the fact that children, in their striving for significance, model themselves upon the individuals around them who are already significant and respected. Every generation learns from its predecessors in this way, and retains what it has learned throughout all the difficulties and complexities to which this striving for power may lead.

The goal of superiority is a secret goal. The presence of social feeling prevents it from appearing overtly – it grows in secret and hides behind an acceptable façade. It must be reaffirmed, however, that this growth would not achieve such tropical luxuriance if we humans understood one another better. If each of us had the power to see through our neighbour's mask to the character behind it, then we should not only be able to protect ourselves better, but also make it so difficult for other people to keep up their striving for power, that it would not be worth their while. Under such circumstances, the veiled struggle for superiority would disappear. It pays us therefore to look into these relationships more closely and make use of the experimental evidence we have gained.

We live under such complicated cultural circumstances that proper schooling for life is made very difficult. People have been denied the chief means for the development of psychological insight. Up to the present day the only function of schools has been to spread the raw materials of knowledge before children and allow them to take what they could or would, without especially stimulating their interest in it. And there are not even enough of these schools. The most important premise for the acquisition of an understanding of human nature has been hitherto much neglected. We too learned to measure human beings in the old school of thought. Here we learned to distinguish good from bad; what we did not learn was how to revise our judgements, and consequently we have carried this misconception into life and are labouring under it to this day.

As adults we are still applying the prejudices and fallacies of our childhood as though they were sacred laws. We are not yet aware that we have been drawn into the confusion of our complicated culture, that we have assumed points of view that true insight would make impossible. In the final analysis, we go about interpreting everything from the point of view of the heightening of our personal self-esteem, and with the aim of boosting our own powers.

SOCIAL FEELING, COMMUNITY SPIRIT AND THE DEVELOPMENT OF CHARACTER

Next to the striving for power, it is social feeling that plays the most important role in the development of character. It is expressed, just as is the striving for significance, in the first psychological stirrings of children, especially in their desire for contact and tenderness. We have previously expounded on the conditions for the development of social feeling; we wish to refer to them briefly here. Community spirit, or social feeling, is influenced both by a person's feelings of inferiority and by the compensatory striving for power. Human beings are very susceptible to inferiority complexes of all kinds. The process of psychological development, the growth of an anxiety that seeks for compensations and security, begins as soon as the feeling of inferiority appears. The rules of child-rearing must take account of our recognition of children's inferiority feelings. These rules may be summed up as follows: do not make life too bitter for children, or let them see the dark side of existence too early. Give them the chance to experience the joy of living. For economic reasons, it may not be possible to apply these rules in all cases. Unfortunately, many children grow up in circumstances of poverty and want. Physical handicaps play an important role too because they can make a normal life style impossible and suggest to children that they need special privileges. It is inevitable that children facing poverty or disablement will feel that life has treated them badly. This in turn gives rise to the great danger that their social feeling will be affected.

We cannot judge human beings except by using the concept of community spirit as a standard, and measuring their thought and action by this standard. We must maintain this point of view because every individual within the body of human society must subscribe to the oneness of that society. We have to realize our duty to our fellow human beings. We are in the very midst of a community and must live by the logic of communal existence. This logic determines the fact that we need certain known criteria for the evaluation of our peers. The degree to which social feeling has developed in any individual is the only univer-

sally valid criterion of human values. We cannot deny our psychological dependency upon social feeling. No human beings are
capable of ignoring their social feeling completely.

For we all *know* we have a duty to our fellow human beings.
Our social feeling constantly reminds us of the fact. This does
not mean that social feeling is constantly in our conscious
thoughts; but it does require a certain amount of determination
to deny it and set it aside. Furthermore, social feeling is so
universal that no one is able to begin any activity without first
being justified by it. The need for justifying each act and thought
originates in our unconscious sense of social unity. At the very
least it is the reason why we seek extenuating circumstances to
excuse our actions. Interestingly enough, social feeling is so fundamental and important that, even if we have not developed this
ability to consider others as fully as most people have done, we
still make efforts to appear as though we had done so. This
means that the pretence of social feeling is sometimes used to
conceal the antisocial thoughts and deeds that are the true
expressions of a personality. The difficulty lies in differentiating
between the false and the genuine; it is this very difficulty that
raises the understanding of human nature to the plane of a
science. We shall now look at several examples that demonstrate
how social feeling may be misused.

A young man once told us how he swam out to an island in
the sea with some companions, and spent some time there. It
happened that one of his companions, leaning over the edge of a
cliff, lost his balance and fell into the sea. Our young man leaned
over and watched with great interest as the fellow went under.
When he thought about this event later, it occurred to him that
he had not considered this behaviour strange. It happened that
the young man who fell into the sea was saved, but as far as the
narrator of the story is concerned, we can affirm that his social
feeling must have been minimal. We shall not change this view
even if we hear that he has never harmed anyone in his life, or
that he has occasionally been a good friend to someone.

Our assumption must be reinforced by further facts. A frequently recurring day-dream of this young man was that he
found himself shut off from all human beings in a pretty little
house in the middle of a forest. This picture was also a favourite

motif in his drawings. Anyone who understands fantasies and also knows his previous history, will easily recognize his lack of community spirit, reaffirmed in his dream. It would be fair to say that his psyche has developed unevenly: he is simply deficient in social feeling.

The following anecdote may show the difference between true and false social feeling. An old lady, while attempting to catch a bus, slipped and fell down in the snow. She could not get up, and a number of people hurried past her without noticing her plight, until a man came and helped her up. At this moment another man, who had been hidden somewhere, appeared and greeted her chivalrous saviour with these words: 'Thank God! I have finally found a decent person. I have been standing here for five minutes, waiting to see whether someone would help the old lady up. You are the first one to do it!' This incident shows how the semblance of community spirit may be misused. By this palpable deception, one man has set himself up as a judge of others. He distributes praise and blame, but has not himself lifted a finger to help.

There are other more complicated cases in which it is not easy to gauge a person's social feeling. The only thing to do is carry out a radical investigation. Once this is done we do not remain in the dark for long. There is the case, for instance, of a General who, although he knew the battle was already lost, caused thousands of soldiers to die unnecessarily. This general claimed he was acting in the interests of the nation, and many people agreed with him. Yet it would be difficult to consider him a good fellow human being, whatever reasons he may have given to justify his behaviour.

In order to judge correctly in these uncertain cases we need a universally applicable standpoint. For Individual Psychology, such a standpoint can be found in the concept of social useful-ness and the general well-being of humanity, the 'common weal'. If we assume this standpoint we can usually decide on particular cases quite easily.

The degree of social feeling shows itself in every activity in which individuals participate. It may be very obvious in their habitual expressions such as the way they look at others, the way they shake hands, or the way they speak. Their whole personality may make an indelible impression, one way or another, which we sense almost intuitively. Occasionally, we unconsciously draw such far-reaching conclusions from a person's behaviour that our own attitude is governed entirely by these conclusions. In these discussions, we are only bringing this intuitive knowledge into the sphere of consciousness, and thus enabling ourselves to test and evaluate it, in order to avoid some grave misconceptions. The value of this bringing into consciousness lies in the fact that we are then less likely to harbour prejudices (which arise when we form our judgements in the unconscious where they are beyond our control and where we have no opportunity of modifying them).

To repeat: no evaluation of the character of individuals should be made out of context. If we wrench isolated phenomena from their life and judge them singly, as one might if one considered only their physical status, or their environment or upbringing, we are bound to jump to the wrong conclusions. This is an important point because it immediately removes a great load from the shoulders of mankind. Greater self-knowledge enables us to behave more sensibly and get more out of life. Our method makes it possible to step in, exert a favourable influence on others, especially children, and save them from a fate that might otherwise overtake them. In this way nobody will be condemned to lifelong misery simply because of an unfortunate family or personal history. If we can only achieve this, it will be a tremendous step forward for our civilization. A whole new generation will grow up unafraid, conscious that it is master of its own fate!

HOW CHARACTER DEVELOPS
Any character traits conspicuous in personalities must be appropriate to the direction in which the psyche of individuals has developed since early childhood. This direction may be a straight line or may be marked by meanders and detours. In the first instance, children strive for the realization of their goal along a direct line, and develop an aggressive, courageous character. The beginnings of character development are usually marked by such active, aggressive traits. But this line is easily diverted or modified.

Difficulties may first become apparent if the forces resisting children prevent them from achieving their goal of superiority by direct attack. Children will attempt in some way to circumvent these difficulties. Their detour, again, will produce specific character traits. Other obstacles to the development of their character, such as physical disadvantages, or repulses and defeats at the hands of those around them, have a similar effect upon them. Further, the inescapable influence of that wider environment, the world, is of great importance. The business of living in our civilization, as expressed in the demands, doubts and emotions of children's family and teachers, ultimately affects their character. All education takes on the method and the attitude best calculated to develop pupils in the direction of the prevailing social life and culture.

Obstacles of every sort are fatal to a straight-line development of character. Where they are present, the paths children will take to accomplish their goal of power will deviate to a greater or lesser extent from the straight line. Where there are no obstacles, the efforts of children will be undeterred, and they will approach their difficulties directly. Let us call them Type A children. In the second case – Type B – we have the picture of an entirely different type of child. They lack Type A's courage. Moreover, they have discovered that fire burns and that not everyone is kindly disposed towards them. Type B will not take the direct route to their goal of recognition and power, but will use a series of detours. How they develop psychologically depends on how far they go out of their way. These detours will determine how cautious they are, whether they are in tune with the necessities of life or merely attempt to avoid them. Type B will not approach their tasks and problems directly. If they become cowardly and timid, refusing to look other people straight in the eye or to speak the truth, it does not mean their aims are any different from Type A's. Two people can act differently, but have the same goals.

Both types may co-exist to a certain degree in the same individual. This occurs especially when children's characters are not fully formed, when their principles are still elastic, when they do not always assume the same path, but retain sufficient flexibility to look for another approach if the first attempt proves inadequate.

An undisturbed communal social life is the first requirement for successful adaptation to the demands of the community. We can easily teach children to adapt so long as their attitude towards their environment is not a hostile one. War within the family can be eliminated only when the parents are capable of minimizing their own striving for power to such a degree that it is not a burden upon children. If, in addition, the parents understand the principles of children's development, they can avoid the development of exaggerated 'straight line' character traits, in which courage becomes impudence, and independence becomes raw egotism. Similarly they will be able to avoid the exaggerated strictness that produces servile obedience. Mistakes of this sort may cause children to be shut in, afraid of telling the truth for fear of the consequences.

Pressure, in child-rearing, is a two-edged sword – it produces the semblance of adaptation. Compulsory obedience is, however, only apparent obedience. Children's psyches reflect their general relationship to their environment. Whether all the obstacles that may conceivably be present act directly or indirectly upon them will also be reflected in their personality. Children are not usually capable of evaluating outside influences; and the adults around them either know nothing of them or cannot understand them. The pattern of the children's difficulties, plus their reaction to the obstacles in their way, constitute their personality.

We can also classify people according to the way they approach difficulties. First there are the optimists. These are individuals whose character development, by and large, has been in a straight line. They approach all difficulties courageously and do not take them too seriously. They retain their belief in themselves and find it fairly easy to maintain a happy attitude towards life. They do not demand too much of life because they have a good sense of self-worth and do not consider themselves neglected or insignificant. Thus they are able to weather the storms of life more easily than others to whom difficulties are only further justification for believing themselves weak and inadequate. In the most difficult situations the optimists stay calm, convinced that mistakes can always be rectified.

Optimists may immediately be recognized by their manner. They are not afraid, speak openly and freely and are neither too modest nor too inhibited. Asked to draw optimists, we would show them with open arms, ready to greet their fellow human beings. They make contact with others easily and have no difficulty in making friends, because they are not mistrustful. Their speech is not laboured; they stand and move naturally and easily. Pure examples of this type are seldom found except in the first years of childhood. There are, however, many lesser degrees of optimism and of ability to make social contacts with which we can be well satisfied.

Quite a different type are the pessimists. They present the greatest educational problems. These are the individuals who have acquired an 'inferiority complex' as a result of the experiences and impressions of their childhood. The difficulties they have experienced have given them the feeling that life is not easy. They always look on the dark side of life because of their pessimistic personal philosophy, which has been nourished by unwise treatment in their childhood. They are much more conscious of the difficulties of life than the optimists are, and it is easy for them to lose heart. Tortured by a feeling of insecurity, they are constantly seeking for support. A cry for help is forever echoed in their behaviour, because they cannot stand alone. As children, they are always crying for their mothers. This cry for their mother can sometimes be heard even in their old age.

The abnormal cautiousness of this type can be seen in their timid and fearful overall attitude. The pessimists forever dwell on the troubles and dangers that may lie just around the corner. Obviously pessimists sleep badly. Sleep, as a matter of fact, is an excellent standard for measuring the development of a human being, for sleep disturbances are an index of great cautiousness and a feeling of insecurity. It is as though these people were always on their guard in order to defend themselves against the threats of life. How little joy in life they have, and how poor their understanding! Individuals who cannot sleep well show a faulty philosophy of life. If they were really correct in their conclusions, if life were as bitter as they believe it to be, then they would not dare to sleep at all! In their tendency to approach the natural phenomena of life in a hostile manner, pessimists betray their lack of preparation for living. There is really no reason why they should not sleep soundly. We may suspect this same pessimistic tendency when we find individuals constantly occupied with checking the locks or worrying about burglars. You can even spot pessimists by their posture when asleep. Pessimists frequently curl up into the smallest possible space, or sleep with the covers drawn up over their heads.

Human beings may also be divided into aggressive and defensive types. The aggressive attacker is characterized by violent movements. People of the aggressive type, when they are brave, elevate courage into foolhardiness to show the world how fearless they are – and thus betray their deep feeling of insecurity. If they are anxious, they attempt to harden themselves against fear. They play the 'tough' role to a ludicrous degree. Others go to great pains to suppress all feelings of tenderness and gentleness because they see such feelings as signs of weakness.

Aggressive people show traits of brutality and cruelty, and, if they tend to pessimism too, all their relationships with their environment are changed, for they can neither sympathize nor co-operate, being hostile to the whole world. Their conscious sense of their own worth may at the same time have reached a very high degree. They may be puffed up with pride and arrogance and self-importance. They exhibit their vanities as though they were actually conquerors, yet the obviousness with which they do all this, and their behavioural excesses, not only disturb their relationship with the world, but also betray their whole character, because all their swagger is built upon an insecure, shifting foundation.

The subsequent development of the aggressive type is not easy. Human society does not look very favourably on such people. The very fact that they are so obtrusive makes them disliked. In their persistent efforts to win the upper hand, they soon find themselves in conflict, especially with others of their own type, who feel compelled to compete with them. Life becomes a series of battles; and when, inevitably, they suffer defeats, their whole procession of triumph and victory comes to an abrupt end. They are easily frightened, lack the stamina for sustained conflict, and are unable to recoup their losses.

Their failure to accomplish their tasks has a stunting influence upon them and their psychological development stops approximately where that of another type, the defensive, begins.

Defenders are the ones who feel threatened. They are constantly on the defensive. They compensate for their feelings of
insecurity, not by aggression, but by anxiety, caution and
cowardice. We may be sure that people do not become defenders
without previously, and unsuccessfully, adopting the aggressive
attitude we have just described. The defensive type is quickly discouraged by setbacks and unpleasant experiences, and easily put
to flight. Occasionally they succeed in disguising their defection
by behaving as though a useful piece of work lay along the line of
retreat.

Thus when they reminisce and fantasize they are merely
trying to avoid the reality that threatens them. Some, who have
not entirely lost their initiative, may actually accomplish
something of value to society. Many artists belong to this type,
having withdrawn from reality and built a boundless world of
fantasy and ideals. They are the exceptions to the rule, for individuals of this type usually capitulate to difficulties and suffer
defeat after defeat. They fear everything and everybody, become
increasingly distrustful, and expect nothing but hostility from the
world.

In our civilization, unfortunately, their attitude is all too frequently reinforced by their bad experiences at the hands of
others. Soon they lose all belief in the good qualities of human
beings and in the brighter side of life. One of the most common
characteristics of such individuals is their constantly critical
attitude, which becomes so exaggerated at times that they are
quick to recognize the most insignificant defect in others. They
set themselves up as judges of humanity without themselves ever
doing anything useful for their fellow human beings. They busy
themselves in criticizing and spoiling the other fellow's game.
Their mistrust forces them into an anxious, hesitating attitude.
No sooner are they faced with a task than they begin to doubt
and to hesitate, as though they wished to avoid every decision. If
we want to portray this type symbolically, we can do so by
imagining a figure with one hand raised to defend itself and the
other covering its eyes, to blot out the danger.

Such individuals have other unpleasant character traits. For
example, those who do not trust themselves never trust others.
Envy and avarice are inevitably developed by such an attitude.

The isolation in which such doubters live usually signifies their disinclination to contribute to the pleasures of others, or to join in the happiness of those around them. Moreover, the happiness of strangers is almost painful to them. Certain members of this group may succeed in maintaining a feeling of their own superiority over the rest of mankind by deceit and dissimulation. In their desire to maintain their superiority at all costs they develop a behaviour pattern so complicated that, at first glance, no one would ever suspect their basic hostility to humankind.

THE OLD SCHOOL OF PSYCHOLOGY

It is true that an attempt can be made to understand human nature without being consciously aware of the direction one's research takes. The usual method is to take a single point in psychological development, and set up 'types' as markers by which to orient ourselves. We could, for instance divide human beings into thinkers and doers. Thinkers are more given to meditation and reflection. They live in a world of fantasy and shun the real world. Individuals of this type are more difficult to jolt into action than those of the second type, the doers. Doers reflect less, meditate hardly at all, and busy themselves with an active, matter-of-fact, down-to-earth approach to the problems of life.

Such types certainly do exist. Yet if we subscribed to this school of psychology, we would soon reach the limit of our investigations, and would be forced, like other psychologists, to be content with affirming that in the one type the power of fantasy, and in the other the ability to work, was better developed. This would hardly be sufficient material for a really scientific statement. We need to discover better conceptions of how these things happen, and whether they had to happen, and whether they can be avoided or mitigated. For this reason such artificial and superficial labelling is not valid for a rational study of human nature, even though the various types, as stated above, actually do exist.

Individual Psychology has concentrated on the development of the psyche at the point where the various forms of psychological manifestation originate: in the earliest days of childhood. It has established that these manifestations, taken together or singly, are coloured either by the predominance of social feeling, or by the struggle for power. With this contention, Individual Psychology has found a key to understanding human beings according to a simple and universally applicable concept. Any human being may be classified according to this key concept, which has an extremely wide field of application. Naturally we need to approach every case with the caution and skilful observation appropriate to a psychologist. With this obvious premise we acquire a standard, and are able to judge whether a psychological manifestation contains a great degree of social feeling and only a muted striving for personal power and prestige, or whether it is predominantly selfish, ambitious, and useful only in creating a sense of superiority. On this basis it is easy to understand more clearly certain character traits that have previously been misunderstood, and to judge them according to their place in the personality as a whole. Moreover, understanding a trait or behaviour pattern in someone gives us a tool with which to modify that individual's behaviour.

TEMPERAMENT AND ENDOCRINE SECRETION

The categories of 'temperaments' are an old classification of psychological phenomena and character traits. It is difficult to know just what is meant by 'temperament'. Is it the quickness with which we think, speak, or act? The power or the rhythm with which we approach a task? On investigation the explanations of psychologists concerning the essence of temperament seem singularly inadequate. We must admit that science has been unable to get away from the concept that there are four temperaments, or humours, a concept that dates back to the dim antiquity in which the study of human nature first began. The division of temperaments into sanguine, choleric, melancholic and phlegmatic dates from ancient Greece, where it was developed by Hippocrates, taken up later by the Romans, and remains today an honourable and sacred relic in our present psychology.

To the sanguine type belong those individuals who experience a certain joy in life. Sanguine people do not take things too seriously and do not let life wear them down. They attempt to see the most pleasant and most beautiful side of every event. They are sad when sadness is proper, without breaking down, and experience pleasure in happy things, without losing their sense of perspective. A careful description of these individuals shows nothing more than that they are reasonably healthy people with no serious defects. We cannot make this assertion about the other three types.

The choleric individual is described in an old poetical work as a person who fiercely kicks aside a stone that lies in the way, while the sanguine individual walks serenely around it. Translated into the language of Individual Psychology, choleric individuals are those whose striving for power is so intense that they react emphatically and violently to every-thing, feeling that they are forced at all times to prove their strength. They rush at every obstacle like a bull at a gate. In reality, these violent feelings begin in early childhood, when feelings of powerlessness are experienced, and it becomes necessary constantly to demonstrate power in order to be convinced of its existence.

Melancholic types make quite a different impression. If melancholics came across the same stone in their path, they would see it, remember all their sins, begin brooding sadly about their past life, and turn back. Individual Psychology sees in them the openly hesitating neurotic who has no confidence in ever overcoming their difficulties or of getting ahead. Melancholics prefer not to risk a new adventure. They would rather stand still than move towards an objective, and if they do set out, they begin every movement with the greatest caution. In their life, doubt plays a predominant role. These types think much more about themselves than about others, which eventually makes it impossible for them to forge adequate relationships. They are so oppressed with their own cares that they spend their time in fruitless introspection and nostalgia.

Phlegmatic individuals in general are strangers to life. They are subjected to experiences without drawing the appropriate conclusions from them. Nothing makes a great impression upon them; they are hardly interested in anything; they make no friends; in short they have almost no connections with life. Of all four types they are probably the ones who are farthest away from the business of living, because of their insensitivity to their environment.

We may therefore conclude that only sanguine individuals can be 'good' human beings. Clearly defined temperaments, however, are seldom found. For the most part one deals with mixtures of two or more. This fact renders the theory of temperament valueless. Nor are these 'types' and 'temperaments' fixed. We frequently find that one temperament dissolves into another. Children can start out as choleric individuals, later become melancholics, and end their lives as classic phlegmatics. Temperament can also be a matter of luck. Sanguine individuals seem to be the ones who have been the least exposed to feelings of inferiority in their childhood. They suffer few physical disadvantages and have not been subjected to any strong irritations. As a result they have developed uneventfully, with a certain love for life that enables them to approach it with confidence.

At this point science comes on the scene and declares: 'Our temperaments are dependent upon the glands of internal secretion.' One of the latest developments in medical science has been the recognition of the importance of endocrine secretions. The glands of internal secretion are the thyroid, the pituitary, the adrenals, the parathyroids, the islands of Langerhans in the pancreas, and the interstitial glands of the testes and ovaries, together with certain other histological structures, whose functions are only imperfectly understood. These glands have no ducts but release their secretions directly into the blood.

The general impression is that all organs and tissues are influenced in their growth and activity by these endocrine secretions, which are carried by the blood to every single cell in the body. These secretions act as activators or detoxicants and are essential to life, but the full significance of these endocrine glands is still not fully understood. The whole science of endocrine secretion is only in its infancy and reliable facts about the function of endocrine secretions are few and far between. But since this young science has demanded attention by claiming that these secretions determine character and temperament, we must say something more about them.

To begin with, let us deal with one important point. In cases of actual endocrine disorder, such as cretinism, in which the thyroid gland is insufficiently active, it is quite true that we also find psychological symptoms, which in the case of cretinism are characterized by an ultra-phlegmatic temperament. Apart from the fact that these individuals appear puffy and bloated, the growth of their hair is abnormal, and their skin is particularly thick, they also show extraordinary slowness and lassitude in their movements. Their psychological sensitivity is markedly low and the capacity for initiative is virtually absent.

Should we now compare such a case with another case that we could diagnose as phlegmatic, although no demonstrable pathological changes in the thyroid gland were present, we should find two entirely different pictures, with entirely dissimilar character traits. We might therefore conclude that there seems to be something in the secretion of the thyroid gland that helps to maintain adequate psychological function; but we cannot go so far as to say that the phlegmatic temperament arises out of an inadequacy in this secretion of the thyroid gland.

The pathologically phlegmatic type is something entirely different from that which psychologists are used to calling phlegmatic. The psychologically phlegmatic character and temperament is entirely distinguished from the pathologically phlegmatic by the previous psychological history of the individual. The phlegmatic types with which we as psychologists are concerned are by no means passive individuals. We are often surprised by the intensity and violence of their reactions. No phlegmatics have been phlegmatic all their life. We shall learn that their temperament is only an artificial shell, a defence mechanism (for which they may have had, conceivably, a constitutionally determined tendency earlier in life) that oversensitive beings have created for themselves, a fortification they have thrown up between themselves and the outer world.

The phlegmatic temperament is a defence mechanism, a purposeful response to the challenge of existence. In this sense it is entirely different from the slowness, laziness and inadequacy of a person whose thyroid gland is seriously defective. Even in those cases where it would seem that only patients whose thyroid glands were once inadequate acquired a phlegmatic temperament, this important and significant point is not overruled. This is not the cause of the whole problem. What is actually involved is a whole complex of causes and purposes, a whole system of internal and external influences, which produce a feeling of inferiority. It is this feeling of inferiority that makes someone develop a phlegmatic temperament to shield themselves from unpleasant insults and injuries to their personal self-esteem. But we are dealing here with a type of whom we have already spoken in general. The deficiency of the thyroid gland is a specific organic defect, and its consequences are important. This handicap gives rise to a more anxious attitude towards life for which individuals attempt to compensate by various psychological stratagems, of which the adoption of a phlegmatic temperament is a well-known example.

We shall be confirmed in our assumption when we take into consideration other glandular problems and examine the temperaments associated with them. Thus there are individuals who have an exaggerated thyroid secretion, as in Basedow's disease, or goitre. The physical signs of this disease are over-activity of the heart, rapid pulse, exophthalmos or bulging eyes, swelling of the thyroid gland, and slight or severe trembling of the extremities, particularly the hands. Such patients perspire easily, and often have digestive problems as a result of the influence of the thyroid secretion upon the pancreas. They are highly sensitive and irritable, and are characterized by a hasty, trembling activity, often associated with well-marked anxiety states. The picture of a typical exophthalmic goitre patient is unmistakably that of an over-anxious person.

To say, however, that this is identical with the picture of psychological anxiety, is to commit a grave error. The psychological phenomena one sees in exophthalmic goitre – the anxiety states, the inability to do certain physical or mental work, the easy fatigue and great weakness – stem not only from psychological causes, but also from organic ones. People who suffer from a neurosis involving hurry and anxiety present a totally different picture. In marked contrast to those individuals whose psychological symptoms are the result of hyperthyroidism, who are, so to speak, drunk on thyroid secretion, neurotics are excitable, hasty, anxious individuals who belong in a completely different category, for their condition is caused almost entirely by their previous psychological experiences. Hyperthyroid individuals certainly show similarities in behaviour, but their activity lacks that element of plan and purposefulness that is the essential index of character and temperament.

Other glands with internal secretions must also be discussed here. The connection between the development of the various glands and the development of the testes and ovaries is especially important. Our contention, which has become one of the fundamental tenets of biological research, is that one never finds endocrine anomalies without also finding anomalies of the gonads, or sex glands. The special relationship between these glands, and the reason for the simultaneous appearance of these disorders, have never been fully understood. In cases of organic defects in these glands, the same conclusions apply as in other organic defects. People whose gonads are inadequate tend also to find it harder to adjust to life, and in consequence have to think up more psychological tricks and defence mechanisms to help them to adjust.

Enthusiastic investigators of the endocrine glands have led us to expect character and temperament to be wholly dependent upon the endocrine secretions of the sex glands. It appears, however, that extensive anomalies in the glands of the testes and ovaries are actually quite rare. Cases of actual pathological degeneration are the exception rather than the rule. There is no particular psychological disorder associated with the defective function of the sex glands that could not also originate – indeed does so much more frequently – in specific diseases of the sex glands. We find no solid medical foundation for a view of character based on endocrine function or dysfunction, as claimed by endocrinologists. It goes without saying that certain stimuli, necessary for the vitality of the organism, arise from the sex glands, and that these stimuli may determine the situation of children in their environment. Yet these stimuli may be produced by other organs as well, and they are not necessarily the basis for a specific psychological structure.

Since putting a value on a human being is a difficult and delicate task, in which an error may mean life or death, we must issue a warning here. Children who come into the world with physical weaknesses and disabilities are sorely tempted to acquire particular psychological tricks and artifices as compensation. But this temptation to resort to artifice can be overcome. There is no physical disability, no matter how serious, which must inevitably, necessarily and irrevocably force individuals to adopt a particular attitude to life. It may dishearten them, but that is another matter. The contrary opinion exists solely because no one has ever attempted to overcome the difficulties in the psychological development of children with physical disabilities. We have allowed them to develop differently from other children, as a result of their disabilities. We have examined and observed them, but not attempted to help them or stimulate them. In short, this means that the new positional or social psychology founded upon the discoveries of Individual Psychology will prove to be more accurate than psychology based on heredity.

TO SUM UP

Before we go on to consider single character traits, let us briefly review the points we have already discussed. We have made the important point that the understanding of human nature can never be learned by examining isolated phenomena that have been taken out of their whole psychological context. To achieve this understanding it is essential to compare at least two phenomena, separated by as long a time span as possible, and connect them within a unified behaviour pattern. This technique has proved very useful. It enables us to gather a whole mass of impressions and condense them, by systematic arrangement, into a sound evaluation of character. If we were to base our judgement upon isolated phenomena we should find ourselves in the same difficulties that beset other psychologists and educators and thus have to fall back on those traditional criteria that have always been found to be useless and sterile. If we can succeed, however, in finding a number of key points where we can apply our system, and join these into a single pattern, we have a system whose general direction is evident, and that will give a clear and complete evaluation of the human being. Only then shall we be standing upon solid scientific ground.

Various ways and means have been discussed whereby such a system can be fashioned, and as illustrations we have used case histories of which we have direct experience ourselves or that might be accepted as familiar examples of human behaviour.

Furthermore, we have insisted that one factor in this system we have created is absolutely essential, and that is the social factor. It is not enough to observe random psychological phenomena. We must always see them in relation to social life. The most important and valuable fundamental thesis for our communal life is this: *The character of human beings never forms the basis of a moral judgement. We prefer to use a social evaluation of how human beings relate to their environment, and of the quality of their relationship to the society in which they live.*

In this elaboration of these ideas we discovered two universal human phenomena. The first is the universal existence of a social feeling that binds humanity together; this social feeling, or community spirit, is at the root of all the great accomplishments of our civilization. These contributions to society constitute the sole criterion by which to measure the social feeling of individuals. We build up a picture of the human psyche by learning how individuals relate to society, how they express their fellowship with humankind, how they make their life meaningful and worthwhile.

A second criterion for the evaluation of character is an examination of those influences that are most hostile to social feeling: the tendencies that strive for personal power and superiority. With these two points of view we can understand how relations between human beings are conditioned by their relative degree of social feeling, as contrasted with their strivings for personal aggrandizement, two tendencies always in opposition to each other. This is the dynamic interplay, the combination of forces, that manifests itself externally in what we call character.

11

AGGRESSIVE
CHARACTER TRAITS

VANITY AND AMBITION

As soon as the striving for significance gets the upper hand, it provokes increased psychological tension. In consequence, the goal of power and superiority becomes increasingly prominent for individuals, who pursue it with great intensity and violence, and live their lives in the expectation of great triumphs. Such individuals lose their sense of reality and lose sight of real life by always being preoccupied with the question of what other people think about them and with the impression that they make on the world. Their freedom of action is circumscribed to an extraordinary degree because of this life style, and their most obvious character trait is vanity.

It is probable that every human being is vain to some degree; yet exhibitions of vanity are not considered good form. Vanity, therefore, goes into hiding or becomes a master of disguises. For example, there is a type of modesty that is essentially vanity in disguise. One person may be so vain as never to consider the judgement of others; another greedily seeks public acclaim and uses it to his or her own advantage.

Taken too far, vanity becomes exceedingly dangerous. Over and above the fact that vanity leads individuals to all kinds of useless activity more concerned with appearance than essence, and makes them think constantly either of themselves, or of other people's opinions of them, the greatest danger of vanity is that it disconnects individuals from reality. They lose their understanding for human relations, and their attitude to life becomes distorted. They forget their obligations as human beings and lose sight of their role in society as a whole. No other vice is so well designed to stunt the free development of human beings as personal vanity, which forces individuals to approach every person and every event with the query: 'What do I get out of this?'

People are wont to obscure this situation by substituting the better-sounding word 'ambition' for vanity or pride. Think how many people you know who pride themselves on their ambition! The concept 'energetic' or 'active' is also frequently used. So long as this energy is actually useful to society we can admit its value, but all too often the terms 'industry', 'activity' and 'energy' are only used to cloak an inordinate degree of vanity.

Vanity quickly inhibits individuals from playing the game according to the rules. Very frequently it makes them disrupt other people's games. Thus those individuals who are unable to satisfy their own vanity are often to be found striving to prevent others from enjoying their own lives to the full. Children whose vanity is still growing show off their bravery in dangerous situations and delight in showing weaker children how powerful they are. Other children who are already discouraged to a certain degree will attempt to satisfy their vanity with all manner of incomprehensible pettinesses. They will avoid the main arena of work and attempt to satisfy their striving for significance by playing a heroic role in some sideshow of life that takes their fancy. The people who are always complaining how bitter life is, and how badly fate has treated them, belong in this category. They are the ones who would have us believe that if only they had not been so badly educated, or if some other misfortune had not happened to them, then they would be leaders. They are constantly making excuses for keeping back from the real firing line of life; the sole satisfaction for their vanity may be found in the dreams they create for themselves.

Average human beings have problems in dealing with such individuals because they do not know how to evaluate or criticize them. Vain people always know how to shift the responsibility for any mistakes onto someone else's shoulders. They are always right; others are always wrong. In everyday life, however, it makes little difference who is right and who is wrong, since the only thing that counts is getting things done and making a contribution to the lives of others. Instead of making this contribution, vain individuals are occupied with complaints, excuses and alibis. We are dealing here with the various psychological stratagems people employ in their attempts to maintain their feeling of superiority at all costs, and to shield their vanity from any insult.

The objection has frequently been made that without strong ambitions the great achievements of humankind would never have taken place. This is a false view from a false perspective. No one is entirely free from vanity; everyone has a certain amount of it. But it is not only vanity that is responsible for channelling individuals' activities in a universally useful direction, nor is it vanity that has given them the strength to carry out their great achievements. Such achievements can occur only under the stimulus of social feeling. A work of genius becomes valuable only in its social context. Any vanity involved in its creation can only detract from its worth – and vanity plays little part in a real work of genius.

In the social atmosphere of our times, however, it is impossible to divorce ourselves entirely from a certain degree of vanity. Our recognition of this fact is in itself a great asset. With this recognition we touch a sore point of our civilization, a cause of permanent unhappiness to many human beings. These are the unfortunate souls who cannot get along with anyone, who are unable to adjust to life because their whole aim is to appear more significant than they are. It comes as no surprise that they are often at odds with everyone, since they are concerned solely with their reputation with other people.

Even when we examine the most complex case, we find that the essential problem has been someone's unsuccessful attempt to satisfy their vanity. When we are attempting to understand a complicated personality, it is important to be able to determine the degree of vanity, the direction that vanity takes, and the instruments with which it gains its ends. Such an understanding will always disclose how harmful vanity can be to social feeling. Vanity simply cannot co-exist with concern for our fellow human beings. These two character traits can never live together because vanity will not allow itself to be subordinated to the needs of society.

Vanity is essentially self-centredness. But its development is constantly threatened by those logical objections that spring from communal life. Social and communal life are absolute and undeniable principles. Vanity, therefore, is forced to go into hiding at a very early period in its development. It assumes a disguise and takes a roundabout route to reach its goal. Vain people will always be a prey to grave doubts surrounding their ability to achieve the victories their vanity seems to demand; while they dream and ponder, time flies. And when time has flown our vain individuals have the excuse that they never had an opportunity to show what they could do.

The sequence of events is usually something like this. Our vain person seeks some privileged position, holds himself apart from the mainstream of life, and, standing apart, watches the comings and goings of the rest of humankind with a certain mistrust; every fellow-creature is an enemy. Vain people must assume positions of offence and defence. Often we will find them deeply in doubt, entangled in important considerations that seem to be logical, and which give them the semblance of being in the right. However in the course of their considerations they waste their opportunities, lose contact with life and society and shirk the tasks that everyone must accomplish.

Observe them more closely and we see a backdrop of vanity, the desire to conquer all reflecting itself in a thousand varied forms. This vanity is evident in their every attitude, their dress, their way of speaking and their contacts with others. In short, wherever we look, we see vain, ambitious individuals who do not care what weapons they use in their fight for superiority. Since manifestations of this sort are not very pleasant, vain people – if they are clever, and realize how they are estranging themselves from society – make every attempt to camouflage the overt signs of their vanity. Thus we may find individuals apparently modest, dressing sloppily and neglecting their appearance in order to indicate that they are not vain! There is a story that Socrates addressed a speaker who had mounted the podium in old and bedraggled clothes with these words: 'Young man of Athens, your vanity peeps out through every hole in your robe!'

There are people who are deeply convinced of their freedom from vanity. They consider only the outside, knowing that vanity lies much deeper. Vanity may be expressed by always hogging centre stage in one's social circle, holding the floor, judging the worth of a social gathering according to one's ability to be constantly in the limelight. Or vain people may refuse to mix in society, and seek to avoid it as much as possible. This avoidance of society may express itself in various ways. Turning down invitations, coming late, or obliging their host to coax and flatter them into coming, are typical signs of vanity. Other individuals go into society only under very definite conditions and show their vanity by being very 'exclusive'. They proudly consider this a laudable trait. Others, again, show their vanity by wishing to be present at all social gatherings.

We must not feel that these details are insignificant; they are very deeply rooted in the psyche. In reality individuals who are guilty of them have not much place in their personality for social feeling; they are more an enemy than a friend of society. It would take the poetical powers of a great writer to portray these types with all their variations. Here, we attempt merely to sketch them out.

One motive is common to all forms of vanity. Vain individuals have created a goal that cannot be attained in this life. They want to be more important and successful that anyone else in the world, and this goal is the direct result of their feeling of inadequacy. We may suspect that anyone whose vanity is well marked has little sense of their own worth. There may be individuals who are conscious that their vanity stems from their feeling of inadequacy, but unless they make fruitful use of their knowledge their mere consciousness of it is of no value to them.

Vanity develops at a very early age. Usually there is something very puerile about it, and as a result, vain individuals always strike us as rather childish. There are various situations conducive to the development of vanity. Perhaps children feel neglected because of a misguided upbringing and are oppressed by a sense of their own smallness and weakness. Other children acquire a certain hauteur from their family tradition. We can be certain their parents, too, assumed such an 'aristocratic' bearing to distinguish themselves from others, and make them feel proud.

A haughty attitude creates a new elite of people born in a family that is 'better' than all other families, has 'better' and 'higher' sensibilities, and feels itself predestined, by virtue of its genealogy, to maintain certain privileges. The demand for such privileges also gives a direction to life, and determines a type of behaviour. Since life is in general fairly unsympathetic to such aspirations, and since people who demand special treatment are usually either antagonized or ridiculed, many of them withdraw timidly and lead an isolated or eccentric existence. As long as they remain at home where they are not responsible to anyone they can maintain their fiction of greatness, and feel themselves reinforced in their attitude by believing that they might have accomplished their purpose if things had been different.

Occasionally, capable, eminent individuals who have developed themselves to the highest degree are found in this group. If they were to share their talents with the world, they might be of some value, but they misuse their abilities in order to delude themselves further. They set impossibly demanding conditions for their co-operation with society. They may, for instance, place impossible conditions on time, saying if only they had done something, learned something or known something earlier, they could achieve more. Or they make alibis out of the nature of things, saying that men and women should act or think differently. Their conditions are impossible to satisfy, even with the best of intentions. We must conclude, therefore, that they are really only excuses, as valueless as hypnotic or intoxicating drugs that free us from the necessity of having to think about the time we have wasted.

There is a great deal of hostility in these people, and they tend to be indifferent to the pain and sorrow of others. This is the mechanism whereby they achieve a feeling of greatness. La Rochefoucauld, a great judge of human nature, said that most people 'can bear the pains of others easily'. Social hostility often expresses itself in the assumption of a sharp, critical manner. These enemies of society are forever blaming, criticizing, ridiculing, judging, and condemning the world. They are dissatisfied with everything. But it is not enough only to recognize the bad, and condemn it. We must ask ourselves: 'What have I done to make these things better?'

Some individuals use their ready wit to elevate themselves above the rest of humanity, etching the characters of others with the sharp acid of their criticism. It is not surprising that such individuals occasionally develop a fine critical technique, for they get plenty of practice. The greatest wits, whose quickness and readiness of repartee are remarkable, are to be found among them. One can do as much damage with a sharp tongue as with any other weapon, and satirists make a profession of putting people down.

The sharp, destructive, over-critical behaviour of such individuals is the expression of a common enough character trait. We have called this the deprecation complex. It clearly pinpoints vain people's target as the worth and value of their fellow human beings. It is an attempt to gain a feeling of superiority by degrading other people. The recognition of another's worth is seen as an insult to the vain one's personality. From this fact alone we can draw far-reaching conclusions, and learn how deeply this feeling of weakness and inadequacy is rooted in their personality.

Since none of us is utterly free from vanity we can apply the same standard to ourselves, even if we cannot uproot, in a short time, the tendencies that thousands of years of tradition have allowed to flourish. It is nevertheless a step in the right direction if we recognize our ensnaring and dangerous prejudices.

We do not genuinely desire to be different from other human beings, nor to seek out those who are different from the rest. We feel that a natural law demands that we stretch out our hands to join, and co-operate with, our fellow human beings. In an age like ours, which demands so much co-operation, there is no longer any place for the strivings of personal vanity. In times like ours, the crass folly of a vain attitude towards life is especially obvious, since we can see every day how pride goes before a fall, bringing the vain into conflict with society or placing them in need of that society's sympathy. At no time has vanity been more objectionable than it is today. The least we can do is search for better forms and outlets for vanity, so that if we must be vain, we can at least exercise our vanity in the direction of the common weal!

The following case is an excellent demonstration of the dynamics of vanity. A young woman, the youngest of several sisters, was very pampered from the earliest days of her life. Her mother was at her beck and call day and night, and fulfilled her every wish. As a result of this attention the demands of this youngest child, who was also very sickly, grew out of hand. Early on she had made the discovery that when her mother was ill, her smallest wish was law. It did not take the young lady long to learn that sickness could be a very valuable asset.

Normal people dislike being ill, but she soon overcame that dislike, and quite enjoyed her occasional illnesses. Soon she trained herself to fall ill whenever she desired it, and especially when she had set her heart on attaining some special object. Unfortunately there was always something she had set her heart on, with the result that, so far as those around her were concerned, she became chronically ill. There are many manifestations of this 'sickness complex' in children and adults who feel their power growing and use their illnesses to hijack their family's attention. For tender, weak individuals the possibilities of this route to power are enormous, and naturally it is just such individuals who use it, having once tasted the concern their relatives show for their health.

In such a situation individuals can play various other tricks to get their own way. To start with, they may not eat enough; as a result they look unhealthy and the family go to great lengths to cook delicacies to tempt them. In the process, the patients develop the desire for someone constantly to shower attendance on them. People like them cannot bear to be alone. Simply by feeling ill, or being in danger, they get the attention they love.

The ability to identify ourselves with a thing or situation is called empathy. Imaginative empathy is demonstrated in our dreams where we feel as though some specific situation is actually occurring. Once the victims of the 'sickness complex' discover this way of exerting power, they easily succeed in producing and conjuring up a feeling of malaise so genuine that we cannot speak of a lie, or distortion, or imagination. We are well aware that identification with a situation can produce the same effect as if that situation were present in actuality. We know that such individuals can vomit, or exhibit anxiety symptoms, just as though they actually were nauseated or in danger. Usually they betray themselves in the manner in which they produce these symptoms. The young woman of whom we were speaking, for instance, declared that she sometimes had a felling as though 'I was going to have a stroke at any moment'.

There are people who can imagine a thing so clearly that they actually lose their balance, and one cannot talk of imagination or simulation. All that is necessary is that one of these professional invalids succeeds once in convincing others with the symptoms of a disease, or at least with so-called 'nervous' symptoms. Thereafter everyone who has once been convinced must remain at the side of the 'patients', take care of them and attend to their well-being. The sickness of fellow human beings calls on the social feeling of every normal person. Individuals of the type we have just described abuse this spirit and manipulate it to exercise their feeling of power.

Their opposition to the laws of society and communal life, which demand far-reaching considerations of one's fellow human beings, becomes very obvious under such circumstances. We usually find that these individuals are unable to share the pain or happiness of others. It will be difficult for them not to infringe the rights of their neighbours; it is not in their interests to be helpful. Occasionally they may succeed in life, as a result of terrific efforts and by virtue of the mobilization of their whole education and culture. More often their efforts will be directed towards attaining only an outward show of interest in the welfare of others. Essentially their conduct is based on pure self-love and vanity.

Certainly this is true of the young woman we have just cited. Her solicitude for her relatives seemed boundless. She became worried if her mother was half an hour later than usual in bringing her breakfast to her room. In such circumstances she was not satisfied until she had wakened her husband and sent him to see if anything had happened to her mother. In the course of time her mother got into the habit of arriving very punctually with the young woman's breakfast.

Much the same thing happened with her husband. Being a businessman, he had to attend to his customers and business associates to some extent, yet every time he arrived home a few minutes late he found his wife almost on the verge of a nervous breakdown, shivering with anxiety, bathed in sweat, bitterly complaining how worried and anxious she had been for his safety. Her poor husband had no choice but to follow the example of her mother and be punctual at all costs.

Some people may say that this woman got no real benefit from her actions and that her victories were very minor ones. We must keep in mind, however, that we have seen only a small part of the picture; her sickness is a danger sign that says, 'Take care!' It is a key to all the other aspects of her life. With this simple device she put everyone around her under her thumb. The satisfaction of her vanity played an essential role in her endless desire to dominate. Imagine the lengths to which such individuals must go to accomplish their purpose! We must conclude that this woman's attitude and behaviour had become an absolute necessity for her when we remember what a high price she was paying for them. She could not rest unless her whims were obeyed unconditionally and punctually. But marriage consists of more than having a punctual spouse. A thousand other aspects of her relationships were affected by the imperious behaviour of this woman, who had learned how to back up her commands with the threat of an anxiety attack. She seemed intensely concerned with the welfare of others, yet they had unconditionally to obey her will. We can draw only one conclusion: her solicitude is an instrument for the satisfaction of her vanity.

It is not unusual to find a psychological urge of this nature assuming such proportions that getting our own way becomes more important than the thing we desire. This is exemplified by the case of a six-year-old girl whose egotism was so limitless she was solely concerned with the gratification of any random whim. Her behaviour was permeated by the desire to show her ability to dominate everyone, and she was usually successful. Her mother, who was very anxious to remain on good terms with her daughter, once attempted to surprise the child with her favourite dessert, saying: 'I have brought you this because I know it is your favourite.' The little girl dropped the plate on the floor, trampled on the cake and cried out, 'But I don't want it when you give it to me, I only want it when I want it.' Another time she overheard her mother wondering whether the little girl would like coffee or milk. The girl stood in the doorway and muttered very clearly, 'If she says coffee I want milk, and if she says milk I want coffee!'

This was a child who spoke her mind openly, but there are many equally egotistical children who do not express their thoughts so overtly. Perhaps all children have this trait to a degree and are at great pains to get their own way, even though they have nothing to gain from it, and may even suffer pain and unhappiness as a result. For the most part these will be the children who have been allowed to get into the habit of having every whim satisfied. Examples of this are not hard to find nowadays. Consequently, among adults we will find more people who are anxious to have their own way than people who desire to help others. Some go so far in their vanity that they are incapable of doing anything that anyone else has suggested to them, even if this is the most obvious course of action and entirely in their own interests. These are the people who cannot wait until another person has finished speaking before raising their voices in opposition. And there are some people who are spurred on by their vanity to such an extent that they actually say 'no!' when they want to say 'yes!'

To have our own way all the time is possible only within the family circle, and not always there. There are some individuals whose contacts with strangers are amiable and easy-going, but never last long. The relationship soon cools. Life being what it is, with human beings constantly thrown together, it is not unusual to find an individual who wins all hearts, then leaves them in the lurch.

Many strive constantly to confine their activities to the circle of their family. This is what happened in the case of our patient described above. Because of her charming personality she was known and loved outside her home as a delightful person. But she did not stay away from home for long. The desire to return to her family was fulfilled by a variety of tricks. If she went to a party she would get a headache and have to leave, because at a social gathering she could not maintain the absolute power she was capable of maintaining at home.

Since this woman could not achieve her main aim in life – the satisfaction of her vanity – except within her family circle, she was forced to arrange something to drive her back to this family whenever necessary. This escalated to the point where she was seized by anxiety and agitation every time she went among strangers. Soon she could not go to the theatre, and finally she could not go out in the street because in these situations she felt

that the world was no longer under her control. The situation
she sought was not to be found outside her family, and particularly not in the street. As a result, she announced her inability to
go out of her home except when accompanied by the members of
her 'court'. This was the situation she loved: to be surrounded
constantly by solicitous people who were concerned with her
welfare. As our examination showed, she had carried this pattern
with her from early childhood.

She was the youngest child in her family, and also the
weakest, the most sickly, and needed more pampering and
cosseting than the others. She seized upon the role of the
pampered child, and would have maintained it throughout her
life if she had not gone too far and broken life's iron rules, which
are sharply opposed to this type of behaviour. Her agitation and
anxiety attacks, which were so marked that no one could deny
their genuineness, betrayed the fact that she had become trapped
by her solution to the problem of vanity. The solution was inadequate; she did not have the will to subordinate herself to the give
and take of social life and thus, finally, the effects of her failure
to solve her problem became so painful that she sought medical
help.

Now it was necessary to dismantle the entire superstructure
of her life, which she had so carefully constructed over many
years. Great resistance had to be overcome, because, though
outwardly she appealed to the doctor for help, essentially she was
not prepared to change. What she really wanted was to keep on
ruling her family as before, without having to pay the price of the
torturing anxiety that attacked her in the street. But she could
not have the one without the other! She was shown how she was
a prisoner within the cage of her own unconscious behaviour,
whose advantages she wished to enjoy, but whose disadvantages
she wanted to avoid.

This example clearly shows how every significant degree of
vanity acts as a heavy burden throughout life, inhibits the full
development of human beings and finally leads to their
breakdown. Patients cannot understand these disadvantages, for
their attention is directed only to the advantages. For this reason
many people are convinced that their ambition, which might
more appropriately be called vanity, is a valuable characteristic.

They do not understand that this character trait makes people constantly dissatisfied, and robs them of their rest and sleep.

Let us add yet another example to prove our point. A young man of twenty-five was due to sit his final examinations. He did not present himself for the examinations, however, because he suddenly lost all interest in the subject. He was haunted by unpleasant feelings; he doubted his own ability and worth and was so riddled with self-doubt that he had finally become incapable of taking the examinations. His childhood memories were permeated with violent reproaches against his parents whose lack of understanding had hindered his development. While he was in this mood he also thought all human beings were valueless and without interest to him. In this way he succeeded in cutting himself off from the world.

Vanity proved to be the driving force that constantly provided him with the excuse to avoid putting himself to the test. Now, just before his final examinations, he was plagued by doubts, tortured by his lack of motivation and his exam nerves, and became perfectly incapable of taking them. All this was of extreme importance to him because if he gave up now, his sense of self-worth would still be intact. He carried his life jacket with him at all times! He felt safe, consoling himself with the thought that it was sickness and misfortune that caused his failure.

We see just another form of vanity in such behaviour, where individuals are reluctant to put themselves to the test. It is vanity that impels them to make their detour at precisely the moment when a decision is about to be made concerning their ability. They think of the glory they would lose if they failed, and begin to doubt their own ability; they have learned the secret of all those who can never trust themselves to make a decision! Our patient's own account of himself shows that he was, as a matter of fact, always one of these indecisive people. Every time the necessity for a decision drew near, he vacillated and weakened. If we concentrate only on the study of movements and patterns of action, this behaviour signifies to us that he desires to stop, to put a brake on his progress.

He was the oldest child and the only boy among four sisters. He was, besides, the only one who was designated for a college education, the high-flyer of the family, of whom great things were expected. His father had never lost an opportunity to spur on his ambition, and never tired of telling him of the great things he would accomplish. This boy's constant goal was to be first and best, but when put to the test he became seized with uncertainty and anxiety, wondering whether he will ever actually accomplish what is expected of him. Vanity comes to his rescue, and points the way to retreat.

This shows us how, in the development of an ambitious vanity, the die is cast and progress is made impossible. Vanity comes to blows with social feeling and there is no escape from their tangled combat. Moreover, we often observe vain people constantly breaking away from their community spirit in their earliest childhood, and attempting to go their own isolated way. They are like people who imagine the layout of a fantasy city, and go walking through it with an imaginary map looking for imaginary buildings in places where they have convinced themselves such buildings are located. Naturally they never find what they are looking for! And the cruelty of reality gets the blame! This is the approximate fate of egotists who attempt to get what they want by the exercise of power, cunning or treachery in all their relationships with their fellow human beings. They watch for the opportunity to show that others are wrong and are inferior to them. They are happy when they succeed in demonstrating, at least to themselves, that they are cleverer or better than other people. But their peers pay no attention to them, merely resisting their efforts. The fight may end either in defeat or victory, but whichever way it goes our vain friends are convinced of their rightness and superiority.

These are cheap tricks that enable anyone to imagine whatever they wish to believe. It may happen, as in our case, that individuals who ought to be studying – who should be subordinating themselves to the wisdom of a book or submitting themselves to an examination that would test their true ability – become exaggeratedly aware of their own deficiencies in the false light in which they view everything. They consequently overrate the situation, and believe that their whole happiness in life, their whole success, is at stake. As a result they work themselves into a state of tension no human being can bear.

For such people every contact acquires the importance of an enormous event. Every action, every word, is valued in terms of their own victory or defeat. It is a continuous battle that eventually drives such individuals, who have made vanity, ambition, and false hope their pattern of behaviour, into new difficulties and robs them of all true happiness. Happiness is possible only when the conditions of life are accepted; but when these real, essential conditions are pushed aside, they block themselves off from all paths to happiness and joy and fail in all those things that give satisfaction and happiness to others. The best they can do is to dream of their superiority and domination over others, despite the fact that they have no way of making their dreams come true.

Even if they really possessed such superiority, they would have no difficulty finding people who would delight in contesting it with them. This cannot be avoided, as no one can be forced to admit to someone else's superiority. What remains is individuals' own mysterious, uncertain judgement about themselves. It is hard to make any contacts with our peers or to reach any real success when we are involved in such a life style. No one wins in this game! The players are constantly exposed to attack and destruction. They have the terrible duty of appearing clever and superior at all times!

It is quite a different thing when the reputation of people is justified by their services to others. Honour then comes to them naturally, and if it is opposed by others, their opposition carries little weight. They can quietly retain their honour because they have not staked everything upon vanity. The difference – the deciding factor – is the egotistical attitude, the constant search for the elevation of one's own personality. A vain person focuses on expectation and acquisition. Contrast a vain person with one who shows a well-developed social feeling, who asks 'What can I give?', and you will see at once the enormous differences in character and in worth.

And so we arrive at a point of view that people have understood for thousands of years. It is expressed in a famous verse in the Bible: 'It is more blessed to give than to receive.' If we reflect on the meaning of these words, which spring from thousands of years' experience of human nature, we recognize that it is the attitude and feeling associated with giving that is meant here. The willingness to give, serve, or help, brings with it a certain compensation and psychological harmony, like the gold of the gods that comes back to the person who gives it away.

On the other hand, acquisitive people are usually discontented, being occupied solely with the thought of what they must still achieve, still possess, in order to be happy. Acquisitive individuals, who never consider the necessities and needs of others, and to whom another's misfortune is a joy, have no room in their mental universe for reconciliation with and acceptance of life. They demand the unbending submission of others to the laws their egotism dictates. They demand a heaven different from everyone else's, a different way of thinking and feeling. Their dissatisfaction and conceit are as much to be condemned as all their other characteristics.

There are other, more primitive forms of vanity found in those people who dress conspicuously, or with self-importance, who deck themselves out for a brave show, in the same way that primitive peoples made an exhibition of themselves by wearing an especially long feather in their hair when they have reached a certain degree of pride and honour. There are a number of human beings who find the greatest satisfaction in always being dressed beautifully and according to the latest fashion. The various ornaments such individuals wear are like battle standards for their vanity. Sometimes this vanity is expressed by erotic emblems, or by tattoos.

In these cases we have a feeling that individuals are striving to make an impression, but can only do so by being shameless. Shameless behaviour lends the feeling of greatness and superiority to some; others appear hard, brutal, stubborn, or isolated to attain this same feeling. In reality these may be individuals who are tender rather than bad mannered, whose apparent brutality is only a pose. In some, we find a seeming lack of feeling that is, in effect, a hostile attitude towards social feeling. Individuals who are motivated by this type of vanity, who desire to play a role in which they triumph and others suffer, would be insulted by any appeal to their finer feelings. Such an appeal would simply cause them to harden their attitude. We have seen cases in which parents approach

children, pleading that they have hurt them by their misbehaviour; in some situations, the children actually gain a feeling
of superiority from these demonstrations of pain.

We have already noted that vanity likes to wear a mask. Vain
people who would like to rule others must first catch them in
order to bind them to themselves. We must not, therefore, allow
ourselves to be entirely deceived by the apparent amiability,
friendliness or approachability of individuals. Nor must we be
duped into believing that they are anything other than belligerent aggressors looking for conquests to help maintain their
personal superiority. The first phase in their battle is to convince
their opponent of their goodwill, and lull them into a sense of
security. In the first phase, that of friendly approach, we are
easily tempted to believe that the aggressor is full of social
feeling. The second stage removes the veils and shows us our
error. These people always disappoint us. We may say that they
are two-faced, but in reality it is just the one face with an
amiable look that proves false in the end.

The manner of approach may even become a sort of sport:
fishing for friends. Signs of utmost devotion may be evident.
These people speak warmly of humanity, and seem to show love
of their fellow human beings in their actions. Yet they usually do
this so blatantly that anyone with any real knowledge of human
nature becomes wary. An Italian criminal psychologist once said:
'When a human being seems too good to be true, when his phi-
lanthropy and humanity assume conspicuous proportions, we
should be on our guard.' Naturally we must apply this with reservations, but we may be quite sure that it is a valid point of view.

In general we can easily recognize such types. Bootlicking is
not pleasant to anyone; it soon becomes uncomfortable, and we
are on our guard against people who flatter in this way. We are
rather inclined to advise ambitious people against this approach
– it is better to choose a different method and a smoother
technique!

In conclusion we will report another case that will show all
the different aspects we have previously discussed, and at the
same time give us an understanding of another phenomenon in
which vanity plays a major role, and that is the condition of
delinquency. The case concerns a brother and sister. The brother,

who was the younger of the two, was considered untalented, whereas his older sister had a reputation for exceptional ability. When the brother could not keep up the competition any longer he gave up. He was pushed into the background, although everyone around him attempted to remove difficulties from his path. He carried a heavy burden with him, which amounted to acknowledging that he was no good at anything. He had been taught from his earliest childhood that his sister would always overcome life's difficulties easily, whereas he was fit only for insignificant things. In this way, because of his sister's advantages, people credited him with an inadequacy that actually did not exist.

Burdened with this great load, he came to school. His was the career of a pessimistically inclined child who sought to conceal his lack of ability at all costs. As he grew older, there also arose the desire not to be forced to play the role of the stupid boy, but to be treated like an adult. By the age of fourteen he had often mixed with grown-ups, but his deep feeling of inferiority was a thorn in his side that forced him to consider how he could best play the role of a full-grown man.

He drifted into the company of prostitutes. He was spending all his money on them, yet his desire to play the grown-up held him back from asking his father for money. He therefore began to steal from his father. He was not at all troubled by these thefts, and felt he had every right to make use of his father's money. This behaviour continued until one day he was threatened with the prospect of a severe failure in school. Such failure would have been evidence of his lack of ability which he dared not broadcast.

At this point he was suddenly struck with pangs of remorse and conscience that interfered severely with his studies. His situation was improved by this because now, should he fail, he would have the excuse that he was martyred by his remorse, and anyone in such a position would fail in their studies. A high degree of distraction hindered him in his work, forcing him to think of other things. A whole day would be spent in this way; when night came, he went to sleep with the impression that he had tried to study, although in reality he paid very little attention to his work. What happened after this also helped him to play his role.

He had to get up early. As a result he was sleepy and tired all day and could not pay any attention whatsoever to his work. Surely nobody could expect him to compete with his sister now! From an outward view it was not his lack of talent that was at fault, but his fatal remorse, his pangs of conscience, which left him no peace. At last he was armed on all sides and nothing could hurt him. If he failed, there were extenuating circumstances, and no one could say that he lacked ability. If he succeeded it would prove that he could do it all along, and that everyone else was wrong.

When we see such tricks we may be sure that vanity is at the bottom of them. In this case we can see how far people can expose themselves – even to the dangers of petty crime – in order to avoid the discovery of an alleged, but not actual, lack of talent. Ambition and vanity provoke such complications and subterfuges in life. They destroy all frankness, and all true pleasures, all true joy and happiness in life, all for what on closer examination turns out to be a mere fallacy.

PLAYING GOD

It is a characteristic of fairy tales, from which all of us have learned so much about human nature, to give examples of the danger of extreme vanity. Let us review one fairy tale that shows in a particularly drastic way how unbridled vanity leads automatically to the destruction of the personality. It is Hans Christian Anderson's story of 'The Vinegar Jar'. In it a poor fisherman lives in a tiny hut. He catches a fish. He gives the fish its freedom, and the fish, in gratitude, grants him a wish. The fisherman wishes for a cottage, and his wish comes true. His dissatisfied, ambitious wife, however, insists that the fisherman must change his humble request and ask for a castle. But one idea leads to another; she sends her husband back to the fish again and again, and demands to be made a duchess, then a queen, and finally, a goddess! The fish, infuriated at her final demand, swims away and leaves them in their humble state forever.

There are no limits to vanity and ambition. It is very interesting to see how in fairy tales, as well as in the overheated imaginings of vain individuals, the striving for power becomes a desire to play God. We do not have to search far to find vain individuals acting exactly as though they were God or at least God's second in command, or expressing wishes and desires that only God could fulfil. This manifestation, the striving for God-likeness, is one extreme of a tendency present in all their activities, and amounts to a desire to project themselves beyond the boundaries of their personality.

There are many examples of this tendency, for example, among the large group of people involved in spiritualism, psychic research, telepathy and similar exploits. These are composed of people who are anxious to grow beyond the boundaries of mere humanity, who want to possess superhuman powers, who wish to remove themselves beyond time and space, and be in communication with ghosts and the spirits of the dead.

If we investigate still further we find that a large section of humanity has the tendency to seek a place at God's right hand. There are still a number of schools whose educational ideal is God-likeness. In former times this was the conscious ideal of all religious education. We can only witness the results of this education with horror. We must certainly look about nowadays for a more reasonable ideal. But it is quite conceivable that this tendency is deeply rooted in humankind. Apart from the psychological reasons, the fact is that a large portion of humanity gets its first conception of the nature of human beings from what have become catch-phrases of the Bible, declaring that man was created in the image of God. We can imagine what important and perilous consequences such an idea may leave in the soul of children. The Bible, to be sure, is a wonderful work that we can constantly read and reread, marvelling at its insight, after our judgement has matured. But let us not teach it to children, at least not without a commentary. Let children learn to be content in this life, without assuming all manner of magical powers and demanding that everyone must be their slave, ostensibly because they were created in the image of God!

Closely related to this thirst for God-likeness is the ideal of the fairy-tale Utopia where every dream comes true. Children seldom depend upon the reality of such fantasy worlds. Yet if we recognize the great interest children take in magic, then we can never doubt how easily they can be allured by it, and how easy it is for them to immerse themselves in fantasies. The idea of a power of enchantment, of a magic influence upon others, is found to a strong degree in some people, and may not be lost until they are very old.

On one point perhaps no one is entirely free from superstitious thoughts: in the matter of the belief that women can cast magic spells over their lovers. One can find many men who act as though they thought they were exposed to the magical influence of their sexual partners. This superstition leads us back to a time when this belief was held much more firmly and literally than today. Those were the days when a woman ran the risk of being branded a witch on the flimsiest pretext, a prejudice that dogged the whole of Europe like a nightmare and influenced its history for many decades. If we recall that a million women were the victims of this delusion, we cannot call it a harmless mistake, but must compare the influence of this superstition with the horrors of the Inquisition, or of world wars.

The satisfaction of our vanity through the misuse of our desire for religious exaltation is another milestone on the road of our striving for God-likeness. We have only to observe how important it may be to individuals who have suffered a mental breakdown to withdraw from other human beings and engage in personal conversation with God! Such individuals consider themselves close to God, who is duty-bound, by virtue of the worshippers' pious prayers and orthodox ritual, to be concerned personally with the worshippers' well-being. Such religious hocus-pocus is usually so far from true religion that it strikes us as being purely psychopathological. We have heard a patient say that he could not fall asleep unless he had said a particular prayer, because if he had not sent this prayer to heaven, some human being somewhere would suffer a misfortune.

To understand the flimsiness of this idea, we need only consider the corollary of his statement. 'If I say my prayer, no harm can come to anyone', would be the proposition in this instance. These are the ways in which someone can easily achieve a sense of magical greatness. Through this paltry trick, people can succeed in convincing themselves that they have prevented another from suffering a misfortune. In the day-dreams of such religious individuals we can find similar tendencies that reach out beyond the capacities of human beings. In these day-dreams we see empty gestures, brave deeds that are quite incapable of actually changing the nature of things, but succeed very well in the imagination of the day-dreamers in keeping them out of touch with reality.

In our civilization there is one thing that does seem to have magical powers, and that is money. Many people believe that you can do anything you like with money. It is not strange, therefore, that in their ambition and vanity they are obsessed with money and property. In this light, their ceaseless striving for the acquisition of worldly goods becomes comprehensible, although to us it seems almost pathological. Again, it is only a form of vanity that attempts, by the heaping up of possessions, to come close to possessing the power of an enchanter. One very wealthy man who, although he had quite enough to satisfy any normal person, continued to chase after money, actually admitted after he had developed a psychiatric disorder: 'Yes, money has a power that draws me again and again!' This man understood it, but many others dare not understand it. Today the possession of power is so closely allied with the possession of money and property, and the striving for money and property seems so natural in our civilization, that no one pays any attention to the fact that many of the individuals who spend their lives chasing after gold are spurred on merely by their vain desire for God-like power.

JEALOUSY
Jealousy is an interesting character trait because it is so widespread. By jealousy we mean not only the jealousy of love relationships, but also the jealousy in all other human relationships. Thus, in childhood, we find children who become jealous in their attempts to be superior. These same children may also develop excessive ambition. Both traits reveal their belligerent attitude to the world. Jealousy, the sister of ambition and a character trait that can last a lifetime, arises from the feeling of being neglected and of being discriminated against.

Jealousy occurs almost universally among children with the arrival of younger brothers or sisters who demand more attention from their parents, and make older children feel like dethroned monarchs. Children who, before the arrival of younger children, basked in the warm sunshine of their parents' love, become especially jealous. The case of a little girl who had committed three murders by the time she was eight years of age, shows to what extremes this feeling may lead.

This little girl was a somewhat backward child prevented from any vigorous activity because she was so delicate. She consequently found herself in a relatively pleasant situation. This pleasant situation changed suddenly when she was six years old and a sister arrived in the household. Her personality changed completely and she persecuted her baby sister with a ruthless hatred. The parents, who could not understand her behaviour, became strict with her, and attempted to show the child the error of her ways.

It happened that one day a little girl was found dead in the brook that passed by the village where this family lived. Some time later another girl was found drowned, and finally our patient was caught just at the moment when she had pushed a third young child into the water. She admitted her murders, was put into a mental hospital for observation, and was finally placed in a reform school.

In this case, the little girl's jealousy of her own sister was transferred to other young children. It was noticed that she had no hostile feelings towards boys, and it seemed that she saw her younger sister in these murdered children. Through her murderous deeds, she had attempted to get her revenge for the neglect she felt she had suffered.

Manifestations of jealousy occur even more frequently when there are brothers as well as sisters. In our civilization the fate of a girl child is not necessarily alluring; they can easily be discouraged if their brother's birth is greeted enthusiastically, and he is treated with greater care and respect and accorded all manner of advantages from which a girl is excluded.

A relationship like this naturally gives rise to hostility. It is not uncommon for an older sister to be loving and motherly to her younger brother, yet psychologically this might not be so different from the case we have just described. If an older girl assumes a motherly attitude to younger children, then she has regained a position of power where she can behave as she wishes: this stratagem enables her to create a valuable asset out of a dangerous position.

Exaggerated competition between brothers and sisters is one of the most frequent causes of family jealousy. A girl may feel neglected and may strive continually to outdo her brothers. Not infrequently, as a result of her industry and energy, she succeeds in outdistancing a brother. Nature comes to her aid in the matter, for a girl develops more quickly in adolescence – both intellectually and physically – than a boy, although this gap slowly diminishes in the course of the next few years.

Jealousy, like Proteus in the legend, can take on a thousand shapes. It may be recognized in mistrust and the setting of traps for others, in critical sizing-up of other people, and in the constant fear of being neglected. Just which of these manifestations comes to the fore depends entirely upon the person's previous preparation for social life. One form of jealousy expresses itself in self-destruction, another expresses itself in energetic obstinacy. Spoiling the enjoyment of others, senseless opposition, the restriction of other's freedom and their consequent subjugation, are some of the Protean aspects of this character trait.

Giving others a set of rules for their conduct is one favourite trick of a jealous person. A characteristic sign of this is when individuals attempt to bind their partner with chains of love, when they build a wall around their loved one, or prescribe what the loved one should see, do and think. Jealousy can also be used to degrade and reproach others. These are only means to an end: to rob others of their free will, to cage them, to chain them down.

A magnificent description of this type of behaviour is to be found in Dostoevsky's story *Netochka Niesvanova*, in which a jealous man succeeds in oppressing his wife throughout her life, thus exercising his dominance over her. Here we see clearly that jealousy is merely an especially well-marked form of the striving for power.

ENVY

Where there is striving for power and domination, there is also envy. The gulf between individuals and their unreachable goal expresses itself in the form of an inferiority complex. It oppresses them and exerts so much influence upon their general behaviour and attitude to life that we have the impression that they are a long way from their goal. This impression is confirmed by their own low evaluation of themselves and their constant dissatisfaction with life. They begin to spend their time in measuring the success of others, in occupying themselves with what others think of them, or what others have accomplished. They are always the victim of a sense of neglect, and feel that they have been discriminated against. Such individuals may in reality be more fortunate than most.

The various manifestations of this feeling of being neglected are signs of an unsatisfied vanity, of a desire to have more than one's neighbour, or simply to have everything. Envious people of this type do not say that they want to have everything, because their social feeling prevents them from thinking these thoughts. But they act as if they want to have everything.

The feeling of envy that increases in response to this constant measuring of our own successes against others' does not help us to be any happier. The universality of social feeling makes envy universally disliked. Very few people, however, do not feel some envy sometimes. None of us is entirely free from it. When life runs smoothly this may not often be evident. But when people are in pain, or feel oppressed, or lack money, food, clothes or warmth, when their hope for the future is darkened and they see no way out of their unfortunate situation, then envy appears.

Our civilization is still in its early stages. Although our ethics and religions forbid feelings of envy, we have not yet matured enough psychologically to eliminate them. We can well understand the envy very poor people feel for richer people. Who can prove that they, in the same situation, would not be envious too? All we wish to say concerning envy is that we must consider it as a factor in the contemporary situation in the human psyche. The fact is that envy arises in individuals, or in groups, as soon as something limits their activity too much. And when envy appears in its most disagreeable, unforgiveable forms, we have no way of eradicating it or the hatred that often accompanies it. One thing is clear to everyone in our society, and that is that we should never put envious tendencies to the test, nor provoke them; and that we should have sufficient tact not to draw attention to any expressions of envy. True, this course of action does little to improve matters. Yet the very least we can demand of individuals is this: that they should not deliberately flaunt any temporary appearance of superiority over others. They may all too easily injure someone by the pointless parade of power.

The origin of the character trait of envy reflects the inseparable connection between individuals and society. No one can raise themselves above society and demonstrate their power over others, without simultaneously arousing the opposition of those who want to prevent their success. It is to avoid envy that we institute all those measures and rules that attempt to establish equality for all. We have come rationally to a conclusion we have felt intuitively: that there is a natural law of the equality of all human beings. This law cannot be broken without immediately producing opposition and discord. It is one of the fundamental laws of human society.

The manifestations of envy are easily recognized: sometimes even in a person's physical appearance. There is sound psychological sense in the figures of speech with which we describe envy. We talk about people being 'green with envy' – suggesting that envy interferes with the circulation of the blood. The physical expression of envy is a peripheral contraction of the capillary blood vessels.

So far as the educational significance of envy is concerned, only one course of action is open to us. Since we cannot entirely destroy envy, we must make use of it. This can be done by channelling it in a useful direction, without disturbing the person's psychological balance. This applies to individuals as well as to groups. In the case of individuals we can suggest an occupation that will elevate their self-esteem. In the lives of nations, we frequently find countries that feel neglected, and envy their more prosperous neighbours. We need to assist these countries to develop their material and human resources, and help them to take a valued place in the family of nations.

Nobody who has been envious all their life is a useful member of the community. Envious people will be interested solely in taking things away from other people, in depriving them and putting them down. At the same time they will tend to find excuses for their failure to reach their goals, and blame these failures on others. They will be fighters and mavericks, who do not value good relationships, who are not concerned about making themselves useful to others. Since they hardly bother to sympathize with the situation of others, they have little understanding of human nature. The fact that their actions cause suffering to others will not move them one whit. Envy can even lead such people to take pleasure in their neighbours' pain.

GREED

Greed is closely related to envy, and the two are usually found together. We do not mean the form of greed that expresses itself in the hoarding of money. There is another, more general form that expresses itself chiefly in a reluctance to give pleasure to other people. Such people are avaricious in their attitude towards society and towards every other individual. Avaricious people build a wall about themselves to keep their wretched treasures safe. Not only is there a close relationship between greed and envy, but we can also see a connection with ambition and vanity. It is not an overstatement to say that all these character traits are often present at the same time. It does not take much psychological insight, therefore, when we have discovered one of these traits, to declare that the others may be present as well.

Almost everyone in today's civilization shows traces, at least, of greed. The best the average person does is to veil it, or hide it behind an exaggerated generosity, which amounts to nothing more than the giving of alms, an attempt, through gestures of generosity, to bolster one's self-esteem at the expense of others.

Under some circumstances it would appear that avarice can actually be a valuable quality. We can, for example, be avaricious of, and thus economical with, our time or labour, and in the process actually do something useful. There is a definite trend today to push 'time-management' into the foreground, demanding that we should all be economical with our time and labour. This sounds very good in theory, but wherever we see this idea applied in practice, we invariably find that some individual goal of superiority and power is being served. This theory is frequently misused, and 'time-management' is directed towards shifting the real burden of work onto the shoulders of others. This activity, like all activity, can be judged only by the standard of its usefulness to society. It is a feature of the age of technology that human beings are treated like machines and are expected to follow laws of life much as machines obey the laws of physics. In the latter case such laws are universally applicable; but in the case of human beings they lead eventually to isolation, loneliness and the destruction of human relationships. It is therefore better for everyone if we adjust our lives so that we would rather give than save. If we all try to live by this rule, and keep the common weal in mind, we cannot go far wrong.

In this connection, let us look more closely at business life. People in the business world have little concern for the welfare of competitors, or much interest in the social feeling that we consider so essential. Some business practices and enterprises are actually based on the principle that the advantage of one businessperson can result only from the disadvantage of another. As a rule there is no punishment for such behaviour even though there is a conscious malicious intention. Everyday business practices that express greed and lack social feeling poison society as a whole.

Even those who have the best of intentions must, under the pressures of the business world, protect themselves as far as possible. It is often overlooked that this personal protection is usually accompanied by damage to someone else. We point these matters out because they explain the difficulty of exercising social feeling under the pressure of business competition. Some solution must be found, so that the co-operation of every individual towards the common weal will be made easier instead of more difficult. As a matter of fact the human spirit has been at work attempting to create a better situation for its own protection. Psychology must co-operate and set about investigating these changes in order to understand not only business relationships themselves, but also the mental processes involved. Only in this way can we know what can best be done for the individual and for society.

HATE

We often find hate to be a characteristic of belligerent people. Tendencies to hate (which frequently appear in early childhood) may achieve a very high intensity, as in temper tantrums, or may appear in a milder form, as in nagging and maliciousness. The degree to which people are capable of hating and nagging is a good index of their personality. They tell us a lot about individuals, for hate and malice leave an indelible mark on the personality.

Hatred directs itself in various ways. It may be pointed towards various tasks that we must perform, against single individuals, against a nation, against a class, against a race or against the other sex. Hate does not always show itself openly. Like vanity, it is a master of disguise and knows how to appear, for instance, in the guise of a generally critical attitude. Hatred may also be seen in the way someone rejects all opportunities for making contact with others. Sometimes an individual's capacity to hate is suddenly disclosed, as if by a flash of lightning. This occurred in the case of a patient who, himself exempted from war service, told us how much he enjoyed reading the reports of the gruesome slaughter and massacre of others.

Crime is a similar manifestation of this. In milder forms, tendencies to hate may play a major role in our social life, appearing in forms that are not necessarily insulting or horrifying. Misanthropy, the form of hatred that betrays a very high degree of hostility to humankind, is one of these veiled forms. There are whole schools of philosophy so full of hostility and misanthropy as to be virtually equivalent to coarser, undisguised acts of cruelty and brutality. A veil is sometimes drawn aside in the biographies of famous people to reveal hatred. It is less important to meditate on the inevitable truth of this statement than it is to remember that hate and cruelty may sometimes exist in artists who need to stand close to humanity if they wish their art to be relevant.

The ramifications of hate can be found everywhere. It would take far too long to discuss them all here. Some occupations and professions, for instance, cannot be chosen without a certain misanthropic attitude. This does not of course mean that hatred is a prerequisite of certain professions. On the contrary, the moment individuals who are hostile to humankind decide on, for example, a military career, all their hostile tendencies are directed so that they fit, at least outwardly, into the social scheme. This happens because they have to adjust to their organization and co-operate with others who have chosen the same profession.

One area in which hostile feelings are particularly well disguised is in 'criminal negligence'. Criminal negligence towards people or property is characterized by the fact that negligent individuals lose sight of all those considerations demanded by social feeling. The legal aspects of this question have caused endless discussion, but have never been satisfactorily cleared up. It is self-evident that an action that might be termed 'criminally negligent' is not identical to a crime. If we place a flower pot so close to the edge of a window ledge that the slightest tremor might cause it to fall upon the head of some passerby, it is clearly not the same as taking that flower pot and actually throwing it at someone. But the criminally negligent behaviour of some individuals is unmistakably related to crime and is just one more key to the understanding of human beings.

In law, the fact that the criminally negligent act is not consciously intended is considered an extenuating circumstance. There is no doubt, however, that an unconsciously hostile act is based upon the same degree of hostility as a consciously hostile one. In observing children at play, we can always see certain children who pay little attention to the welfare of others. We may be certain that they are not friendly towards their peers. We should wait until we have further evidence to support it, but if we find that whenever a particular child is involved in a game with other children, something is bound to go wrong, then we have to admit that this child is not taking the welfare of his or her playmates to heart.

Negligence is widespread in families, in school and in life in general. We can find it in most of our institutions. Every now and again negligent people find their way into the headlines. Naturally they do not go unpunished; the behaviour of inconsiderate people usually have unpleasant consequences for them. Sometimes this punishment follows only after many years: 'The mills of the gods grind slowly.' It may be so long afterwards that the connection between cause and effect is not understood, hence the complaints about an undeserved misfortune! The evil fate itself may be ascribed to the fact that others, unable to bear their inconsiderateness any longer, have given up on them and withdraw from their company.

Despite any apparent justification for acts of criminal negligence, it will be found on closer inspection that they are the expressions of an essential dislike of people. For instance, motorists who exceed the speed limit and knock someone down will excuse themselves by pleading an important appointment. We recognize in them someone who values their petty personal affairs above the lives of others, so that they discount the dangers to which they expose them. The disparity between someone's own interests and the welfare of society gives us an index of their hostility to the human race.

12

Non-Aggressive
Character Traits

Those character traits that are not openly hostile towards humanity, but give the impression of hostile isolation, may be grouped among non-aggressive human character traits. It would seem that the stream of hostility had been diverted; we have the impression of a psychological detour. Here we have individuals who never harm anyone, but who withdraw from society, avoid all contact and fail, because of their isolation, to co-operate with their fellow human beings. The tasks of life, however, can be accomplished for the most part only by working together. Individuals who isolate themselves may be suspected of the same hostility as those who wage open and direct war on society. There is an enormous field to be researched here; we shall examine in greater detail several of its outstanding features. The first trait we must consider is timidity and withdrawal.

WITHDRAWAL
Withdrawal and isolation appear in a variety of forms. People who withdraw from society speak little or not at all, do not look other people in the eye, and are inattentive when spoken to. In even the simplest social relations they exhibit a certain coldness that alienates them from other people. Coldness is in their actions and mannerisms, in the way they shake hands, in their tone of voice, in the way they greet or refuse to greet others. With every gesture they seem to be distancing themselves from the rest of the world.

In all these mechanisms of isolation we find an undercurrent of ambition and vanity. These people attempt to raise themselves above others by accentuating the differences between themselves and the rest of society; but the most that they can gain is an imaginary glory. A belligerent hostility is evident in the seemingly harmless attitude of these social exiles.

Isolation may also be a trait of larger groups. Everyone knows entire families whose lives are hermetically sealed against approaches from the outside. Their hostility, their conceit and their belief that they are better and nobler than others, is unmistakable. Isolation may be a trait of classes, religions, races or nations, and it is sometimes an extraordinarily illuminating experience to walk through a strange town and see how, in the very structure of homes and dwellings, whole social strata isolate themselves from others.

There is a deep-rooted tendency in our culture that allows human beings to isolate themselves into nations, creeds and classes. Conflict, expressed in outdated, impotent traditions, is the only result. It further enables some individuals to make use of latent divisions to set one group against another, in order to satisfy their personal vanity. Such a class, or such an individual, considers itself especially distinguished, values its characteristics most highly, and is preoccupied with demonstrating the faults of other people.

Those who work so hard to accentuate the differences between classes or nations do so chiefly to heighten their own personal vanity. If disastrous events ensue, such as world wars and all their consequences, these people will be the last to take the blame for provoking them. Hounded by their own feelings of insecurity, these troublemakers attempt to achieve a sense of superiority and independence at the cost of others. Isolation in their own tiny universe is their sorry fate; it goes without saying that they are not capable of progress or of contributing to the culture of our civilization.

ANXIETY

Misanthropists often complain of anxiety. Anxiety is an extraordinarily widespread trait; it accompanies individuals from earliest childhood to old age. It embitters their life to a marked degree, distances them from all human contacts and destroys their hope of building up a peaceful life or making fruitful contributions to the world. Fear can touch every human activity. We can be afraid of the outer world, or afraid of the world within ourselves.

One person avoids society because she is afraid of it. Another may be afraid to be alone. Among anxious people we will also find those familiar individuals who think more of themselves than of their fellow human beings. Once someone assumes the point of view that life's difficulties must be avoided, they are inviting anxiety in, and once in, it will reinforce that point of view. There are people whose first reaction to something new is always anxiety, whether it is simply moving house, parting from a companion, starting a job or falling in love. They are so out of touch with life and with their peers that every change of situation is accompanied by fear.

The development of their personality and their ability to contribute to our common welfare are markedly inhibited by this trait. Anxiety does not necessarily mean trembling and running away. It can be revealed in the dragging of one's feet over a problem, approaching a situation hesitantly, or looking for an excuse to avoid it. For the most part fearful individuals are not aware that their anxious attitude comes to the surface every time a new situation appears.

It is very interesting to find people who are constantly thinking of the past or of death. Dwelling on the past is an unobtrusive and therefore very popular means of constraining ourselves. Fear of death or sickness is a typical characteristic of people who are seeking an excuse to avoid all duties and obligations. They loudly proclaim that all is vanity, that life is woefully brief and that no one can know what will happen. As we have seen, such individuals may avoid all tests because their pride prevents them from submitting to a trial that would disclose their real worth.

The consolation of heaven and the hereafter has much the same effect. For individuals whose real goal lies in the hereafter, the business of life in this world becomes an irrelevant struggle, an insignificant phase of development. With such other-worldly types we find that it is the same god, the same goal of superiority over others for which they strive, the same overweening pride and ambition that leave them ill-equipped for life.

We find anxiety in its first and most primitive form in children who are terrified when they are left alone. They are not satisfied, however, when someone comes to them; they are really concerned with wielding their power. If a mother leaves anxious children alone, they call her back with evident anxiety. This gesture proves that nothing has changed. It does not matter whether the mother is there or not. The children are far more concerned with pressing her into their service. This is a sign that the children have not been allowed to develop any independence but have developed the habit, through mistaken upbringing in early childhood, of making demands of service on other people.

The expressions of childish anxiety are universally known. They become especially evident in the dark, which cuts children off from the world. Their scream of anxiety links them with the world again. They are no longer alone and forgotten. If someone hurries to them, they are happy, because they are demonstrating their power. They want the light on. They want someone to sit with them, play with them and so on. As long as they are obeyed, their anxiety is dispelled, but the moment their sense of superiority is threatened they become anxious again, and use their anxiety to strengthen their position of power.

There are similar phenomena in the lives of adults. There are individuals who do not like to go out alone. We can recognize them in the street from their anxious gestures and the anxious looks they cast about them. Some people will not move from one place to another, others seem to be running along the street as if pursued by an enemy. Perhaps you have been approached by someone of this type who has asked you to help them cross the street. Such people are not invalids! They can walk quite easily, and are usually quite healthy, but in the face of an insignificant difficulty they are struck with anxiety and fear. Occasionally their anxiety and insecurity begin the very moment they leave the house.

Agoraphobia, or the fear of open spaces, is an interesting phenomenon. Agoraphobia sufferers can never shake off the feeling that they are the victims of some malign persecution. They believe there is something distinguishing them from other people. Fear of falling (which simply indicates to us that they have an exalted opinion of themselves) is a symptom of this attitude. In the pathological forms of fear, the same goals of power and superiority may be seen.

For many people anxiety is an obvious device to compel someone to be close to them and take care of them. Under such circumstances, no one can leave the room in case the sufferer becomes anxious again! Everyone must rally round. In this way one person's anxiety affects everyone else. Everyone has to come to these sufferers, who in turn need go to no one and so become ruler of all they survey. The only way to conquer fear of other people is through strengthening the bonds that bind individuals to humanity. Only when we are conscious of belonging to the one human family can we go through life without anxiety.

Let us add an interesting example taken from the days of the 1918 revolution in Austria. At that time a number of patients suddenly declared that they were unable to attend their consultations. Asked for their reasons, they said things like, 'These are such uncertain times; you can never tell what kind of people you will meet. If you are dressed better than the others you can never tell what will happen.'

Those were of course troubled times, yet it is remarkable that only certain individuals drew these conclusions. Why were these the only people to do so? This did not happen simply by chance. Their fear was the result of the fact that they had never had any contact with human beings. They therefore felt insecure under the unusual political circumstances, whereas others, who felt that they belonged to society, felt no anxiety and went about their business as usual.

TIMIDITY

Timidity is a milder but equally noteworthy form of anxiety; what we have said of anxiety applies equally to timidity. Whatever relationships you place timid children in, their timidity may enable them to avoid contacts, or break them off when they are made. The feeling of inferiority, and the sense of being different from others, inhibits these children from finding any joy in making new contacts.

Timidity is a characteristic of those who feel that every task facing them is especially difficult; of people who have no confidence in their ability to achieve anything. As a rule this trait is evinced by slow movements, and a reluctance to get to grips with a test or task, or even to approach it at all. People who find urgent business elsewhere when they should be applying themselves to some particular problem belong to this group. Such individuals suddenly discover that they are totally unsuited to the profession they have chosen, or they think up all manner of ridiculous objections to practising it. Apart from slow movements, timidity is also expressed in an excessive preoccupation with safety and preparation, activities aimed solely at evading all responsibility.

Individual Psychology has termed the complex of questions surrounding this extraordinarily widespread phenomenon, 'the problem of distance'. It has created a standpoint from which to judge human beings and assess how far they are from solving the three great problems of life. The first of these problems, or 'tasks of life', is the question of social responsibilities, the relationship between the 'I' and the 'you', the question of whether they have helped or hindered contact between themselves and their fellow human beings. The second problem is the problem of profession or occupation, and the third is the problem of love and marriage. By examining how far people are from solving these problems, we can draw far-reaching conclusions about their personality. At the same time we can use the data we have gathered in this manner to aid us in our understanding of human nature.

The kinds of timidity described above may be caused by a desire on the part of individuals to separate themselves from their life's tasks. There is, however, a brighter side to the dark pessimism we have described. We may assume that individuals chose their position entirely because of the attractions of this brighter side. It lies in the fact that, if they approach a task ill-prepared for it, then there will be extenuating circumstances if they fail, and their vanity and self-esteem will remain intact. The situation becomes safer; they are like tight-rope walkers who know there is a safety net beneath to break their fall.

Consequently, if they fail in their task through inadequate preparation, their self-esteem is safe, because they can call on a whole battery of excuses to explain their failure. Had they not started late, or had they been better prepared, success would have been certain. In this way it is not a personal defect that is at fault, but some petty circumstance for which they cannot be expected to take responsibility.

But if they succeed, their success is all the more brilliant. For if someone performs their duties conscientiously, no one is surprised if they accomplish their aim; their success seems a foregone conclusion. If, on the other hand, they begin too late, work only a little, or are quite unprepared, yet still solve their problem, they then appear in quite another light. They become prodigies who do with one hand what others can only do with two!

THE DETOUR SYNDROME

The above are examples of the advantages of psychological detours. Yet the detour syndrome betrays not only ambition, but also vanity, and points to the fact that individuals like to play a heroic role, at least to themselves. All their activity is directed towards personal glorification, so that they may appear especially important or powerful.

Now let us consider other individuals who wish to avoid facing up to the three problems or tasks we have described above, and who bring forward all sorts of objections, with the result that they do not approach the problems at all, or only in a very hesitant manner. On their detours they become involved in all life's eccentricities, such as laziness, frequent changes of occupation, petty crime and the like. Some people express this attitude towards life in the way they carry themselves; they have a flexible, sinuous gait. This is surely not accidental. With some reservations, we can evaluate them as individuals who want to avoid problems by making detours around them.

A case taken from real life will show this plainly. It is the case of a man who clearly demonstrated his disappointment with life in boredom and thoughts of suicide. Nothing gave him any pleasure, and his whole attitude proclaimed his world-weariness. A consultation revealed that he was the eldest of three sons of an exceptionally ambitious father who had gone through life with unfailing energy, achieving considerable success. The patient was the favourite child, and was expected to follow in his father's footsteps. The boy's mother died when he was very young but, possibly because his father was very protective, he got on very well with his stepmother.

As a firstborn son, he worshipped power and force uncritically. Everything he did bore the marks of an imperial attitude.

He graduated from high school at the top of his class, then after graduation he took over his father's business and behaved like a generous benefactor. He had a kind word for everyone. He treated his workers well, paid them the highest wages and was always amenable to reasonable requests.

A change came over him after the Austrian revolution of 1918. He began complaining bitterly about the unruly behaviour of his employees. What they had requested and received in former days, they now demanded as a right. He was so embittered that he became obsessed with the idea of giving up his business.

Thus we see him making a wide detour on the power front. Usually he was a benevolent boss, but the moment his power relationships were disturbed he was unable to play the game. His philosophy was disrupting not only the smooth running of his factory, but also the smooth running of his life. If he had not been so ambitious to prove himself master in his own house, an indirect approach might have been successful. But for him the only thing that counted was domination by personal power. The logical development of social and business relationships made such personal domination practically impossible. As a result he lost all pleasure in his work and in life itself. His tendency to withdraw was both a complaint about his demanding employees and an attack on them.

But his vanity could only take him so far. He was immediately involved in the contradictory elements of the situation that had blown up. Because of his one-sided development, he lost the ability to change his mind and to devise a new plan of action; he had become incapable of further development because his only goal had been power and superiority. To this end he had allowed his vanity to become the predominant trait in his character.

If we inspect the relationships in his life we find that his social skills were thoroughly inadequate. As we might expect, he had gathered about him only those who recognized his superiority and obeyed his will. At the same time he was sharply critical, and since he was intelligent, he sometimes succeeded in making very telling, derogatory remarks. His sarcasm soon drove people away and he was without a single real friend. He compensated for this lack of contact with human beings by surrounding himself with pleasures of every other kind.

But his personality really disintegrated when he approached the problem of love and marriage. Here an all-too-predictable fate overtook him. Love demands companionship and commitment, and has no truck with imperious behaviour. Since he always had to be in command, he had to choose his marriage partner accordingly. Yet the power-crazed personality will never choose a weak, easily dominated individual as his partner, but will seek one who must be conquered and reconquered so that each conquest appears as a new victory. In this way two like-minded individuals are drawn to one another, and their marriage is an unbroken chain of battles. This man chose a woman who in many ways was even more imperious than he was. True to their principles, each seized every conceivable weapon in order to achieve and maintain domination of the other. Thus they grew farther and farther apart. They did not dare divorce each other, since each hoped for an ultimate victory, and refused to withdraw from the battlefield of their marriage.

Our patient's state of mind is clearly indicated by a dream he had at this time. He dreamt that he spoke with a young woman who looked like a servant girl and reminded him of his bookkeeper at the office. In his dream he addressed her and said, 'But you see, I am of noble blood.'

It is not difficult to understand what thought processes were taking place in this dream. For one thing, there is the way he looks down upon other human beings. Everyone appears to him like a servant, uncultured and inferior, especially if the person in question happens to be a woman. We must remember in this connection that he is at war with his wife, so that we can assume that his wife is symbolized by the figure in the dream.

No one understands our patient very well, and he understands himself even less, because he is constantly going about with his nose in the air, seeking in vain for his unattainable goal. His separation from the world is paralleled by the arrogance with which he demands recognition of his nobility, although this is quite unjustified. At the same time he fails to appreciate the worth of others. Neither love nor friendship can find a place in this philosophy.

The arguments that are used to justify such psychological detours are usually distinctive. For the most part they are reasons that in themselves are quite rational and understandable, but in reality they apply to other situations, not the immediate one. Our patient decides, for instance, that he must socialize more. He joins a club in which he wastes his time in drinking, card playing and similar useless activities. He believes this is the only way in which he can gather friends about him. He starts to come home late at night, is sleepy and tired the next morning, and claims that if he must cultivate society he should not be expected to have energy left for other things. This rationalization might pass muster if at the same time he paid more attention to his work. Instead, his socializing keeps him away from the front line – exactly as we might have expected. Obviously he is in the wrong, even though he uses rational arguments!

This case proves clearly that it is not our objective experiences that lead us away from the straight path of development, but our personal attitude towards those experiences and our evaluation of events. We are dealing here with the whole sphere of human error. This case, and similar cases, show a chain of errors and the likelihood of further errors. We must attempt to examine them in conjunction with the whole behaviour pattern of individuals, to understand their errors of judgement and to overcome them with appropriate advice. This process is very similar to education, which also consists of the removal of errors.

Development in the wrong direction based on an error of perception can lead to tragedy. We must admire the wisdom of the ancient Greeks, who either recognized this fact, or had a presentiment of it, when they spoke of Nemesis, the avenging goddess. The misfortunes individuals suffer as a result of a flawed development clearly show the consequences of pursuing personal power instead of the common weal. The cult of personal power forces them to approach their her goal indirectly, without consideration of the interests of their fellow human beings, and at the expense of an unremitting fear of defeat. At this point in the development of individuals we usually find the nervous symptoms that have arisen with the specific purpose of preventing sufferers from accomplishing some task. These symptoms serve to tell them that every step forward involves extraordinary dangers.

Society has no place for deserters. A certain degree of adaptability and co-operation are necessary in order to play the game of life. We need to be helpful, and not assume leadership simply for the purpose of ruling. We all know individuals who socialize, conduct themselves well and do not disturb others, but who are unable to form real friendships because their striving for power prevents them. It is not surprising that others cannot warm to them. These sorts of people are not convivial. They will prefer a dialogue to an open discussion, and will show their true character in seemingly insignificant things. They will for instance go to great lengths to prove themselves right, even when their rightness is of little concern to others. The subject itself may be of little importance to them as long as they can prove themselves to be in the right, and others in the wrong. Again, at the point of detour, they show puzzling symptoms; inexplicable tiredness, pointless hurrying, insomnia, loss of concentration – all kinds of complaints. In short we hear nothing from them but complaints for which they can give no adequate reasons. They seem to be sick, they are 'nervous'.

In actual fact all these are devices for diverting attention from the symptoms that show what they are really scared of. It is no accident that they have chosen these weapons. Think of the stubborn intransigence of individuals who are afraid of that natural phenomenon, night! We can be sure that they have never been reconciled with the business of living on this earth. Nothing else would satisfy their ego but to do away with night! They demand this as a precondition for their adjustment to a normal life. But by setting this impossible condition they betray themselves. They are saying 'no' to life.

All nervous manifestations of this sort originate at the point where nervous individuals become frightened of the problems they must solve, problems that are really no more than the necessary duties and obligations of everyday life. When these problems appear on the horizon they look for excuses to approach them more slowly, or under extenuating circumstances. They may even look for an excuse to avoid them altogether. In this way they simultaneously avoid those obligations necessary

for human society and injure not only their immediate environment but, in a larger context, everyone else. If we understood
human nature better, and were able to keep in mind the inex-
orable process that produces these tragic results sooner or later,
we might long ago have made the excuse of such symptoms
impossible.

It does not pay to attack the logical and immutable laws of
human society. Because of the long time lapse, and the innumerable complications that may occur, we are seldom able to
pinpoint the connection between mistakes and their consequences and draw illuminating conclusions. Only when we allow
a whole life's behaviour pattern to unfold before us, and inten-
sively study the history of a human being, are we able, with
much care, to gain insight into these connections and to point
out where the original mistake was made.

ABSENCE OF SOCIAL GRACES
There are people who show a character trait that we might
describe as a tendency for ill-mannered or uncivilized behaviour.
Those who habitually bite their nails, pick their noses or gobble
their food belong in this class. The significance of these habits is
obvious when we observe greedy people. They are voracious
eaters, and so noisy! Enormous mouthfuls of food disappear down
their throat. What remarkable amounts they get through, and so
quickly, and so often! We have all seen people who are not
happy unless they are eating.

Another manifestation of this lack of manners is dirtiness
and disorderliness. Here we do not mean the lack of formality of
people who have a lot of work to do, or the natural disorder one
can occasionally find when someone is hard at work. The kind of
people we mean usually do little useful work and are constantly
surrounded by muddle and filth. These are individuals who seem
to revel in dirt and disorder, and we could not imagine them
without this distinctive trait.

These are only some of the characteristics of uncivilized
human beings. They clearly show us that they are not playing
the game according to the rules, and would really prefer to
remove themselves from other human beings. People who
indulge in these and other uncouth acts lead us to believe that

they have little use for their fellow human beings. Most uncivilized behaviour begins in childhood, for hardly any children develop in a straight line. Some adults have simply never overcome these childish traits.

At the basis of these manifestations of uncivilized behaviour is a more or less well-marked disinclination to relate to fellow human beings. Uncivilized individuals wish to create a distance between themselves and life and are not inclined to co-operate. It is easy to understand why such people are not amenable to well-meaning exhortations to give up their uncivilized ways. For when people are unwilling to play the game of life according to the rules, they are, as a matter of fact, behaving quite logically. They could hardly have hit on a better way of alienating other people than by biting their nails or going about in stained clothes. Such antisocial behaviour effectively bars them from holding a position in which they are subject to criticism and competition and the judgement of others? What better way could they find of retreating from love or marriage, than presenting an unattractive aspect to the world? They lose out in the competition as a matter of course, and at the same time they have an excuse in that they always blame it on their absence of social graces. 'What couldn't I do if I didn't have this bad habit!' they exclaim, but in an aside they whisper their excuse, 'Unfortunately, I have it, however!'

Let us look at one case in which a bad habit became an instrument of self-defence and was used to dominate other people. It is the case of a twenty-two-year-old woman who was a bed-wetter. She was the next to last child in her family, and because she had been a weak and sickly child she enjoyed the particular solicitude of her mother, on whom she was exceptionally dependent. She had managed to chain her mother to her by day and by night, through anxiety attacks during the day and nightmares and bed-wetting at night. At the beginning this must have been a triumph for her, a balm for her vanity. With her misbehaviour she succeeded in monopolizing her mother at the expense of her brothers and sisters.

This young woman was exceptional also in that she could not be persuaded to make friends or attend school. She was particularly anxious whenever she had to leave the house. Even when she grew older, and had to run errands in the evening, walking along after dark was agony to her. She came home thoroughly exhausted and anxious, and told all sorts of terrible stories of the risks she had run. We can see how all these traits signified just one thing: this young woman wanted to remain constantly at her mother's side. However, since financial circumstances would not allow this, a job had to be found for her. She was finally persuaded to take up a position, but after only two days her old bed-wetting problem returned and forced her to give it up. Her mother, who did not understand the true meaning of her illness, reproached her bitterly. The young woman attempted suicide and was taken to hospital, and her mother then swore never to leave her again.

All these things – her bed-wetting, her fear of the dark, her terror of being alone, and her attempted suicide – were directed towards the same goal. To us they mean: 'I must stay close to my mother', or 'Mother must pay constant attention to me!' In this way the socially unacceptable behaviour of bed-wetting acquires a valid meaning. Now we can recognize that human beings may be analysed according to such bad habits. At the same time we see that such inappropriate behaviour can be rectified only when we understand patients entirely and in their social context.

By and large, we usually find that childish bad habits are directed towards gaining attention from the adult world. Children who want either to play a grand role or to show grownups how weak and incapable they are, will make use of them. The common habit of behaving very badly in front of visiting strangers has a similar meaning. The best-behaved children sometimes seem to be possessed of the devil as soon as a guest enters the house. These children want to play a role and do not stop their attempts at doing so until they have achieved their purpose in a way that seems satisfactory to them. When such children grow up they will attempt to evade the demands of society by some such behaviour, or they will attempt to frustrate the common weal by disrupting the group. An imperious, ambitious vanity is hidden beneath all such manifestations. Only the fact that these manifestations are varied and well disguised prevents us from recognizing clearly what their cause is, and to what end they are directed.

13

OTHER EXPRESSIONS
OF CHARACTER

MOOD AND TEMPERAMENT

Psychologists are mistaken if they believe that those human beings whose attitude to life and its tasks is very dependent upon their mood, or temperament, owe this quality to heredity. The tendency to be moody and temperamental is not inherited. It occurs in overly ambitious, and therefore hypersensitive natures whose dissatisfaction with life expresses itself in various evasions. Their hypersensitivity is like an outstretched feeler with which they test every new situation before they finally approach it.

It would seem however, that there are some people who are always in an extremely cheerful mood. They go to great lengths to live their lives in a happy atmosphere, laying stress on the brighter side of life. Cheerfulness, like everything else, varies in its degree. There are some people who are always carefree and jolly. There is something very touching in their childlike enthusiasm. They do not shirk their tasks, but approach them in a light-hearted, youthful way. They tackle their problems as though they were games or puzzles. There is perhaps no type of person more appealing and charming in his or her approach to life.

But there are some who carry their cheerfulness too far, who approach even serious situations in the same childish manner. Sometimes this approach is so inappropriate to the seriousness of life that we find it worrying. Seeing such individuals at work, we get the impression that they are really rather irresponsible and do not take difficult situations sufficiently seriously. As a result they are kept away from the really difficult tasks, which in any case they tend to avoid of their own accord.

Yet we cannot take leave of this over-optimistic type without paying a certain tribute to it. Such people are always pleasant to work with and provide a welcome contrast to those who go about with gloomy faces. Cheerful people can be won over much more easily than the sad and discontented pessimists who see only the dark side of every situation they meet. We have already drawn attention to the fact that we can easily measure the social feeling of individuals by learning to what extent they are prepared to serve, help and give pleasure to others. The talent for bringing pleasure to others makes people interesting to us. Happy people approach us more easily and we perceive them as more sympathetic.

It seems we instinctively sense that a cheerful temperament, when not taken to extremes, is an indicator of a highly developed social feeling. There are people who can remain optimistic, who do not go about looking anxious and careworn, who do not unload their worries onto every stranger. They are quite capable, when in the company of others, of communicating this cheerfulness and making life more beautiful and meaningful. One can sense that they are good human beings, not only in their actions, but in their approach, their speech, their concern for our interests, as well as in their whole external appearance, their clothes, their gestures, their happy disposition and their ready laughter.

That perceptive psychologist, Dostoevsky, said: 'We can judge a person's character much better by his laughter than by any boring psychological examination.' Laughter can make connections or break them. We have all heard the aggressive laughter of those who find humour in other people's misfortunes. Then there are some people who are totally unable to laugh, because they stand so far back from the natural bond that links all human beings that they lack the ability to give or receive pleasure. There is another small group of people who are utterly incapable of giving joy to anyone else because they are concerned only with souring every encounter. They go through life as though they wanted to douse every light. They do not laugh at all, or only when forced to do so, or when they wish to adopt the semblance of bonhomie.

The mystery of the emotions of sympathy and antipathy is thus made clear. At the opposite extreme from the sympathetic type are the chronic killjoys and spoilsports. They see the world as a vale of sorrow and pain. Some individuals go through life as though they were bent by the weight of a great load. Every little difficulty is made much of, and the future is always black and depressing; they never miss an opportunity, when others are happy, of delivering doleful Cassandra-like prophecies of doom. They are pessimists through and through, not only on their own behalf but on everyone else's. If someone in their vicinity is happy, they become restless and attempt to find a gloomy side to the situation. This they do, not only with their words, but with disturbing actions. In this way they prevent others from living happily and from enjoying a fellowship with humanity.

MANNER OF SPEECH

The thought processes and manner of expression of some people may make a truly indelible impression and give us a further insight into them. For example, in every culture there are thoughts and words that are unacceptable in polite company. Their vulgarity and coarseness echo in people's speech and sometimes frighten even the speakers themselves. This type of language shows a speaker's lack of imagination and judgement.

Other people think and speak as though their mental horizon were circumscribed by mottoes and proverbs. You know in advance what they will say. They sound like cheap novels, and their speech is full of slang and jargon. They demonstrate a lack of empathy with others when they answer every question with a catch-phrase or slang expression, and think and act according to the clichés of the tabloids and movies. Needless to say there are many people who cannot think in any other way, thus revealing a stunted psychological development.

SCHOOLROOM BEHAVIOUR

We frequently meet people who give the impression that their development ceased somewhere in their school career, never progressing beyond the 'elementary' stage. At home, at work and in society, they behave like schoolchildren, eagerly listening and waiting for a chance to speak up. They are always anxious to answer any question raised at a gathering, as though they are keen to show they have done their homework on the subject and are seeking for a good school report to prove it.

The key to these people is the fact that they feel safe only in structured situations. They are anxious and insecure whenever they find themselves in a situation in which schoolroom behaviour would be inappropriate. This trait appears at all intellectual levels. In its least likeable forms, the individual appears dry, austere and unapproachable, or assumes the role of the all-knowing one, appearing to understand everything immediately or seeking to pigeon-hole everything according to predetermined rules and formulae.

PEDANTRY AND PREJUDICE
An interesting example of this scholastic type is to be found in the people who attempt to catalogue every activity and every event according to some rigid principle. They believe in this principle and cannot be persuaded to relinquish it, nor would they be comfortable if they found something that could not be interpreted according to its rules. They are the dry-as-dust pedants. We have the impression that they feel so insecure that they must squeeze all of life and living into a tiny cage of rules and formulae, lest it overwhelm them. They avoid situations for which they have no rule or formula, and they are insulted and displeased if anyone plays a game whose rules are unfamiliar to them. It goes without saying that one can exercise a great deal of power by the use of this method. Think for instance of the innumerable cases of antisocial 'conscientious objectors'. We know that these over conscientious individuals are moved by overweening vanity and an inflexible desire to dominate.

Even if they are good workers, the pedants' attitude is obvious. They show no initiative, become narrowly circumscribed in their interests and are full of senseless fads and whims. Some may develop a habit of always walking on the outside edge of stairs, for example, or avoiding the cracks in the pavement. Others cannot be diverted from a familiar path at any cost. All these types lack sympathy for the real issues of life. In working out their principles they waste an enormous amount of time and energy, and sooner or later they get completely out of tune both with themselves and with their environment. The moment they encounter an unfamiliar problem they fail entirely, because they are not equipped to solve it. They believe that nothing can be done without rules and magic formulae, and they will religiously avoid all change.

It will even be difficult for them, for instance, to get used to spring because they have spent so long adjusting to winter! The beckoning of the outside world that comes with warmer weather awakens a fear that they will have to make more contacts with other people; and they feel unhappy as a result. These are the individuals who complain that they feel ill in the spring. Since they can only adjust to new situations with great difficulty, we will find them in jobs that demand little initiative. No employer would place them in any other position. These are not hereditary or unchangeable manifestations, but stem from a misguided attitude towards life, which has taken so firm a grip on their psyches that it entirely dominates their personalities. In the end such individuals cannot free themselves from their own prejudices.

SUBMISSIVENESS

People who are characteristically servile and submissive are equally ill-adapted to jobs that demand initiative. They are only comfortable when obeying someone else's command. Servile individuals live by the rules and laws of others, and this type seeks out a position of servility almost compulsively. This attitude can be found in the most varied of life's relationships. One can surmise its existence in a person's bearing, which is usually somewhat bent and cringing. These are 'yes-men'. We see them bending forward in the presence of others, listening carefully to everyone's words, not so much to weigh and consider them, but rather to carry out their commands and to echo and reaffirm their sentiments. They consider it an honour to appear submissive, sometimes to an unbelievable degree. These are people who take a real pleasure in subjugating themselves to others. Far be it from us to say that those who wish to dominate at all times are an ideal type, yet we must also show the negative aspects of the life of those who find submissiveness to be a true solution to their life's problems.

But it is fair to say that there are many for whom submission appears to be a law of life. By this we do not mean professional servants, but women. That women must be submissive is an unwritten but deeply rooted law to which a number of people subscribe as if it were a fixed dogma. They believe that women are put on earth to be submissive. Such superstitions have poisoned and destroyed countless human relationships, yet they cannot be weeded out. There are, even among women, many believers who feel that the submission of the female is an eternal law they must obey, but no one has ever gained anything by such a viewpoint. Moreover, sooner or later someone complains that if a woman had not been so submissive everything would have turned out better!

Quite apart from the fact that the human spirit will not endure submission without revolt, a submissive woman sooner or later becomes dependent and socially parasitic, as one of our cases illustrated. This was a woman who married a famous man for love. Both she and her husband subscribed to the dogma of female submission. In time she had become simply a machine for which there was nothing but duty, service and more service. Every independent gesture vanished from her life. Those around her had become accustomed to her submission, and did not especially object, but their silence did not help the situation.

This case did not reach a crisis because it occurred among relatively cultured people. But if we consider that to a large section of humankind the submission of women is their pre-ordained destiny, we can understand how much conflict this view can cause. When a husband expects this submission as a matter of course, he is likely to take offence at any moment, because in reality such total submission is impossible. But there are some women to be found who are so permeated with the spirit of submission that they seek out the most imperious or brutal men. Sooner or later this unnatural relationship degenerates into open war. We sometimes get the impression that what these women really want is to ridicule the idea of the submission of women and prove to everyone how misguided it is.

We already know the way out of these difficulties. When a man and woman live together, they must live under the conditions of companionable division of labour in which neither partner is subjugated. If, for the time being, this is only an ideal, at least it gives us a yardstick by which we can measure the cultural progress of an individual.

The question of submission plays a role not only in the relationship of the sexes, where it burdens the masculine sex with a thousand insoluble problems, but it also plays an important role in the life of nations. Ancient civilizations built up their whole economic structure on the institution of slavery. Perhaps most of the people who are alive today originated in slave families, and hundreds of years passed during which two classes of people lived in absolute estrangement from and opposition to each other. Today, indeed, the caste system still survives among certain peoples, and the principle of submission and subordination still exists.

In ancient times it was customary to believe that work was degrading and belonged properly to slaves. The master did not demean himself with common labour. Not only was he a leader of men, but a personification of all worthwhile traits. The ruling class consisted of the 'best', as the Greek word *Aristos* signifies. Aristocracy was domination by the 'best', but this 'best' was determined entirely by power, not by the evaluation of virtues and qualities; evaluation and classification occurred only among slaves. The aristocrat was the one who held the power.

In modern times our point of view has been influenced by our history of slavery and aristocracy. Even the great thinker Nietzsche advocated rule by the best and the subjugation of everyone else. There are still human beings today who have become so servile that they are happy only when they can be grateful to someone else. They seem to be forever apologizing for their very existence in the world. We must not be deceived into believing that they do this gladly. For the most part they are extremely unhappy.

It is difficult to expunge from our thinking the division of human beings into master and servant, and to consider everyone as absolutely equal. However, the need to bring human beings closer to one another has robbed the institutions of slavery and aristocracy of significance. The mere existence of a new point of view, of the absolute equality of every human being, is an advance, and a safeguard against future errors in our conduct.

IMPERIOUSNESS

In contrast to the servile individuals we have just described are the imperious individuals who must always be dominant. They are concerned with only one question all through life: 'How can I be superior to everyone?' This role carries all manner of disappointments with it.

To a certain degree the imperious role may be useful, if it is not accompanied by too much aggression and hostility. Wherever an organizer is required an imperiously minded individual will appear. They seek out positions where commanders and managers are needed. In times of unrest, for example, when a nation is in revolution, such characters come to the fore, and quite understandably so, for they have the right demeanour, attitudes and desires, and usually also the necessary preparation, to assume the leader's role. They have been accustomed to command in their own homes. But no game satisfies them unless they can play the king, the ruler or the general, and among them are individuals who are incapable of doing the slightest thing if someone else is giving the orders. They become excited and anxious as soon as they have to submit to another's commands.

In quiet times, one finds such individuals heading small groups, whether in business or in society. They are always in the foreground because they push themselves forward and have plenty to say. So long as they do not violate the rules of the game of life, we can have no objection to them, but we cannot subscribe to the excessive value that society places on such individuals today. They too are only fallible human beings, for they cannot perform well in the rank and file and do not make the best of team-mates. All their lives they strain to the utmost and can never relax until they have proved their superiority in some way.

BAD LUCK

It is a psychological truism that whoever gets into difficulties with the absolute truth and logic of communal life, will sooner or later feel the repercussions. Often the individuals who make these profound mistakes do not learn from experience, but view their misfortune as an undeserved personal disaster. It takes them their whole life to demonstrate what bad luck they have had, and prove that they have never succeeded in anything, because everything they have laid their hands upon has ended in failure. Such unfortunates tend even to be proud of their ill-luck, as though some supernatural power had caused it. Examine this point of view more closely and you will find that vanity is rearing its ugly head again! These people act as though some sinister deity is singling them out for persecution. In a thunderstorm they believe that the lightning will strike only them. They are afraid that burglars will choose their house. If any misfortune is to occur they are certain that they are the ones it will touch.

Only people who consider themselves the centre of the universe can exaggerate like this. It seems the opposite of selfishness to be constantly pursued by misfortune, but actually a stubborn vanity is at work when such individuals feel that all hostile powers are intent on wreaking vengeance upon them. They are the individuals whose childhood was embittered by a belief that they were the prey of robbers, murderers, ghosts and vampires, as though all these people and apparitions had nothing better to do with their time.

It is to be expected that their attitude will be expressed in their outward bearing. They walk as though under pressure, bent over so that no one can mistake the heavy load under which they labour. They remind us of those caryatids who supported the Greek temples and spent their existence holding up porticos. These people tend to take everything so seriously and judge everything so pessimistically, that it is not hard to understand why things often go wrong for them. They are persecuted by bad luck because they embitter not only their own lives but also those of others. Vanity is at the root of their misfortune. Being especially unlucky is one way of feeling important!

RELIGIOSITY

Some of these chronically misunderstood people retreat into religion, where they proceed to do exactly as they did before. They complain and commiserate with themselves, and shift their burdens onto the shoulders of a benevolent God. They think only about themselves. It is therefore natural for them to believe that God, this extraordinarily honoured and worshipped being, is concerned entirely with serving them and is responsible for their every action. In their opinion God may be brought even closer to them by artificial means, such as through particularly zealous prayer or other religious rites. In short, the dear Lord has nothing else to do but to be occupied with their troubles and pay a great deal of attention to them. There is so much heresy in this type of religious worship that if the old days of the Inquisition were to return, these religious fanatics would probably be the first to be burned at the stake. They approach their God just as they approach their fellow human beings, complaining, whining, yet never lifting a finger to help themselves or to better their circumstances. Co-operation, they feel, is an obligation only for others.

The case history of an eighteen-year-old girl demonstrates the lengths to which this vain egotism may go. She was a very good and industrious child, though very ambitious. Her ambition expressed itself in her religion, in which she performed every rite with the utmost piety. One day she began to reproach herself for having been too unorthodox in her beliefs, for having broken the commandments and for entertaining sinful thoughts from time to time. As a result she spent the whole day violently accusing herself with such vehemence that everyone assumed she had taken leave of her senses. She spent her time kneeling in a corner, bitterly reproaching herself; yet no one else was allowed to reproach her for a single thing. One day a priest tried to remove the burden of her sin by explaining to her that she had never really sinned, and that her salvation was certain. The next day this young girl went up to him in the street and screamed at him that he was unworthy to enter a church because he had taken such a burden of sin upon his shoulders.

We need not discuss this case further, but it illustrates how ambition breaks into religious matters, and how vanity makes individuals believe themselves a judge of virtue and vice, purity and corruption, good and evil.

14

FEELINGS AND EMOTIONS

Feelings and emotions are accentuations of what we have previously described as character traits. Emotions express themselves in a sudden flow under the pressure of some conscious or unconscious necessity. Like character traits, they have a definite goal and direction. We might call them psychological developments within a definite time limit. Feelings are not mysterious phenomena that defy interpretation; they occur wherever they are appropriate to the given life style and predetermined behaviour pattern of individuals. Their purpose is to modify the situation of the individuals in whom they occur, to their benefit. They are accentuated, vehement movements that occur in individuals who have abandoned other mechanisms for achieving their purpose, or have lost faith in any other means of attaining their goal.

We are dealing again with individuals who, burdened by a feeling of inferiority and inadequacy that forces them to gather all their powers together, make more strenuous efforts than would otherwise be necessary. By the forece of these exertions they believe they can get into the limelight, and prove themselves victorious. We cannot have anger without an enemy; we cannot conceive of the emotion of anger without considering also that its purpose is a victory over this enemy. In our culture it is still possible to achieve our aims by means of this exaggerated behaviour. We would have fewer outbursts of temper if it were not possible to achieve some goal in this way.

Individuals who do not have sufficient confidence in their ability to achieve their goal tend not to give up their aim because of their feeling of insecurity, but rather to approach it with greater efforts and with the aid of additional feelings and emotions. In this way individuals, stung by a sense of their inferiority, gather their powers together and attempt to win a desired objective in a manner reminiscent of a brutal, uncivilized savage.

Since feelings and emotions are closely bound up with the very essence of personality, they are not the unique characteristics of a few individuals, but are to be found more or less uniformly among all people. All individuals are capable of showing some particular emotion if they are put into an appropriate situation; we might call this capability the faculty for emotion. The emotions are such an essential part of human life that we are all capable of experiencing them.

As soon as we have gained a fairly good understanding of human beings, we may well be able to imagine their usual feelings and emotions without ever having actually come into contact with them. It is quite natural that so deeply rooted a phenomenon as a feeling or emotion shows its effect upon the body, since body and mind are so intimately allied. The physical phenomena that accompany feelings and emotions are indicated by various changes in the blood vessels and in the respiratory apparatus, for example in the appearance of blushing, pallor, rapid pulse rates and variations in breathing.

DISJUNCTIVE FEELINGS

Anger
Anger is the feeling that most typifies the striving for power and domination. Its purpose is the rapid and forceful destruction of every obstacle in the way of the angered person. Previous research has shown us that angry individuals are those who are striving for superiority by every possible application of all their powers. The striving for recognition occasionally degenerates into real power-madness. Where this occurs we expect to find individuals who respond with violent outbursts to the slightest occurrence that might detract from their sense of power. They believe (perhaps as a result of previous experiences) that they can best get their own way, thus conquering their opponents, by this method. This procedure does not stand on a very high intellectual level, yet it works in a majority of cases. It is not difficult

for most people to remember how they have won back their prestige or got their own way through an occasional outburst of fury.

There are occasions when anger is largely justified, but we are not considering such cases here. In discussing the use of anger we are referring to individuals in whom this feeling is always present and is a habitual, well-marked response. Some people systematically use their anger for their own ends, because they have no other way of approaching a problem. They are usually haughty, highly sensitive people who cannot bear anyone to be their superior or even their equal, who must themselves be superior in order to be happy. Consequently they are continually on guard in case anyone comes too close to them or does not value them highly enough. Distrust is the character trait most frequently allied with this kind of sensitivity. They find it impossible to trust their fellow human beings.

Other, closely related character traits go along with their anger, sensitivity and mistrust. In extreme cases one might find, for example, exceptionally ambitious individuals shying away from every serious task, incapable of ever adjusting to society. Should they be denied anything, they only know one method of response. They announce their protest in a manner that is usually very painful for everyone else. They may, for instance, shatter a mirror or destroy an expensive vase. We cannot really accept their apologies if they afterwards attempt to excuse themselves by saying that they did not know what they were doing. The desire to express themselves by destructiveness is plainly evident, for they always destroy something valuable and never confine their rage to worthless objects. A plan of some kind must have been behind their action.

Although this method achieves a certain success on a small scale, as soon as the context becomes wider it loses its effectiveness. Consequently, these habitually angry people soon find themselves in conflict with the whole world.

The external signs of anger are so common that we have only to think of the word 'fury' to call up a mental picture of an irascible people. Their hostile attitude towards the world is clearly evident. The feeling of anger signifies an almost complete negation of social feeling. The striving for power is so bitterly expressed that even killing an opponent is not too difficult to imagine. We can practise our knowledge of human nature by analysing the various emotions and feelings we observe, since feelings and emotions are the clearest indications of character. We must classify all irascible, angry, acrimonious individuals as enemies of society and enemies of life. We must again call attention to the fact that their striving for power is rooted in their feeling of inferiority. No human beings confident of their own power need to show these aggressive, violent reactions and gestures. This fact must never be overlooked. In paroxysms of rage, the whole pattern of inferiority and superiority appears with utter clarity. It is a cheap trick whereby one person's self-esteem is raised at another person's expense.

Alcohol is one of the most important triggers of rage and anger. Very small quantities of alcohol are often sufficient to produce this effect. It is well known that the action of alcohol deadens or removes the inhibitions of civilization. Intoxicated individuals act as if they had never been civilized. In this way they lose control of themselves and all consideration for others. When they are not intoxicated they may, with great effort, be able to hide their hostility to humanity and inhibit their unfriendly tendencies. Once they are intoxicated their true character is expressed. It is by no means coincidental that people who are out of tune with life often take to alcohol. They find in this drug a certain consolation and forgetfulness, as well as an excuse for their failure to attain what they desire.

Temper tantrums are much more frequent among children than among adults. Sometimes an insignificant event is sufficient to throw a child into a temper tantrum. This arises from the fact that children, as a result of their greater feeling of inferiority and their lack of experience, show their striving for power in a more transparent manner. Angry children are striving for recognition because every obstacle they meet appears exceptionally difficult, if not insurmountable.

A deep-seated feeling of anger, when it goes beyond the usual behaviour of swearing and rage, may cause physical as well as psychological injury to the person who is angry. It is worth adding a note in this connection on the nature of suicide.

Suicide is often an attempt to hurt relatives or friends, and to avenge oneself for some perceived defeat.

Grief

Grief occurs when individuals cannot console themselves for a loss or deprivation. Grief, along with the other feelings, is a compensation for the experience of displeasure or weakness, and amounts to an attempt to secure something better. In this respect its value is identical with that of a temper tantrum. The difference is that it occurs as a result of other stimuli, is marked by a different attitude, and uses a different method.

The striving for superiority plays a role in the excesses of grief, just as in all other feelings. Whereas anger is used to raise the self-esteem of individuals while degrading their opponents, and is thus directed against someone, grief amounts to an actual shrinkage of the psychological horizons, which is a prerequisite to their subsequent expansion in which the grieving individuals achieve their personal elevation and satisfaction. But this satisfaction takes the form of a kind of outburst, a reaction against the social environment, although in a different manner from that of anger. The grieving individuals complain, and with their complaint express their opposition to their fellows. Natural as sorrow is in the nature of humanity, its exaggeration is a hostile gesture against society.

The elevation of grief-stricken individuals is achieved through the attitude of those around them. We all know how these individuals find their position alleviated by the way others hurry to help them, sympathize with them, support them, encourage them and otherwise contribute to their welfare. If people feel relieved after crying, it is because they have achieved a kind of elevation by setting themselves up as plaintiffs against the existing order of things. The more plaintiffs demand of their environment because of their grief, the more obvious their claims become. Grief becomes an irrefutable argument that places a binding duty upon the friends, neighbours and family of these individuals. This feeling clearly indicates the struggle to pass from weakness to superiority, and the attempt to retain one's position and evade a feeling of powerlessness and inferiority.

Disgust

The affect of disgust is socially disruptive too, although less so than the other feelings. Physically, disgust occurs when an unpleasant sight or smell causes a certain stimulus in the stomach walls. Mentally, disgust consists of tendencies and attempts to 'vomit' matter out of the psyche. It is here that the disruptive nature of disgust becomes apparent. Disgust is a feeling of aversion. The grimaces that accompany it signify contempt for everything and everyone, and an attempt to solve a problem by a gesture of rejection.

This feeling can easily be misused by being made an excuse for removing ourselves from an unpleasant situation. It is easy to simulate a feeling of nausea, and once it is conjured up we must, of necessity, escape from the particular situation in which we find ourselves. No other feeling can be artificially produced as easily as disgust. With a little practice, anyone can learn to feel nauseous to order. Thus a harmless feeling becomes a powerful weapon against society, or a reliable excuse for withdrawing from it.

Fear

Fear is one of the most significant phenomena in the life of human beings. This feeling is complicated by the fact that it is not only a disjunctive emotion, but like sorrow it is capable of creating a one-sided bond with one's fellows. A child escapes from a situation because of fear, and runs to the protection of someone else. The mechanism of fear does not directly demonstrate any superiority – indeed, it seems to denote a defeat. When we are afraid, we try to make ourselves as small as possible, but it is at this point that the other side of this feeling, involving a simultaneous thirst for superiority, becomes evident. Fearful individuals flee to seek the protection of others, and attempt to strengthen themselves in this way until they feel capable of meeting and triumphing over the dangers to which they feel exposed.

With fear, we are dealing with a phenomenon that is a deeply rooted organic function. It is a reflection of the primitive fear that seizes all living creatures. Humans are especially subject to this fear because of their weakness and insecurity in the natural scheme of things. So inadequate is our inborn knowledge of the difficulties of life that children can never reconcile themselves with it unaided. Others must contribute whatever they lack. Children sense these difficulties as soon as they come into the world and the world begins to make its demands on them. There is always a danger that they will fail in striving to compensate for their insecurity, and develop a pessimistic philosophy as a result. Their most significant character trait becomes, therefore, a certain thirst for the help and consideration of those around her. The farther they are from solving life's problems, the more cautious they are. If ever such children are forced to do something on their own, they carry with them everything they need for their retreat. They are always poised for flight, and naturally their most common and obvious character trait is the feeling of fearfulness.

We see the beginnings of confrontation in the way fear is expressed, perhaps indirectly and without open aggression. We sometimes gain a particularly clear insight into the workings of the psyche when pathological degenerations of this feeling occur. In these cases we see clearly how fearful individuals reach out for a helping hand, and seek to draw other people towards them and chain them to their side.

Further study of this phenomenon leads us to considerations we have already discussed when looking at anxiety. In this case, we are dealing with individuals who demand support from someone, who need someone to pay attention to them at all times. Their relationship becomes similar to that of a master and slave, as if someone else had to be present to aid and support the anxious person. If we investigate this further we find many people who go through life demanding special attention. They have lost their independence to such an extent (as a result of inadequate and defective contact with life) that they demand exceptional privileges with extraordinary vehemence. No matter how much they seek out the company of others, they have little real social feeling. Let them show fear and fright, and they can establish their privileged position again. Fear helps them to both evade the demands of life and enslave all those about them. Finally fear worms its way into everyday relationships, and becomes an individual's most important instrument of domination.

The Misuse of Emotion

No one understood the meaning and value of feelings and emotions until it was discovered that they were valuable instruments to overcome a sense of inferiority and to elevate the personality and obtain recognition. The faculty of showing emotion has a wide application in the life of the psyche. Once children, feeling neglected, learn that they can tyrannize their environment through fury or tears or fearfulness they will test this method of obtaining domination again and again. In this way they will fall easily into a behaviour pattern that allows them to react to insignificant stimuli with their typical emotional response. They use their emotions whenever they suit their needs. Preoccupation with emotion is a bad habit that occasionally becomes pathological. When this has developed in childhood we find adults who constantly misuse emotions. Such individuals utilize anger, grief and all the other feelings in a dramatic way, as though they were puppets. This valueless and often unpleasant behaviour robs emotions of their true value. Play-acting with emotions becomes a habitual response whenever such an individuals are denied anything or whenever the dominance of their personality is threatened. Grief may be so violently expressed that it becomes distasteful: it is too loud, too showy, too histrionic. We have seen people who give the impression that they are competing with everyone in the amount of grief they can display.

The same misuse can be made of the physical accompaniments of emotion. It is well known that there are people who allow their anger to react so strongly upon their digestive systems that they vomit when they are angry. This mechanism expresses their hostility all the more transparently. The emotion of grief is similarly associated with a refusal to eat so that the grieving person actually loses weight and really looks 'the picture of sadness'.

We cannot ignore these types of misuse, because they affect other people. The moment a neighbour expresses concern for the sufferer, the violent reactions we have described above tend to cease. There are, however, individuals who crave the expression of other people's friendliness to such an extent that they keep up their grief or fear indefinitely, because in this condition they feel an enhanced sense of self-worth, thanks to the many expressions of friendship and sympathy from their friends and neighbours.

Even though they engage our sympathies to varying degrees, anger, grief, disgust and fear are disruptive emotions. They do not bring people closer together. In fact they drive people apart by damaging their social feeling. Grief, it is true, can bind people together, but this union does not develop normally if both parties do not contribute equally. It reflects a distortion of social feeling when, sooner or later, the comforter has to contribute the greater share.

CONJUNCTIVE FEELINGS

Joy

Joy is the feeling that most effectively bridges the distance between people. Joy does not allow isolation. Expressions of happiness, as shown in the seeking out of a companion, in an embrace and so on, arise in human beings who want to join together, or to enjoy something together. It is conjunctive in the sense that it is a movement towards unity, the reaching out of a hand, a radiation of warmth.

Admittedly, we are once again dealing with human beings who are attempting to overcome a feeling of dissatisfaction, or of loneliness, in order to attain a measure of superiority, or move along our frequently demonstrated line from less than happiness to more than happiness. As a matter of fact, joy is probably the best way to overcome difficulties. Laughter, with its liberating energy, its powers of release, goes hand in hand with joy and represents, so to speak, the keystone of the feeling. It reaches out beyond the personality and engages the sympathies of others.

But laughter and happiness may be misused for personal ends. For example, one patient who was afraid to show his feelings of powerlessness and insignificance showed signs of joy at the report of a serious earthquake. When he was sad he felt powerless; he therefore rejected sadness and attempted to approach the opposite feeling, joy. Another abuse of happiness is *schadenfreude*, the expression of joy at the pain or misfortune of others. Joy that arises at the wrong time or in the wrong place, that denies social feeling and destroys it, is a disjunctive feeling, an instrument of conquest.

Sympathy

Sympathy is the purest expression of social feeling. Whenever we find sympathy in human beings we can generally be sure that they are mature individuals with a social conscience, because sympathy is a good yardstick of how far human beings are able to identify with others.

Perhaps more widespread than the genuine feeling is its conventional misuse. This consists of posing as an extremely public-spirited, exaggeratedly sympathetic individual. Thus there are people who crowd to the scene of a disaster to achieve a mention in the newspapers and get themselves noticed without actually doing anything to help the victims. Others seem to take a delight in tracking down people suffering a misfortune. Professional sympathizers and alms-givers will not easily give up their activity, for they are actually building a feeling of their own superiority out of the sufferings of the miserable or poverty-stricken victims whom they purport to be helping. As that wise judge of human nature, La Rochefoucauld, said: 'We can always find a measure of satisfaction in the misfortunes of our friends.'

A mistaken attempt has been made to relate our enjoyment of tragic drama to this phenomenon. It has been said that the onlooker feels superior to the characters on stage. But this is not true for most people; our interest in dramatic tragedy originates for the most part in a desire for self-knowledge and self-instruction. We do not lose sight of the fact that it is only a play, and we make use of the experience to give us an added impetus in our approach to life's problems.

Humility

Humility is a feeling that is simultaneously conjunctive and disjunctive. This feeling is also part of our relationship with the world around us, and as such is not to be separated from our psyche. Human society would be impossible without a measure of humility and modesty to make us conscious of the need for co-operation.

Humility occurs whenever it seems that the value of one's personal qualities is about to be questioned, or where one's conscious self-esteem might be lost. This feeling is strongly communicated to the body, and results in the expansion of the peripheral capillaries. Congestion in the skin capillaries, or blushing, occurs, usually on the face, but there are some people who blush all over.

Humility can also be an attitude of withdrawal. It can become a gesture of self-isolation, bound up with slight depression, which amounts to a readiness to flee from a threatening situation. Downcast eyes and coyness are preparations for flight, revealing that humility, like other feelings, can be disjunctive if misused.

Some people become embarrassed so easily that all their relationships with other people are spoilt by this disjunctive trait. Its value as a means of achieving isolation becomes obvious when it is exaggerated in this way.

15

GENERAL REMARKS ON
CHILD-REARING AND EDUCATION

Finally let us add a few remarks on a theme we have occasionally touched upon in our previous considerations. It is the question of education's influence on the development of the psyche, at home, at school, and in life in general, .

There is no doubt that contemporary child-rearing in the family nurtures the striving for power and the development of vanity to an extraordinary degree. Everyone can give an example of this from personal experience. To be sure, the family as an institution has great advantages, and it is hard to imagine an institution better adapted to the care of children than a family environment in which they are properly brought up. The family is the institution best fitted for the survival of the human race, especially when ill-health is involved. If parents are also good educators, with the necessary insight and ability to recognize faults in their children's development as soon as they appear, and if, furthermore, they are capable of correcting these faults with proper guidance, we would be happy to state that no institution could be better fitted for the nurturing of well-adjusted human beings.

Unfortunately, however, parents are generally neither good psychologists nor good teachers. Various degrees of a pathological family egotism seem to dominate child-rearing today. This egotism demands that the children of one's own family should be especially cherished and regarded as extraordinarily precious, even at the cost of other children. Such education in the home therefore commits the gravest of psychological errors in brainwashing children with the false idea that they must be superior to everyone else.

Intrinsic to this phenomenon is the typical family pattern based on the leadership and superiority of the father. This is where the damage begins. This fatherly authority has only the flimsiest of ties with the feeling of human community and social interdependence. Only too soon, the experience of paternal authority seduces an individual into an open or secret resistance to social feeling. Revolt is rarely attempted openly. The greatest danger of an authoritarian upbringing lies in the fact that it gives children an ideal of power and shows them the advantages that go with the possession of power. The children grow greedy for domination, and become vain and ambitious for power. Now all children want to reach the top; all children want to be respected, and sooner or later demand the same obedience and submission that they have seen accorded to the most powerful individual they have known. A belligerent attitude to their parents and the rest of the world is the inevitable result of on the development of such false expectations.

Under the prevailing formative influences in the home, it is practically impossible for children to lose sight of the goal of superiority. We see it in small children who like to play at 'big people', as we may see it in the later life of individuals whose thoughts or unconscious recollections of their childhood show clearly that they treat the whole world as though it were still their family. If they are thwarted, they tend to withdraw from a world that has become hateful to them.

It is true that the family is also well adapted to foster social feeling in children. But if we remember the strong influence that the striving for power has, and the conspicuous presence of authority in the family, we find that in this setting social feeling can only be developed to a certain degree. Children's first movements towards love and tenderness are concerned with their relationship to their mother. Perhaps this is the most important experience children can have, for in this experience they discover the existence of another entirely trustworthy person. They learn the difference between 'I' and 'you'. Nietzsche has said that 'everyone fashions the picture of his beloved from his relationship with his mother.' Johann Heinrich Pestalozzi, the Swiss educational reformer, has also shown how a mother is the ideal that determines children's future relations with the world. The relationship with the mother, indeed, determines all subsequent activities.

It is the function of the mother, therefore, to develop social feeling in the child. The eccentric personalities we see among children arise out of their relations with their mothers, and the direction this development takes is an index of the mother–child relationship. Wherever the mother–child relationship is unsatisfactory, we usually find certain social defects in the children. Two types of mistake are most common.

The first error arises when a mother does not properly perform her motherly role, and her children fail to develop any social feeling. This defect is very significant and has many unpleasant consequences. The children grow up like strangers in a strange land. If we wish to help such children, the only way to do it is to re-enact the role of their mother, which children have somehow missed in the course of their development. This is the only way we can, so to speak, make fellow human beings out of them.

The second mistake is probably more common. The mother is motherly, yes; but she plays her role in such an exaggerated, emphatic manner that the children are unable to develop any social feeling beyond the mother. This mother allows the love that has developed in the children to express itself entirely towards her. That is to say, such children are interested only in their mother, and exclude the rest of the world. It goes without saying that such children lack the basis for social development.

There are many other factors apart from the relationship with the mother that play an important role in growing up. A happy babyhood helps children find their place in the world. If we bear in mind what difficulties most children have to fight against, and how few of them can reconcile themselves with the world in the first years of their life, or find it a pleasant place to live, we can see how extraordinarily significant children's first impressions are. These are the signposts indicating the way they should go in the world. Now let us remember that a number of people come into the world as sickly babies and experience only pain and sorrow. Let us remember, too, that most children do not have a childhood entirely calculated to make them happy. Now we can easily understand why so few children grow up well-disposed towards life and society, and why so few are motivated by true social feeling.

In addition, we must take into account the exceptionally important influence of mistakes in upbringing. A stern, authoritarian upbringing is quite capable of quenching any natural *joie de vivre* that children may have, just as an upbringing that removes every obstacle from the path of children and surrounds them with a hothouse atmosphere 'acclimatizes' them, so to speak, so that when they are adults, they are incapable of living in any conditions more blustery than the tropical warmth of their family.

We see therefore that education in the family, in our society and civilization, is not well adapted to developing those public-spirited 'citizens of the world' that we might wish for. It is too likely to foster vain ambitions, and the desire for personal aggrandizement.

What institution exists that is capable of compensating for errors in the early development of children, and helping them to adjust more happily to the world? The answer is school. But closer examination shows that school, as it exists today, is not well adapted to this task either. Few teachers today will claim that they can always recognize a child's emotional difficulties and correct them under present school conditions. Teachers are quite unprepared for this task. It is their business to work through a certain curriculum with their pupils, without daring to concern themselves too much with the human lives they are dealing with. The fact that there are far too many children in each class further militates against the proper accomplishment of the teaching task.

Is there no other institution capable of correcting the defects of family upbringing? Some might suggest that life itself is this institution. But life, too, has its own limitations. Life is not capable of fundamentally changing a human being, although it may sometimes appear to do so, for the vanity and ambition of human beings will not allow it. No matter how many mistakes people make, they will either blame the rest of humankind, or feel that their situation is irrevocable. We very seldom find anyone who has come up against obstacles or taken a wrong turning, and stopped to consider where they went wrong. Our analysis of the misuse of experience, in a previous chapter, illustrates this point.

Life itself cannot affect any essential change. This is psychologically comprehensible because life is dealing with the finished products of humankind: human beings, who already have their own sharply focused viewpoints, all striving for power. On the contrary, life is the worst teacher of all. It has no consideration, it does not warn us, it does not teach us; it simply reject us, and lets us perish.

We can draw only one conclusion: the only institution that we can hope to use to affect change is the school. We might make our schools capable of this function, if they were not misused. Up to the present time it has always been the case that individuals who gained control of a school used it as an instrument for the fulfilment of their own vain and ambitious plans. We hear demands today for the old régime to be re-established in schools. Did the old régime ever achieve any good results? How can an authoritarian approach that has always been found to be harmful suddenly become valuable? Why should authoritarianism in school be good when we have seen that authoritarianism in the home, where the situation is theoretically more favourable, achieves only one thing: universal rebellion against it?

Any authority that is not spontaneously recognized, but has to be forced upon us, is a sham; true authority and discipline come from within. Too may children come to school with the feeling that teachers are no more than state employees. It is impossible to impose a rigid régime on such children without this leading to unfortunate consequences for their psychological development.

Even though teachers know their duties, which are deeply rooted in the logic of life, they cannot force children to accept this logic. The only possible way forward lies in avoiding any confrontation, so far as possible, and treating children not as the objects of education, but as the subjects; as though they were mature individuals on an equal footing with their teachers. Then it would not be so easy for children to fall into the error of believing that they were under pressure, or being neglected, and thus obliged to engage in a battle with their teachers. It is from this belligerent attitude that the false ambition of our culture, which characterizes our thinking, actions, and character traits to such a large extent, inevitably develops. Authority must not depend upon force – it must be based solely on social feeling.

School is an institution all children experience in the course of their psychological development. It must, therefore, meet the demands of healthy psychological growth. Only a school that is in sympathy with its pupils' psychological needs can truly be called a good school, and only such a school can be regarded as offering an education for social life.

CONCLUSION

We have attempted to show in this book that the psyche is not determined by hereditary factors. Its development is entirely conditioned by social influences. On the one hand the demands of the organism must find fulfilment, and on the other the demands of human society must be satisfied. It is in this context that the psyche develops, and under these conditions that it grows.

We have investigated this development further and have discussed the capabilities and faculties of perception, recollection, feeling and thought. Finally, we have considered traits of character and emotions. We have shown that all these phenomena are connected by indivisible bonds; that on the one hand they are subject to the rules of communal life, and on the other they are influenced by individual striving for power and superiority. The two forces work on each person's psyche and express themselves in a specific, individual and unique pattern. We have shown how the individual's goal of superiority, modified by social feeling (according to the degree of its development), gives rise to specific character traits. Such traits are in no way hereditary, but are developed in such a way that they fit into the pattern of personal psychological development, and lead in a consistent direction to the goal that is constantly present, more or less consciously, for everyone.

A number of these character traits and feelings, which are valuable indicators for the understanding of a human being, have been discussed at some length, whereas others have been passed over. We have shown that a degree of ambition and vanity appears in all human beings, according to their individual method of striving for power. In its expression we can clearly discern an individual's struggle for superiority and observe its particular manifestation. We have also shown how exaggerated ambition and vanity prevent a person's orderly development: the growth of social feeling is either stunted or made quite impossible. Because of the disturbing influence of these two traits, not only is the evolution of social feeling inhibited but power-hungry individuals follow a path to their own destruction.

This law of psychological development seems to us irrefutable. It is a vital guideline for any human beings who wish to determine their own destiny consciously and openly rather than allow themselves to be the victim of dark and mysterious psychological forces. Our research takes the form of experiments in the science of human nature, a science that cannot otherwise be taught or cultivated. The understanding of human nature seems to us indispensable to every person, and the study of this science the most important activity of the human mind.

GLOSSARY
OF KEY TERMS

Individual Psychology The study of the individual as an indivisible whole, as a unitary, goal-directed self, which in the normal, healthy state is a full member of society and a participant in human relationships.

Inferiority complex Feelings of inferiority or inadequacy that produce stress, psychological evasions and a compensatory drive towards an illusory sense of superiority.

Life style A key concept in Individual Psychology: the complex of the personal philosophy, beliefs and characteristic approach to life of individuals, and the unifying feature of their personality. The life style represents the creative response to early experiences of individuals, which in turn influence all their perceptions of themselves and the world, and thus their emotions, motives and actions.

Masculine protest A reaction, by either sex, to the prejudices of our society about masculinity and femininity. A man's behaviour may constitute a protest against the demands made on him by the myths of male superiority; a woman's may be a protest against the denigration of femininity and the limitations placed on women.

Misguided behaviour An attempt to compensate for a feeling of inadequacy or insecurity in an indirect manner, based on a mistaken 'private logic'.

Organ inferiority A physical defect or weakness that often gives rise to compensatory behaviour.

Other sex Adler's term for 'opposite sex', emphasizing that male and female are not opposite but complementary.

Pampering Over-indulgence or over-protectiveness of children, stunting the development of their self-reliance, courage, responsibility and capacity for co-operation with others.

Psyche The mind, the whole personality both conscious and unconscious, which directs personal drives, gives significance to perceptions and sensations, and originates needs and goals.

Social feeling (or social interest) Community spirit, the sense of human fellowship and identity with the whole of humanity that entails positive social relationships. For Adler, these relationships should incorporate equality, reciprocity and co-operation if they are to be constructive and healthy. Social feeling begins with the ability to empathize with fellow human beings, and leads to the striving for an ideal community based on co-operation and personal equality. This concept is integral to Adler's view of the individual as a social being.

Tasks of life The three broad areas of human experience that each individual must confront: the tasks of pursuing a socially useful profession or occupation; of building fruitful human relationships; and of fulfilling one's role in love, marriage and family life.

BIBLIOGRAPHY

BOOKS BY ALFRED ADLER

The Case of Miss R: The Interpretation of a Life Story. New York: Greenberg, 1929

The Education of Children. Chicago: Regnery Gateway Ed, 1970

The Neurotic Constitution. New York: Arno Press, 1974

The Pattern of Life. New York: Rinehart & Co, 1930

The Practice and Theory of Individual Psychology. New York: Harcourt, Brace & Co, 1927

Problems of Neurosis: A book of case histories. New York: Harper Torchbooks, 1964

Social Interest. Oxford: Oneworld Publications, 1998

What Life Could Mean to You. Oxford: Oneworld Publications, 1998

Understanding Life. Oxford: Oneworld Publications, 1997

BOOKS ABOUT ALFRED ADLER AND HIS WORK

H. L. & Rowena R. Ansbacher (eds). *The Individual Psychology of Alfred Adler: A systematic presentation in selection from his writings.* New York: Harper Torchbooks, 1964

P. Bottome. *Alfred Adler: A Portrait from Life.* New York: Vanguard, 1957

D. C. Dinkmeyer, D. C. Dinkmeyer, Jr., & L. Sperry. *Adlerian Counseling and Psychotherapy.* Columbus: Merrill Publishing Company, 1987

R. Dreikurs. *Fundamentals of Adlerian Psychology.* Chicago: Adler School, 1953

B. Handlbauer. *The Freud–Adler Controversy.* Oxford: Oneworld Publications, 1998

G. Manaster & R. Corsini. *Individual Psychology: Theory and Practice.* Chicago: Adler School, 1982

H. Orgler. *Alfred Adler: The Man and His Work.* New York: Capricorn Books, 1965

INDEX

adaptation, 28–9, 32–3, 36–8
Adler, Alfred, 9–10
  central insights, 10–14
adolescence, 41, 125, 180
affection, 43–4, 46, 58, 73, 77
ageing, 122
agressive type, 30–1, 146
agoraphobia, 191
alcohol, 55, 215
Alexander the Great, 13
aloneness, fear of, 190–1, 201
ambition, 52–4, 91–2, 127, 211, 214
  antisocial, 71–2
  and vanity, 158, 159, 175, 229–30
Anderson, Hans Christian: *The
  Vinegar Jar*, 175
anger, 212, 213–16, 219–20
animals, 35, 61
antipathy, 203–4
anxiety, 18, 76, 139, 146, 147, 153,
  164–6, 189–92, 200–1, 205, 218
aptitude, 111–12
aristocracy, 129, 208
assessment, 45–6, 102–3, 111–113,
  132
attention, 42, 85–6, 218–219
attitudes, 33, 47, 75, 115–16, 147
Austrian Revolution (1918), 192, 195
authority, 224, 226, 227–8
avarice, 183–4

babyhood, *see* childhood
Basedow's disease, 153
bed-wetting, 200–1

behaviour
  patterns, 19, 21, 22, 30–1, 47
  childhood, 18–19
  on life graph 74–82
  schoolroom, 204–5
  shameless, 172–3
  uncivilized, 199–200
Bible, 95, 126, 128, 19–30, 171–3,
  176
blushing, 222
bootlicking, 173
brutality, 61, 146, 172–3
business life, 184

cautiousness, 145
celibacy, 117
character, 139–42
  good, 38
  evaluation, 142
  and social feeling, 139
  traits, 19, 113–14, 229–30
    aggressive, 157–87
    childhood, 18–19
    criminal, 137
    development of, 73–4, 135–8,
  142–8
    family, 131
    feminine and masculine, 109
    non-aggressive, 188–201
    type formation, 40–1
characteristics, psychological, 83–103
cheerfulness, 202–3
childhood
  babyhood/infancy, 31, 39–41,

225-6
  early, 11-13, 18-19, 66-8, 225-6
  later, 68-73
child-rearing, 106-7, 116-17, 223-8
  errors, 67-8
  pressure in, 144
  rules, 139
  see also upbringing
children
  aloneness, fear of, 190-1
  bad habits of, 83, 201
  development of, 83, 142-5
  disabled, 45, 66, 139, 154-5
  effect of obstacles on, 41-5
  egotistical, 166-8
  eldest, 80-2, 117, 129, 169-70
  empathy in, 60
  fantasy in, 57-9
  fear of aloneness in, 190-1
  goals of, 18,44
  inferiority in, 58
  isolation in, 45
  jealousy in, 178-180
  only, 130-1
  pampered, 12, 43-4, 163-9
  problem, 67
  psyche of, 32-3, 39, 106
  second, 129-30
  security in, 32-3
  self-fulfilment of, 10-11
  and society, 39-46, 132
  temper tantrums of, 215
  timid, 192
  vanity in, 158
  youngest, 126-8, 168
choleric type, 150, 151
Cicero, Marcus Tullius, 100-1
civilization, human, 32, 35, 115
  mistakes of, 122-3
cleanliness, excessive,118, 121
clumsiness, 42, 115-16
co-eduation, 124-5
'common weal', 141
communal life, 30, 34-5, 104-5,144,
  156
  need for, 35-6

community spirit, *see* social feeling
compensation, striving for, 70-1
competition, 127-8, 180
confrontation, 218
consciousness, 27, 90, 142
consideration, appeal for, 78-82
cretinism, 152-2, 153
crime, 137, 185
criminal negligence, 87, 186-7
cruelty, 61, 146, 172-3

dark, fear of, 200-1
Darwin, Charles, 35
day-dreams, 57, 140-1
  religious, 177-8
deafness, 48, 137
daeth, fear of, 190
deception, 23
defenders, 147
delinquency, 173-5
delirium, 55
deprecation complex, 163
destructiveness, 214
detour syndrome, 193-9
difficulties, avoidance of, 32-3
dirtiness, 199-200
disabilities, 13, 48, 136
  in children, 45, 66, 139, 154-5
  disadvantage of, 41-2
  physical, 72-3, 154-5
discouragement, 99-100
disgust, 217
disobedience, 62-3
disorderliness, 199
distraction, 86-7
distrust, 30-1, 214
division of labour, *see* labour, division
  of
doers, 148
domination, striving for, 78, 79,
  98-100, 104-5, 195
  inchildren, 32, 40
  in men, 106-10
  in peers, 131-2
Dostoevsky, Feodor Mikailovitch, 203
  Netochka Nievanova, 180

The Idiot, 89–90
dreams, 59, 82, 94–102, 196
  see also day-dreams
Dreikurs, Dr Rudolf, 11
dress, conspicuous, 172

education, 19, 20, 22, 132, 143
  co-education, 124–5
  inadequate, 23–4
  influence of, 61–2, 70, 223, 226–8
  only child's, 130
  receptivity to, 647
  religious, 176
  youngest child's, 127
  see also schools
egotism, 166–9, 170, 21
  pathological family, 223–4
emancipation movement, 124
emotions, 43, 212–22
  misuse of, 219–20
empathy, 20, 24, 59–61, 164, 204
endocrine secretions, 151–4
Engels, Friedrich, 34–5
environment, material, 41–2
envy, 180–3
equality, 80–108
errors, 21–2, 197
  behavioural, 76–82
exaltation, religious, 177

fairy tales, 111, 126, 175–6
family, 63, 126–32, 167–8, 223–6
  power in, 106–7, 129
  unreasonable demands of, 41
fantasy, 51, 57–9 141
  chilhood, 57–9
father, as power symbol, 106–7, 224
fear, 189–90, 190–1, 200–1, 217–19
feelings, 212–22, 229–30
  conjunctive, 220–2
  disjunctive, 231–20
  see also inferiority; social feeling
fictions, psychological, 69
foresight, 57, 59–60
forgetfulness, 87
Freud, Sigmund, 9, 10, 46

friendship, lack of, 195–6
Furtmüller, Carl, 38

games, 83–4, 186
gangs, 62
glands, 151–4
goal-directness (teleology), 28–33,
  47–8, 68–9, 84, 135
  in childhood, 18–19, 44, 66–7,
  69–71
God, 210–11
  playing, 175–8
Goethe, Johann Wolfgang von:
  'Marriage Song', 97–8
gonads, 154
grandeur, 58, 63, 110
greed, 193–4
  for food, 199
Greeks, ancient, 95, 149, 197, 208
grief, 216, 219, 220

hallucinations, 51–6
handicap, *see* disabilities
happiness, 220–1
hate, 185–7
hauteur, 161–2
hearing, defective, 48, 137
heredity, 31–2, 118, 131, 136–7, 229
heroic ideal, 93–4
Hitler, Adolf, 13
hostility, 40, 42, 100, 162, 179,
  185–7, 189
humility, 221–2
hyperthyroidism, 153–4
hypnosis, 63–5

ideal state, concept of, 31
identification, power of, 59–61
illusion, 55
imagination, 49, 51–6, 58–9, 68, 83,
  178
imperiousness, 209
impressions, 65
inadequacy, 212–13
inattention, 86–7
Individual Psychology, 29, 61, 69, 83,

103, 141–2, 148–50
infancy, *see* childhood
inferiority
  in children, 58, 127, 139, 145
  complex, 66–82, 139, 145
    and envy, 180–1
  feeling of, 36, 98–100, 153, 212–13
    compensation for, 13
  organ, 13, 40–1
  of women, alleged, 110–14, 116,
    122
influence, of others, 61–3
insecurity, 36, 68, 70, 145, 147
intelligence, 102–3
  tests, 102–3, 111–12, 112–13
interest, 86
invalids, professional, 165
isolation, 100
  in children, 45
  and withdrawal, 188–9

jealousy, 30–1, 178–83
joy, 220–1
judgement, moral, 132
Jung, Carl Gustav, 9

knowledge, 20–1, 137

La Rochfocauld, 162, 221
labour, division of, 36, 39, 104–5,
  207–8
laughter, 203, 220
laziness, 44, 136
Lichtenberg, G. C., 94–5
life
  graph of, 31, 74–82
  limitations of, as teacher, 226–7
  preparation for, 83–4
  problems of, 193
  skills, 83, 89
life style, 18
locomotion, *see* movement
logic, 37
love, 42–3, 46, 193, 196
luck, bad, 209–10

magic, 176–7
male dominance, 106–10
marriage, 78, 96, 97–8, 108, 193
  against parental advice, 51–4
  and feminine role, 117, 119–21
Marx, Karl, 34–5
masculine protest, 114
masculinity, 109–10, 115
matriarchy, 107, 111
melancholic type, 150, 151
memory, 50–1
menopause, 122
mind, human, 36–7
misanthropy, 185–6, 189
misguided behaviour, 15
mistakes, 21–2, 76–82, 197
mistrust, 42, 137, 147–8
mobility, *see* movement
money, 178
mood, 202–11
mothers, 52–4, 113, 116–21, 200–1,
  224–5
movement, 27, 29–30, 42, 47–8

nail-biting, 90, 199
nervous symtoms, 17–18, 115–16,
  117–21, 153, 165, 197–9
Nietzche, Friedrich, 208, 224
nose-picking, 90, 199

obedience, 62, 63, 109, 144
obstructiveness, 89
occupation, 193
opposition, 85
optimism, 23, 33, 144–5, 202–3
organ(s)
  inferiority, 13, 40–1, 45
  sensitivity of, 48–9

pampering, 43
paradise, 83
parents, 12–13, 42–3, 51–4, 100
past, dwelling on, 190
pedantry, 205–6
perception, 49–50
personal effectiveness, 11

pessimism, 23, 145–6, 204
    of children, 23, 41, 45
Pestalozzi, Johann, Heinrich, 224
phlegmatic type, 150, 151, 152
play, 83–4, 186
power, 40, 195
    family, 106–7, 129
    striving for, 63, 948–102, 104–5,
        156–7, 230
        and anger, 213–16
        in children, 57–9
        in fairy tales, 175–6
        fantasy as, 57–8
        laziness as, 136
        opposition to, 69–71
        pathological, 71–2
        over peers, 131–2
prejudice, 112–13, 122–3, 138, 205–6
privileges, 108, 114, 161–2
psyche, 19, 20, 27–33, 47–9,
    83–4,156, 229
    of children, 32–3, 39, 106
    foundations of, 18
    function of, 27–8
psychology, old school of, 148–9
psychiatry, 17

recognition, desire for, 68, 137
re-education, 22
relationships, 9–10, 195
    mother–child, 117–21, 200–1,
        224–5
    sexual, 123–4
    social, 22–3, 34–8, 43–4, 46
religion, 35, 176, 177–8, 210–11
resignation, attitude of, 115–16
responsibilities, 44–5, 193
restlessness, 48
revolt, 114–16, 224
ridicule, 68

Sand, George, 114
sanguine type, 149–50, 151
schadenfreude, 221
schools, 138, 226–8
    behaviour in, 204–5

see also education
science, 23
security, 32–3, 36–8
self-discovery, 75
self-estimation, 70
self-evaluation, 'constant of', 12, 70
self-expression, 84
self-fulfillment, 10–11, 39
senses, 48, 49, 137
sex glands, 154
sexual relationships, 123–4
sickness, 190
    complex, 164–6
Simonides, 100–1
sinners, reformed, 23–4
slavery, 208
sleep, 96, 145–6
    hypnotic, 63–5
    see also dreams
social feeling (community spirit), 10,
    14, 38, 58, 104, 170, 229
    in character development, 87, 132
        misuse of, 140–1
    in children, 46, 132
    development of, 87, 132
    distortion of, 41
    extent of, 68–9, 139–42
    and family, 224–5
    as guage of character, 139–40
    and superiority goal, 229–30
    and sympathy, 211
    universal existence of, 156
social graces, 199–201
social inhibitions, 91
social life, 34–5, 35–6, 104–5, 144,
    156
social relationships, 22–3, 34–8, 43–4
    in children, 46
social usefulness, concept of, 141
society
    and the child, 39–46, 132
    place in, 105
Socrates, 160
speech, 37–8, 46, 204
stereotype, feminine, 114–16
stimuli, 65

bbornness, 90
bmissiveness, 62, 63–4
  of women, 109, 111, 206–8
suggestion, 65
suicide, 194, 201, 215–16
superiority goal, 68–74, 138, 156
  in children, 32–3
  and grief, 216
  opposition to, 68–74
  and social feeling, 229–30
  and upbringing, 224
superstition, 176–7, 207
support, demand for, 218–19
sympathy, 203, 221

tasks of life, 193
teleology, *see* goal-directness
temperament, 202–11
  categories, 149–51
tenderness, 42–3, 224–5
tension, 122–4
thinkers, 148
thyroid gland, 152–3
time-management, 183–4
timidity, 192–4
tools of survival, 35–6
transformation of human beings, 22
truth, absolute, 34–5

unconscious, 9, 87–94
unreality, aspects of, 57–65
upbringing
  authoritarian, 224, 226
  family, 63
  mistakes in 43–4, 93–4, 226
  strict, 45, 73, 99–100, 116
  see also child-rearing
utopia, 176

vanity, 71, 88, 157–75, 195, 229
  and bad luck, 210
  examples of, 163–71, 173–5
  and religion, 211
Virgin Mary, 52–4
vision, defective, 48

weakness, 65, 116
  trading on, 40–1
wit, 162–3
withdrawal, 188–9
women, 105–6, 107, 108, 111
  alleged inferiority of, 110–14, 116,
    122
  emancipation of, 124
  and rejection of role, 114–16,
    117–22
  submissiveness of, 109, 111, 206–7